50
Classic Walks
in the Pennines

Terry Marsh

Published by Sigma Leisure - an imprint of
Sigma Press, 1 South Oak Lane, Wilmslow, Cheshire SK9 6AR, England.

British Library Cataloguing in Publication Data
A CIP record for this book is available from the British Library.

ISBN: 1-85058-400-1

Typesetting and Design by: Sigma Press, Wilmslow, Cheshire.

Cover design: The Agency, Wilmslow

Cover photograph: On the Pennine Way, Mozie Law (Cheviot Hills) – *Terry Marsh*

Printed by: Manchester Free Press

Disclaimer: the information in this book is given in good faith and is believed to be correct at the time of publication. No responsibility is accepted by either the author or publisher for errors or omissions, or for any loss or injury howsoever caused. You must judge your own fitness, competence and experience.

Contents

A Portrait of The Pennines

What images present themselves when you think of "The Pennines"? Would it be "the floundering in glutinous peat bogs, the stumbling in soggy heather, the squelching in muddy fields" gloomily depicted by Wainwright in his *Pennine Way Companion*? Or perhaps "the wildest, most barren and frightful" landscape encountered by Daniel Defoe? Or do you immediately think of Areas of Oustanding Natural Beauty, or of one of the three national parks – the Peak, the Yorkshire Dales and Northumberland? Or majestic sweeps of rolling moorland stretching as far as the eye can see; the liquid bubbling of curlew, the evocative call of golden plover, great swathes of sunlit purple heather or autumnal light on bracken-brown hillsides; long sculpted escarpments and weird weathered rockforms; the ever present sound of running water, meandering, racing, tumbling, crashing this way and that from along the watershed of our country?

I was born little more than a "spit an' a throw" from the Pennines of South Lancashire, but it was not until I had flirted with the grander designs of the mountains of Wales and Lakeland that I "discovered" them. And here, cultivated in the belief that the Pennines held little appeal, I found to my surprise and delight a tapestry rich of colour, woven from an unimagined variety of threads, some dramatic and awe-inspiring, some serene or hauntingly wild, others gentle and of simple beauty. And if indeed beauty rests in the eye of the beholder, how short-sighted, I concluded, must be some of those who ventured here before me.

Geographers will tell you that the Pennines are neither a chain nor a range of mountains, but simply a broad uplift, and that what many might regard as Pennine country means quite different things in different places.

To compound this identity crisis, even the name "Pennine" is of doubtful origin, a literary forgery in fact. In 1747, a Professor of English in Copenhagen, Charles Bertram, claimed discovery of a 14th century document describing Britain in Roman times. Britain, the document said, was divided by a chain of mountains called the Penine Alps. This led later geologists to adopt the name "Penine", which subsequently acquired an additional "n". Bertram's document turned out, however, to be a forgery, although he may well have been inspired by Camden's definition of the Pennine chain contained in *Britannia*: "It runs like as the Apennine in Italy, through the middest of England, with a continued ridge, rising more with continued tops and cliffs one after another ever as far as Scotland. Here they are called 'Mooreland', after a while the Peak, Blackstone Edge, the Craven, the Stainmore and at length Cheviot." This south-north description is typical of many early representations of the Pennines, and simply reflects that the first explorers came from the south: today, with modern "explorers" arriving from all directions, there is no longer any justification for this approach, so we can adopt a simple top-down order.

Geology

To the geologist the Pennines represent a veritable wonderland. The principal rocks were formed during the Carboniferous Period, a time that began about 350 million years ago and lasted for 80 million years, a mere week's work on the evolutionary timescale. Three main geological divisions occur – limestone, millstone grit and coal measures. In a series of domestic upheavals these divisions were folded upwards and exposed to millions of years of erosion by wind, water and ice. Virtually all of the coal and most of the millstone was swept from the hilltops, though enough gritstone was left behind, sticking out of the landscape like bones from the frame of a hungry cow, to form the distinctive scenery of the High Peak, for example. The remaining limestone, formed in a Carboniferous sea at a time when Britain lay somewhere south of the equator, was then ravaged by the action of ice and water to produce deep dales, caverns and gorges.

Remnants of earlier formations also occur. Volcanic action formed part of Derbyshire and the Cheviot Hills of Northumberland, and the fine basaltic rocks of the Whin Sill intruded in the strata over an area stretching from the Farne Islands to Upper Teesdale, where they are responsible for the dramatic falls of High Force and Cauldron Snout, the crags of High Cup Nick and the undulations favoured by the engineers who determined the formidable line of Hadrian's Wall.

The geological structure is monoclinal, the rocks for the most part abruptly cut off in the west, but tilted gently towards the east. After the Carboniferous Period came the greatest era of earth movements, the Permian times (207-230 million years ago). It was during this era, for example, that the domed shapes of the Howgills were swept to one side by a complicated process of faulting, isolated like crumbs fallen from a table from the main carpet of the landscape. It is to Craven, however, that we must go in search of the oldest rocks, for here, at Chapel-le-Dale and Horton-in-Ribblesdale, are to be found the ancient slates with bands of grit, known as Ingleton granite.

It was the geological housekeeping of the Permian times that formed the massive, elongated ridge which is the principal feature of the Pennines today. Once it reached considerable height, only to be denuded and moulded by the agents of erosion to the softer, rounded aspect familiar to everyone. But it is the variety injected into the geology by local peculiarities which presents the fascination. In Upper Teesdale, limestone has had its structure changed by baking in molten basalt, and later weathered to form the "sugar" limestone favoured by alpine flora, which explains why visitors to Teesdale will find the Nature Conservancy Council at pains to protect this spectacular heritage. Not far away molten material has cooled and hardened to form the Great Whin Sill, and to give us quite remarkable scenery. Other hot rocks, rising from the earth's depths cooled and became galena (lead ore) and barytes, providing man with a living for many years.

Early Times: Nature in the raw

Before man, however, there is a picture of a much younger Pennine landscape, roamed by animals now associated with tropical Africa – elephant, lion and hyena. Later, as the climate cooled woolly rhinoceros appeared, to be followed, during the tundral conditions after the last Ice Age, by animals normally found beyond the Arctic Circle – reindeer, Arctic fox and hare, elk and lynx.

About 10,000 years ago, the Ice Age finally released the land from its freezing embrace. Year by year the glaciers relinquished their claim on the high corries, leaving behind indelible scars. Miraculously life returned; low scrubby trees, heather, pine, willow, birch and juniper, somehow found purchase in the hostile earth, stretched scrawny fingers to the kindling sun and gave shelter to seedling oak and elm, hazel, lime and beech. Gradually the trees gained dominance and spread across the sea of heather a thick forest in which a wealth of wildlife found refuge. Above the trees, high on the mountainsides, grew an immensely rich carpet of grasses, heaths and sedges.

This, while it lasted, was nature in the raw. And it lasted only until man appeared on the scene.

The arrival of man

First, about 8,000 to 10,000 years ago, Mesolithic man ventured into the virgin land, hunting parties summered on the hillsides and fished the glacial lakes, fired the trees to clear the forests, and pursued game which they chased with dogs and sought to kill with stone-headed spears and bows and arrows. Camps were made, providing a base only for so long as suited ancient man's precarious way of life, the great forests receding as man made his inroads, regaining ground and flourishing again as seasons changed and the uncertain people passed on.

It was the nomadic Bronze Age men who first made any real impact on the landscape. Spreading to Europe from the east by about 1500 BC, Bronze Age man brought tools and weapons that were as different from the flint spears and fragile arrowheads of Mesolithic man as were the people themselves. With him came not only hunting dogs, but cattle, sheep and goats to graze the landscape and so halt the forest's natural regeneration. Rain, beating down on the cleared landscape, washed all goodness from the soil. No longer could the ground support trees, and so nature went into reverse, trees succumbing to scrub, and scrub to grass. But the reversal was not entirely complete, for heather somehow managed to cling to life in the thin, acid soil, spreading where once it had spread before, this time unhampered by foundling trees. And so, by processes unknown to him, ancient man created the moors and uplands as we know them today.

Yet we cannot lay the blame at any one door, for those few trees that survived Bronze Age man merely fuelled Iron Age man's furnaces. The Vikings, the Romans, the Normans, all took their toll in creating the open moorland that forms the greater part of the Pennine landscape.

Later centuries saw the growth of farming, and an increase in the number of villages and hamlets. Angles and Danes populated the valleys, while the Norse peopled the higher ground. All three left a legacy of place-names: Anglian place-names are suffixed by *ley* (a clearing) or *tun* (a farmstead), while Danish names end in *by* and *thorp*. The Norsemen provided us with the names *fell, beck, moss, heath* and *gill*.

Later, after the removal of the forests had imposed artificial boundaries where none had existed or were needed, dry-stone walls started to appear, imposing a sometimes idiotic regularity, fuelled by the decrees of desk-bound Enclosure Commissioners whose straight line dictates were transferred to the ground with often ludicrous results.

Even so, in spite of all that has happened to it there is no escaping the uniqueness of a landscape that man now seeks in ever-increasing numbers for his recreation.

The Backbone of England

As a schoolboy mnemonic, the description of the Pennines as "the Backbone of England" has its place. Indeed, they were the backbone, too, in an industrial sense, providing many with work during and for some time after the period of the Industrial Revolution.

But it is a rather disjointed backbone, with individual vertebrae sticking out rather awkwardly from the main north-south spine. As a watershed they peter out somewhere north of Cold Fell, but ever since the concept of a "Pennine Way" was first mooted in 1935 by the late Tom Stephenson it has been customary to include the Cheviot Hills, in Northumberland and just across the border in Scotland. In any case, Camden's description embraced the Cheviot, and these two authorities combined are good enough for me!

At its northerly end, then, rise the tawny hills of the Cheviot, spreading themselves across the border and descending gently southwards, through the ancient hunting forests of Kielder and Wark, to rise again in the wild country of the Northern Moors. Here, the heights vie with those across the broad Eden valley in Lakeland, reaching, in Cross Fell summit, the highest point in the Pennines.

As the hills roll on to the dales of Yorkshire, so, out on a limb, rise the domes of the Howgills, in many ways imitated further south in the projecting vertebrae of the Forest of Bowland, Pendle, and the West Pennine Moors. After the Yorkshire Dales, the Pennines begin to show the ravages of man's industry rather too plainly as they progress across the Aire Gap, where limestone gives way to millstone grit, and on south until the land drops into the windswept South Pennine plains of Lancashire and Yorkshire.

Finally, tugging at the skirts of the great conurbations of Manchester and Sheffield, the Pennines enter the land of the Peak, where yet again the geological changes hold great sway. Here the millstone of the Dark Peak ends in the limestone undulations of Derbyshire's White Peak before the whole massive sprawl of mountain uplands and lowlands sinks gently to rest northwest of Derby.

The Cheviot Hills

By almost any standards the Cheviots are minor hills; The Cheviot itself barely exceeds the 800-metre mark. But this should not tempt anyone venturing on to them to underestimate their capacity for embracing the conditions and rigours of higher mountains, nor their ability to beguile and trap the unwary; not without reason do the armed forces have a military training area here.

The principal axis is southwest to northwest, extending from near Newcastleton in Scotland on the Liddel Water to Wooler, some 65 kilometres (40 miles) away on the edge of the coastal plain. In places, at Carter Bar and Note o' the Gate, the north-south axis degenerates to a mere col, but around The Cheviot itself stands considerably deeper, about 25 kilometres (15 miles) from, for example, Peat Law beside the Coquet to Kirk Yetholm, that traditional end of the northbound Pennine Way.

Though outcrops of rock are few and far between, and the highest ground a peaty morass to vie with the worst clutches of Kinder and Bleaklow, much of the range is excellent walking country. Views are extensive, taking in both the Irish and North Seas, the Pentland Hills, the Lammermuirs, the Eildons, and, on good days, the southern highlands beyond the Forth.

The Northern Moors

The mountain uplands that rise between the Cheviot Hills and the Yorkshire Dales spread themselves across too broad a landscape to have acquired any true generic name. Most walkers know of Cross Fell, Cauldron Snout, High Cup Nick, High Force, and similar honey pots, but the region is almost 50 kilometres (30 miles) wide in places, and much the same from its most northerly summit, Cold Fell to the Stainmore gap: 2500 square kilometres (900 square miles) of wild and beautiful moorland.

Within this comparatively unknown area lies the largest concentration of hills in England outside the Lake District, and while it does not boast the status of a national park (though there are those who think it should), a sizeable chunk has been designated an Area of Outstanding Natural Beauty. Here, in these bleak moorland heights, it has been suggested that the valleys rather than the hills form the attraction. Certain it is that no walker keen on broadening his or her horizons should turn aside from a skirmish or two with the hills of the Northern Moors.

Some parts (AONB notwithstanding) are affected by access controls: Mickle Fell, for example, forms part of the Warcop Military Training Area, and vast areas are actively managed grouse moors with all the attendant obligations such conditions impose on walkers. But there is ample room for everyone, and anyone venturing there will find the Northern Moors too big to ignore, too wild to take for granted.

The Howgills

Possessing a geological affinity with the low fells around Windermere in Lakeland, and owning none of the moorland bog usually associated with the high summits of the Pennines, the Howgills are unique, a diversion from the main thrust of our north-south trail.

Their name comes from a small hamlet in the Lune valley, supplanted by Ordnance Survey cartographers to give to a fairly well-defined group of hills a collective name, and quite fortuitously, too, for neither "the Sedbergh Fells" nor "the Lune Hills" has quite the same ring. "Howgill" derives from two old Scandinavian words, one of the Old Norse (*haugr*, meaning "hill" or "mound"), the other Old West Scandinavian (*gil*, meaning "ravine"). Combine the two meanings and it becomes easy to see why "fells", as in "Howgill Fells" is surplus to requirements – tautology, in fact.

Wherever you walk in the Howgills you are certain to encounter springy turf underfoot, outcrops of rock being few, and occurring only at Cautley Spout and in the confines of Carlin Gill. This is free range country, the fells, unrestricted by walls and fences, sporting surprisingly few trees, rise abruptly from glaciated valleys, their sides folded into deep, shadowy gullies, their tops a series of gentle undulations. This is a region inhabited by free-roaming cows, black-faced Rough Fell sheep and long-haired wild fell ponies, and a delight to travel.

The Yorkshire Dales

The Yorkshire Dales, which also embrace the southerly section of the Howgills, share with the Peak, the distinction of being the best known parts of the Pennines. And that fine distinction is fashioned by the underlying rock, limestone, the most dominant of rock types throughout the whole of the Pennines. Everywhere limestone shapes the land forms, etching out the fine detail of the countryside, shaping fine towering cliffs, and the curious beds of limestone pavement. And even out of sight, underground, the influence is still there, forming tortuous labyrinths that extend over great distances and undermine the very foundations that support this unique and irreplaceable beauty.

The greater part of the Dales has been embraced within the jurisdiction of the Yorkshire Dales National Park, though the boundaries seem to have been arbitrarily drawn in places, and exclude the whole of Nidderdale (though this was in 1994 declared an Area of Outstanding Natural Beauty), the upper Eden valley lying between the heights of Mallerstang Edge and Wild Boar Fell, Middleton and half of the Howgills, all of which have unmistakeable "Dales" characteristics.

Central to the Dales, at least for walkers if not geographically, are the Three Peaks – Whernside, Ingleborough and Pen y Ghent. Less well known are the remote dales of Walden, Kingsdale and Barbondale, and Coverdale, an offshoot of Wensleydale.

In spite of the preponderance of limestone, other rocks do occur and provide a frequently changing scene; limestone gives way in places to the gritstone which occurs so noticeably in the Peak, craggy escarpments relax into soft-shouldered fells, and high mountains surrender benignly to rolling moorland. All around lies evidence of the titanic struggle between land and the elements – ravines, steep-sided gills, waterfalls, all testify to the power of glaciers and water, water with the capacity, it seems, to disappear and reappear almost at will as the age-old underground plumbing pursues its mysterious course.

But perhaps the most prominent feature of the Dales are the ubiquitous stone walls, fashioned often by the hands of men dispossessed under the Enclosure Acts of the eighteenth and nineteenth centuries, and now mute testimony to a dying skill and bureaucratic skulduggery. Later, the Industrial Revolution brought mills and mines and quarries, some of which still scar the landscape but provide a treasure trove of delight for the industrial archaeologist, and later still came the modern invasion, tourism.

The Forest of Bowland, Pendle and the South Pennines

The Forest of Bowland (pronounced "Bolland") stretches west from the Yorkshire Dales to within a mere 16 kilometres (10 miles) of the Irish Sea, leaving free just enough ground to facilitate the major north-south lines of communication along the western side of England. Many travellers therefore unavoidably pass these moulded domes, yet few could attach a generic name to the group, even fewer identify individual summits, and fewer still recognise this as one of the Pennines' two Areas of Oustanding Natural Beauty.

Separating themselves into two distinct groups the hills on the west circle around the head of Wyresdale to meet at the popular Trough of Bowland, while to the east, a region little known to walkers, they stretch away to far off Ingleton and Dales country. Regrettably, much of the areas is out of bounds to walkers, bearing shades of Tom Stephenson's *Forbidden Land*, land owners keeping the high grounds private for the grouse-shooting fraternity. Some access agreements have been made, but much, of considerable interest to the walker, is still unavailable. For all that the walking in Bowland is good, and the views among the best in the Pennines.

South beyond the Ribble, which marks the southern boundary of Bowland, rises Pendle Hill, an isolated mound long steeped in tales of witchcraft following famous trials in Lancaster in 1612, when nineteen luckless souls were found guilty and hanged.

Further south, pressing against the northern reaches of the Peak, we enter the industrially-tormented moors of the South (and West) Pennines, where man's hand on the landscape has been as certain as the landscape's own forces upon man. For here, as the land made possible the mills and fabricated the social history of the place, so too did it cultivate its customs, relationships and attitudes, often described as dour.

The South Pennines are harsh moors where the lovely orange and gold crystals of millstone grit have oxidised to a black that makes your eyes hurt, and portrays, falsely, a land of darkness and dirt even on the brightest day. Few peaks in the South Pennines are remote from the great conurbations of Lancashire and Yorkshire wherein arose the pioneers of mining, weaving and spinning, for everywhere they are traversed by moorland roads, and riven by sylvan deans and cloughs carved long ago by ice. And it is this very accessibility which has long provided the people of the South Pennines with high, refreshing oases from the turmoil and hardships of industrial life.

The Peak

Being the most southerly region of the Pennines, the Peak was the first to attract the attention of early travellers, many arriving, even in the seventeenth century, to see "the Wonders of the Peak". With the arrival of the railways in the nineteenth century, a day trip to this land, famous in court circles as a place of exile for recalcitrant wives, was within the reach of everyone who could afford the fare.

Influenced largely by its geological structure, the Peak divides itself into the High Peak and the Low Peak, also, because the former is predominantly fashioned from gritstone and the latter from limestone, known as the Dark Peak and the White Peak. The old name for the district is Peakland, or "Peaclond" as it appeared in the Anglo-Saxon Chronicle for 924, and means "the land of the hill dwellers". In those times of early history the district lay on the northern edge of the Kingdom of Mercia, and those who lived here were called "Pecsaetna", meaning hill dwellers.

The southern and to the early visitors the most approachable half of the region is a gently undulating plateau of limestone among which numerous towns and villages have grown up in a strange and delightful harmony. Splendid spa towns evolved where natural mineral water issued from the earth, notably Buxton and Matlock, and it is here that the region is seen at its best, in Dovedale, and the Derwent and Wye valleys.

Further north, the High Peak lies within easy reach of millions resident in the great conurbations of Lancashire, Cheshire and Yorkshire. Here gritstone predominates, and the moorland is cloaked in a rich shroud of heather and bilberry and tough, resilient grasses. But it is the ubiquitous peat which impresses on the mind, especially on a fist visit, and it takes time to appreciate the subtleties, of line and shape, colour and hue, and contrasts which bring devotees to the Peak time and time again in preference to other more superficially attractive regions. Often, for example, it is the very bleakness of the peaty moorland plateaux which emphasises the verdant loveliness of the valleys and fringes, giving the whole a satisfying sense of completeness.

And finally . . .

As with any book, this contribution is very much one man's statement, an expression of gratitude, an appreciation in words and photographs of some of the finest walking country in Britain. It lies centrally placed to our nation, accessible from all directions, rich and varied, benign and savagely powerful, an inspiration, a panacea, and a place of enjoyment.

May your enjoyment echo mine, and may all your *Classic Walks in the Pennines* have happy endings.

Notes and Advice for Walkers

None of the walks suggested in this book present technical problems in good weather conditions, especially in summer. The vast majority may also be tackled in winter by competent walkers. Some of the walks traverse bleak and often featureless moorland where mist becomes a major hazard.

For all the walks I have assumed that readers possess navigational skills, are conversant with map and compass technique, and know how to clothe and protect themselves effectively. In winter, with snow and ice on the ground, an ice-axe is an essential item of equipment, but it is useless without the knowledge to use it properly. And there may be times and places when crampons will greatly facilitate progress. To venture into the world of the Pennines without meeting these basic requirements is foolhardy.

Maps: Each walk carries details of appropriate Ordnance Survey (or other) map(s), and is supported by a diagrammatic map outlining the walk.

Various maps are available to the walker, and with one exception, these are all produced by Ordnance Survey. These are:

Landranger Maps: these are produced to a scale of 1:50,000 (1¼ inches to 1 mile or 2cm to 1km), and are all-purpose maps. Landranger maps, of which 204 are required for the whole country, each cover an area 25 x 25 miles (40 x 40km), i.e. 625 square miles (1600 square kilometres); only 11 or so are needed for the walks in this book. All Landranger maps contain Rights of Way information, such as footpaths and bridleways, and the maps are available in both flat and folded form, the latter proving a handy size to carry in pockets or rucksacks.

Outdoor Leisure Maps: cover popular leisure and recreation areas of the country, and are packed with detail invaluable to the serious walker. They are to a scale of 1:25,000 (2½ inches to 1 mile or 4cm to 1km). These, too, are available flat or folded and most cover an area of approximately 195 square miles (500 km^2). Six OLMs are appropriate to the walks in this book.

Historical Maps: show the position of buildings and monuments and layout of the roads of the time, overlaid in colour against modern plans. Each map includes informative text and is illustrated with colour photographs. Only one of this series is appropriate to this book, that on Hadrian's Wall, in which the folds of the map are cleverly arranged so that only one section of the Wall is revealed at a time. This map is to a scale of 1:25,000.

Pathfinder Maps: are also to a scale of 1:25,000, and since 1989 completely cover the country. There are 1373 in total, most covering an area 20km east to west and 10km north to south. Where the area of a Pathfinder Map is completely covered by an Outdoor Leisure Map, then the Pathfinder Map may not be available. Elsewhere they provide a useful and detailed addition to any walker's equipment, and in this book are especially useful in the Howgills.

Harveys Walker's Maps: were originally conceived for the Karrimor International Mountain Marathon, but have proved tremendously popular with less energetic walkers. Unlike other maps, the Harveys Maps are waterproof, being produced on a material appropriately called 'Duxbak'. As a result, the map is stronger when wet, but not indestructible. Each map is based on a completely new survey carried out from air photographs, followed by extensive field checking by a team of mapmakers, with special attention being paid to footpaths. Land use is categorised, differentiating between open moorland, cultivated farmland, thick commercial plantations and open woodland, and land form is shown by detailed contours and different descriptions for boulders, scree, marsh, peat hags, groughs, crags, etc. The maps, many of which also contain a brief Visitor Guide, are produced to a scale of 1:40,000, and are available from most outdoor shops and from Harvey Map Services Ltd., 12-16 Main Street, Doune, Perthshire, FK16 6BJ. The maps which cover the Peak District and the Howgills are appropriate to walks in this book, though others are added to the series.

Throughout the book, where Outdoor Leisure Maps are appropriate to a walk, all subsequent reference in the text relates to features which may only be found on the OLM.

Distances and Ascent: are approximate and have been rounded up or down, but they are sufficiently accurate to allow calculation of times using Naismith's or other rules.

Paths: There are numerous paths throughout the Pennines, but it should be noted that *any reference to paths or other lines of ascent does not imply that a right of way exists.*

Access: The author has walked without challenge throughout the Pennines for many years, and most walkers will enjoy the same liberty. This general freedom, achieved and maintained only by considerate walkers, should not be interpreted as a licence to clamber over walls and fences indiscriminately causing damage, or to tramp through fields of crops. While to travel anywhere on the hills and moors with a dog that is not held on a leash is inviting the wrath, rightly so, of those who own the land and earn a living from it.

Gear for walking: At certain times of the year some parts of every walk in this book are affected by rain, becoming muddy or peaty. For this reason proper footwear in the form of leather boots is recommended; canvas and suede boots, especially the modern lightweight boots, are however more than adequate most of the time, but cannot cope with the worst conditions. For these times and conditions a spare pair of socks or two in your rucksack will mean you can change to dry footwear, if necessary.

Flashy climbing breeches, as such, are not needed. Any warm trousers capable of withstanding wind and (some) rain are ideal, but not jeans, which are too restrictive, very uncomfortable when wet and take a long time to dry. The modern lightweight trousers made specifically for outdoor use are excellent, and tougher than they look.

Upper body inner clothing which supports the layer principle of insulation need not be the pricey garments found in equipment shops. Very often a couple of old sweaters serve just as well, but it is important to have a good quality outer garment, windproof and waterproof, for both the upper and lower body, and of that there is a vast array. My maxim has always been to find the most expensive garment I can afford, and then buy something a little more expensive – investment in good quality mountain clothing saves lives! It is essential to maintain an even body temperature; this may be affected by damp and cold and could lead to hypothermia, a serious and potentially fatal condition.

Up to twenty per cent of body heat loss escapes via the head, so it is a good idea to wear a cap or balaclava, no matter how daft you think you look.

All the walks in this book may be easily accommodated within a few hours, but time enough to justify a day-sack to carry drinks and food, spare clothing, emergency rations, first aid kit, a torch, whistle, map and compass.

Walk 1: Kirk Yetholm to Harthope Valley

Maps: (1) OS Landranger 1:50,000 series: Sheet 74 — Kelso, and Sheet 80 — Cheviot Hills and Kielder Forest area (on a clear day you can manage without Sheet 80); (2) Harveys Walker's Maps: Eastern Cheviots, and Western Cheviots.

Start: The Border Inn, Kirk Yetholm. GR 827282.

Distance: 21 kilometres (13 miles)

Ascent: 1070 metres (3510 feet)

Type of walk: An exhilarating and testing walk, initially along the Border, leaving it at its highest point to do battle with the infamous Cheviot bogs before descending into the delectable Harthope Valley. Not being a circular walk, transport problems will need to be resolved, but by extending the walk to Wooler a return to Kirk Yetholm may be made by bus.

Border battles, bog and beauty bountiful

No doubt the Pennine Way Old Boys' Club Annual Reunion, if it existed, would have daunting tales to recount of the day that included The Cheviot, be it the first or the last. Undeniably, The Cheviot traverse is a challenge, with problems and difficulties magnified tenfold if it comes at the end of a two or three-week trek. Even then, I suspect that on reflection most walkers would still have enough about them to appreciate what The Cheviot and its acolytes have to offer, for this is delectable walking country, and the long traverse from Kirk Yetholm to the Harthope Valley an immensely rewarding affair. Whether it ever becomes a love affair will depend largely on you.

Rising as a mighty frontier to form the border between England and Scotland, the Cheviot Hills viewed from afar dappled in sunlight seem like a modest assortment of gentle green domes that might be found elsewhere in the Pennines. In fact, geologically, they are quite different from other Pennine hills, having been formed almost 400 million years ago by intense volcanic activity of immense ferocity, an epoch hallmarked by gigantic outpourings of volcanic lava. Later, a dome of magma formed beneath the volcanoes, and where these two rock masses, the magma and the lava, met the intensity of the heat produced a harder ring of rock, a Metamorphic Aureole of "baked" andesite. Much of this rock was eroded away by ice, but rock tors still project above the surrounding terrain, aligned north to south to accord with the direction of the ice flows. Being formed of the same rock, andesite, the Cheviots, in one respect at least, have much in common with the Andes of Western South America, and it is but a short step to speculate that in aeons past the Cheviot Hills may well have resembled the Andes, before the powers of erosion set about their work. Certainly, there is ample evidence that the range once formed an island in a shallow sea, and later rose as a massive headland overlooking the immense river that fashioned the sandy coastlands of Northumberland.

The fact that the Cheviots were a frontier significantly affected the way they developed. No one, for example, can avoid noticing how barren the hills are, a state which denotes a troubled episode in man's history of the region, one that began with an attack on Scotland by Edward I in 1295 and which endured for more than 300 years until the Union of the Crowns in 1603. Had the turbulence of this period never happened there can be little doubt that its agriculture and civilisation would have advanced at a more rapid pace. But the centuries of trouble bred insecurity, as war became a fact of life; the land and its people became impoverished and hard with only the most powerful landowners able to protect themselves. The Border regions degenerated into a vast wasteland of lawlessness, where house burning, cattle theft, and the massacre of whole families by marauding moss troopers were common occurrences.

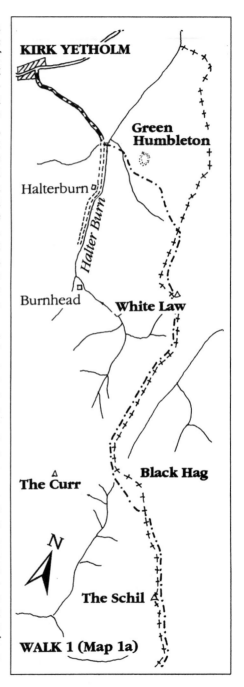

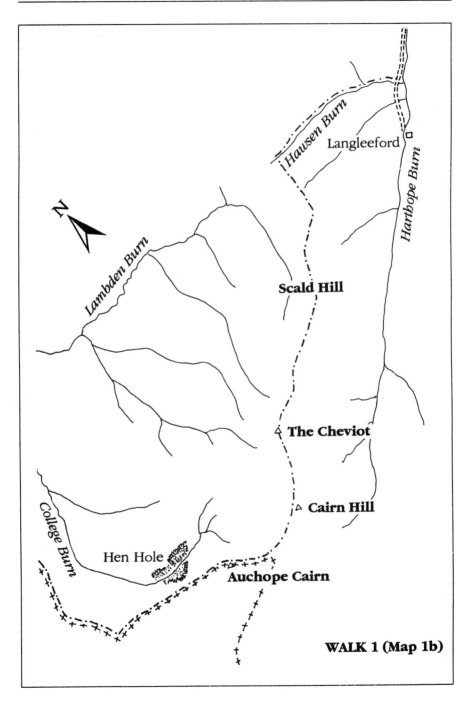

Hawsen Burn

Langleeford

Harthope Burn

N

Lambden Burn

Scald Hill

△ **The Cheviot**

△ **Cairn Hill**

College Burn

Hen Hole

Auchope Cairn

WALK 1 (Map 1b)

Now, almost 400 years later, the borderlands still betray the murderous signature of war.

Kirk Yetholm, where our walk begins, nestles peacefully in the Bowmont Valley, its tranquillity disturbed only by the ragged caravans of Pennine Wayfarers that debouch from the hills, or the fewer visionaries who up-end convention and set off south. Throughout much of its length the signposting of the Pennine Way favours those heading north, often posing for others fundamental questions of direction.

We begin up the lane leading away from the Border Inn, a lane flanked by hawthorn and walls etched white, gold and green by lichen and mosses. Wild flowers grow in abundance and in spring and early summer the scent of yellow broom hangs heavily in the morning air. We soon cross a narrow ridge that undulates to The Curr, and is worthy of exploration itself, containing as it does the remains of a fort on Wildgoose Hill. Ahead of us rises Green Humbleton, a minor grassy hill, but also sporting an Iron Age hill fort, our way passing south of it. But first we encounter a cattle grid and shortly leave the road to ford the shallow Halter Burn. Another burn, Shielknowe Burn (not named on 1:50,000 maps), flows on our right, leading us around Green Humbleton until the tempting form of Coldsmouth Hill appears away to the left. We now follow a green track to a gated fence where we cross the Border into England for the short stretch to Whitelaw Nick, a conspicuous neck of land between White Law and its minor neighbour.

White Law is a spot worthy of a moment's pause; although of modest elevation, the summit holds a commanding position overlooking, northwest, the Tweed Valley to the Lammermuir Hills and northeast the Bowmont Valley we have just left and the Till. East of north, between the two rivers, lies Branxton where in 1513 the Battle of Flodden Field brought about the conclusive defeat of the Scots. Far away in the distance is Berwick-upon-Tweed and the North Sea, while to the east rise the foothills of the Cheviots, Hare Law, Newton Tors, Easter Tor and Yeavering Bell. The latter, seen from White Law in twin-peaked profile, is one of the most important archaeological sites in the region being encircled by a stone rampart within which are traces of 130 circular huts dating to the Iron Age. Below it lies the site of the Anglo-Saxon palace of Ad Gefrin, court of Aethelfrith and Edwin, kings of Northumbria. Much nearer lies Great Hetha, yet another Iron Age hill fort and evidence enough that between two and three hundred years ago these hills were far less sparsely populated than now.

At Whitelaw Nick we return to Scotland, not that we really needed to leave it, and after a short descent begin a superb, airy and gradual ascent over Steel Rig, grassy and firm underfoot. A path finally directs us to the col between Black Hag and The Curr, and in a short while a ladder-stile, left, affords a return to England for the final pull to the strange rocky summit of The Schil.

The Schil is one of the finest summits in the Cheviot Hills, and its rocky topknot provides an exhilarating panorama.

Remaining with the Border we now press on towards Auchope Cairn, Cairn Hill and The Cheviot. To the east the exquisite College Valley insinuates itself into the folds of The Cheviot, ultimately absorbed into the dark embrace of Hen Hole. This valley affords an excellent circular ascent of The Cheviot (see Walk 3), and from the spot known as Red Cribs the two walks share the same route until well beyond Scald Hill, northeast of the summit.

The pull up to Auchope Cairn is not unduly tiring, but the summit is a bleak and forbidding place, the start of an uncomfortable conflict with peat bog. The good sense not to attempt this walk after prolonged wet weather will offer a reasonable prospect of outmanoeuvring the worst clutches of the ensuing assembly of quagmires by deviations left or right; the even better sense to leave the whole outing until the ground is frozen within winter's grip will speed progress across otherwise unhappy terrain. For all that, my records tell me that over the years I have only ever visited The Cheviot during June and July, and have yet to experience personally any of the nastiness to which I refer. Alas, there are sufficient tales by others to confirm in me a belief that the stretch from Auchope Cairn to The Cheviot possesses quite a repertoire of dirty tricks.

The summit of The Schil

Note: In recent times, footpath restoration work (on-going at the time of writing) is solving most of the boggy problems between Auchope Cairn and The Cheviot.

Here, on Auchope Cairn, bird watchers may well spot snow buntings and peregrines, as well as the more customary wheatears, curlew and golden plover.

Finally, the fence from Auchope Cairn joins one ascending from Windy Gyle and

King's Seat and another setting off for Cairn Hill and The Cheviot, all reliable guides in poor visibility. Nearby, and worth the short diversion on a nice day, a little outcrop of rocks on the western slope of the hill is known as the Hanging Stone, and in the days when this region was governed by Marcher Lords it marked the boundary between the Middle March and the East March. Where these three fences meet is the highest point on the Union boundary, a distinction signified by a tall post.

All around the ground in spring and summer is dotted with the flowers and leaves of a wide range of ground-hugging plants – cowberry, bilberry, cloudberry, crowberry and heather – a passing study of which will consume the time needed to plod across Cairn Hill, following a fenceline, and on to the summit of The Cheviot itself. Off to our right the summits of Comb Fell and Hedgehope Hill (see Walk 2) rise above the unseen head-waters of Harthope Burn; due south, Cushat Law and Bloodybush Edge overlook the source of the River Breamish, backed by the conifers of Kidland Forest (see Walk 4).

From the summit of The Cheviot, its trig pillar, now approached by a pavement of slabs, looking rather forlorn above the surrounding morass, the onward route to Harthope Valley could not be simpler. Conveniently, a fence sets off northeast descending easily to the col below Broadhope Hill which separates the waters of Hawsen Burn and Lambden Burn. A slight re-ascent, as if making for Broadhope Hill, and we soon encounter a gate at which we turn right (east) to scamper down the bracken-clad banks of Hawsen Burn to gain the valley about one kilometre south-west of Langlee Farm. If making for Wooler, the ensuing walk out along the road is no hardship, and in spring quite delightful.

Walkers with no taste for the bogs of The Cheviot will find that by heading east of south across untracked ground from the top of Cairn Hill, they will reach the col northwest of Comb Fell, from where an easy and enjoyable descent may be made into Harthope, passing en route Harthope Linn, favoured by trout, wagtails and dippers. Strong walkers could do worse than consider tackling Comb Fell itself, progressing then to Hedgehope Hill before pursuing a steep and grassy descent along the boundary of Threestoneburn Wood until a change of direction is needed (indistinct path) to head for Long Crags and Housey Crags, from where the valley is easily achieved: a demanding addition, but well worth the effort.

Walk 2 : Linhope Spout and Hedgehope Hill

Maps: (1) OS Landranger 1:50,000 series: Sheet 80 – Cheviot Hills and Kielder Forest, and Sheet 81 – Alnwick and Morpeth; (2) Harveys Walker's Map: Eastern Cheviots

Start: Hartside Farm, Breamish valley. GR 977162. Very limited roadside parking.

Distance: 18 kilometres (11.25 miles)

Ascent: 685 metres (2245 feet)

Type of walk: A rough and energetic walk over wild and lonely fells; few pathways exist, and those that do are apt to disappear. Essentially a circuit for strong walkers, the hills are a long way from help should it be needed.

Of which memories are woven

Walkers ploughing along the dedicated line of the Pennine Way on a clear day, or diverting from it to take in the summit of The Cheviot, cannot fail to notice and perhaps wonder about the promising hills that rise to the south; these are Hedgehope, Comb Fell, Cushat Law and Bloodybush Edge, rough, remote hills, no place for a Sunday picnic.

Much of the land further south is embraced by an artillery range making access limited. But lovely river valleys have pressed themselves into the folds of the hills since time immemorial, and these afford excellent incursions, proving to be the threads from which our fondest memories might be woven. One such is the Breamish, carved by a river that finds its source on the high shoulders of these four fine hills, and works its way eastwards and north to join the Till near Wooler.

To many the Breamish valley is the jewel of the Northumberland National Park, and though busy over summer weekends, is seldom uncomfortably crowded. But perhaps it is at its best in late May or early June when the broom is sweeping the air with its heavy, heady perfume. Access to the valley is gained not far north of the village of Powburn by a minor road that effectively terminates at Ingram, where there is a national park information centre and a delightful church tucked away among the trees in a setting worthy of Constable.

For most people Ingram is an adequate base from which to explore the surrounding

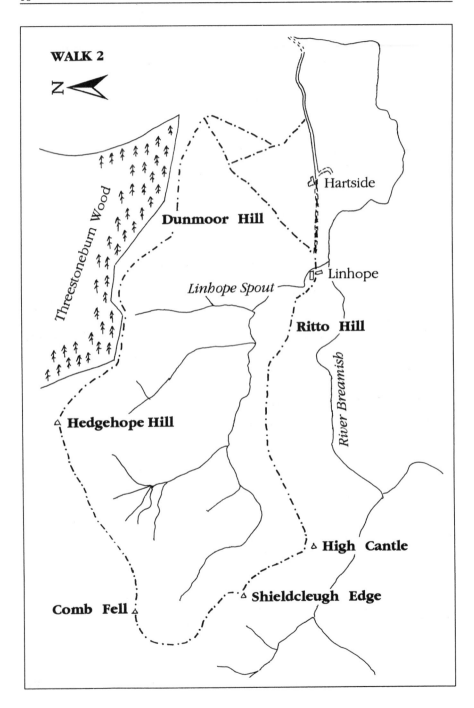

hillsides. Close by, on Ingram Hill, are ancient round barrows, numerous Romano-British settlements, and traces of several promontory forts. The road, a shadow of its former self, continues, however, beyond Ingram and enters a splendidly rugged region, squeezing tightly through Breamish gorge with Brough Law pressing down hard on its course from the south, and possessing two massive stone ramparts dating from 400 BC.

Hedgehope Hill

The public road into Breamish finally ends at Hartside Farm, and here cars must be left. There is very limited space at the side of an already narrow road, so care must be taken not to cause obstruction.

Ignore the road heading south, which if followed on foot would lead us to High Bleakhope Farm, one of the remotest farms in England, and follow instead the good track leading us to Linhope Manor, concealed by a cloak of exotic trees and rhododendrons. The track continues to the waterfall of Linhope Spout where Linhope Burn plunges in a cascade of white water over a huge rock step into a deep, dark pool surrounded by birch trees and moss-covered rocks. All around the hills rise serenely, bracken-clad and burnished gold in autumn, and this has to be one of the most idyllic spots, enclosing the Spout in a leafy oasis, its waters foaming ferociously after rain.

Climb west now, away from the Spout, and on to Ritto Hill, beyond which a long steady plod takes us to High Cantle, perched above High Bleakhope Farm. Now we head northwest, rising in rough steps of close-cropped grass and heather seamed by peaty troughs that offer excellent shelter for a short break, the abundant vegetation playing host to a few varieties of damsel and dragonfly. To the south the peak of Wether Cairn is prominent, while Cushat Law and Bloodybush Edge take on a bolder form, their summits rising above the Forestry Commission plantations of Kidland Forest.

Shielcleugh Edge forms the first step up, followed by Coldlaw Cairn where the granite outcrops have a pink tinge about them. For much of the way a dilapidated fenceline has accompanied us, and on Coldlaw Cairn it takes another twist ascending northeast above the Harthope col to Comb Fell, an innocuous twin-topped summit, its highest point, unmarked, lying on the flat mound nearest Hedgehope Hill. The fence here guides us to Hedgehope, down at first and then ascending quite steeply on springy turf, through heather and cloudberries to the large summit cairn and trig. The view is one of the finest in the Cheviot Hills, the summit being overtopped only by the highest tops of The Cheviot massif across the Harthope Burn. But Hedgehope Hill undoubtedly has the finer form, a bold profile from any direction.

A descent southeast from the top of Hedgehope Hill soon encounters the boundary of Threestoneburn Wood which may be followed over Dunmoor Hill to the rocky topknots of Cunyan Crags. A steep southerly descent now will intersect a bridleway running southwest to Linhope Manor, by which way we may make our return to Hartside Farm, or by the bridleway heading directly for Greensidehill, where we rejoin the road about one kilometre east of Hartside.

Walk 3 : The Cheviot via College Valley

Maps: (1) OS Landranger 1:50,000 series: Sheet 74 — Kelso, with just a small amount on Sheet 80 — Cheviot Hills and Kielder Forest (2) Harveys Walker's Map: Eastern Cheviots

Start: Hall in College Valley, near the junction of the roads to Mounthooly and Goldscleugh. GR 888252. Room to park cars off the road.

Distance: 19 kilometres (12 miles)

Ascent: 625 metres (2050 feet)

Type of walk: The approach through College Valley is one of the finest walks in the Cheviot Hills. It begins along a metalled roadway that later degenerates into a broad track and then a narrow path before climbing to the Border ridge between Auchope Cairn and The Schil. Here the going is inclined to be boggy and best tackled during dry weather or when the ground is frozen. The summit of The Cheviot should not be contemplated after prolonged wet weather — you may never come back! The height gain while considerable comes in easy instalments, mostly confined to the stretch between the head of the College Valley and Cairn Hill.

Of freebooters, battles and peat

When, after years of walking elsewhere, the enthusing reports of friends and my own curiosity finally lured me to the far northeastern corner of England that contains the Cheviot Hills it was love at first sight, and I cursed myself for having wasted so much time in prodigal pursuit of pathways in more popular walking areas. To my delight I discovered these gently-fashioned hills were a catharsis for me, reviving a jaded palate that had travelled the length and breadth of Britain and Ireland, and well into Europe, too. Standing on the summit of The Cheviot itself, gazing far across the wild beauty of Northumberland and into the Borders Region of Scotland, I began to understand what my friends had meant. This, I decided, was what I wanted for Christmas!

Fittingly, the eponymous Cheviot is the highest point of the range, its shapely dome always seeming to grace the skyline no matter where you find yourself. Yet far from boasting a fine monarchical topknot of rock the summit is a vast peat bog: rainwater, unable to penetrate the underlying granite, prevents the proper decomposition of heather, moss and grasses, forming, as a result, a ubiquitous black peat. It is this preponderance of peat which has earned The Cheviot an unfortunate, and in my view ill-deserved, reputation, for there is far worse and far more on Kinder and Bleaklow at the other end of the Pennine Way, without The Cheviot's abundance of attractive valleys as surrounding compensation. A modern, flagged pavement now eases progress considerably. A modern, flagged pavement now eases progress considerably.

Ironically, 300 million years ago, this great sprawling mound was an active volcano on the southern shores of the Devonian land mass, but not now. No doubt when Daniel

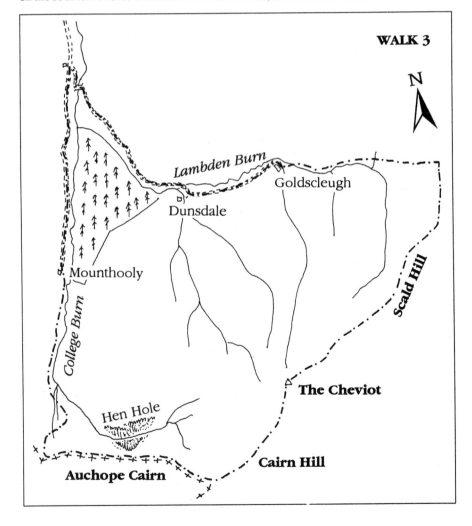

Defoe ascended The Cheviot in 1728, expecting in his hyperbolic naivety to encounter a knife-edged ridge, he was disappointed (or relieved) by what he found. Yet as ever he allowed his imagination to run riot, and you would think from all his exaggerations he had spent the time in the French Alps at least.

The Cheviot via College Valley

Pennine Wayfarers, nearing the end of their journey, may hold a differing view, but the softly-shapen Cheviot Hills have a relaxing and untroubled air about them. Alas, it was not always so. Before the Union of the Crowns in 1603, the border was divided into the East, Middle and West Marches, each under the charge of a warden whose unenviable task it was to keep order in the area. A Memorandum of 1579 suggests that the decay of the English Marches was due to raids by the Scots, neglect of horses and arms, castles and forts being in unworthy hands, and deadly private feuds between many of the families, made worse by intermarrying. The reality, in terms of who did what to whom, has honours about even, with a fair bit of international squabbling to boot!

Not surprisingly, the whole region abounds in legends and folklore. Close by The Cheviot itself stands Hen Hole, a massive and impressive corrie and gorge gouged from the rocks during the Ice Age, and down which College Burn now cascades in a fine series of waterfalls. Fairies, it is claimed, once lived among the dank and mossy clefts by the falls, where alpine plants and saxifrage cling tenaciously to the rocks; huntsmen were lured to their deaths by strange music, and Black Adam of Cheviot, a notorious freebooter, had his lair there. On one occasion he is said to have invaded a wedding party at Wooperton, robbed the guests and *stabbed* the bride. In a slightly different version he is said to have *ravished* the bride; either way the bridegroom, Fletcher, was none too happy, and pursued him back to Hen Hole where, in attempting to jump the gorge, both men fell to their deaths.

"They tottered on the vera brink
O' that precipice so high;
Black Adam clung unto a rock,
For he feared sic death to die.

Slowly right owre then they fell
For Fletcher his hold did keep;
A minute and their twa bodies
Went crashing doune the steep

There was a splash as the water flew
Half up the rugged dell;
The torrent rushed and the water gushed
As a' was dethely still."

Life in the Cheviot Hills, however, was not always murder and mayhem. When Sir Walter Scott spent the autumn of 1791 at a farmhouse at Langleeford he wrote to a friend: "All the day we shoot, fish, walk and ride; dine and sup upon fish struggling from the stream, and the most delicious heath-fed mutton, barn-door fowls, pies, milk-cheese etc., all in perfection; and so much simplicity resides among these hills, that a pen, which could write at least, was not to be found about the house . . . till I shot the crow with whose quill I wrote this epistle."

In many ways Scott says it all, a place of quiet calm, yet breathing a history as savage as any place, invaded, plundered, fought over by the people for whom these noble mounds were the hills of home.

The ascent to The Cheviot through the College Valley is typical of the rare beauty of the region, and one to be savoured. As if to restrict the numbers of those allowed to enjoy this sanctum, consent is required if you wish to take a vehicle into the valley, which is private. The valley is open to approximately 12 motor vehicles on any day except between the middle of April and the end of May when lambing is taking place. Permits may be obtained from Messrs. Sale and Partners, 18 – 20 Glendale Road, Wooler, Northumberland, NE71 6DW, who explain that the restriction on numbers is to keep the valley unspoiled, and because there are still a great number of people who enjoy walking in a traffic-free environment.

It is possible to drive along the valley as far as Mounthooly, but for a satisfying circuit, leave your car near the hall, an isolated building at GR 888252, and proceed along the roadway from there. Beyond Mounthooly a track courts College Burn, deteriorating finally to a narrow path leading directly into Hen Hole. There is a scrambly route through this chasm, but you are then faced with a larger share of bog-bashing than is necessary, when there is an alternative route available.

Follow instead the line of the footpath shown on the 1:50,000 map which runs on south and then east, making for a gash on the hillside, known as Red Cribs (not named on maps). The name comes from the colour of the soil, and was mentioned as long ago as 1597 as "Gribbheade, a passage and hyeway for the theefe." There are still signs of an old drove road linking the valleys on either side of the border.

A number of indistinct paths bring you finally to the Scottish border fence which may be easily followed first to Auchope Cairn, and then on to the fence junction (GR 896194) at which the border makes a sharp dog-leg to the west. Here a less prominent fence runs initially eastwards and then northeastwards in a gradual ascent to the trig, built on a high plinth, marking the summit of The Cheviot. The final section is bare peat crossed by a paved way. Formerley, it was a virtually impassable quagmire when wet.

A return the way you came is simple enough, and could be combined with a slight extension to visit The Schil, but a better line is to stay with the fence, following it northeastwards to the col between Lambden Burn and Hawsen Burn, and there to turn west making for Goldscleugh, eventually joining a good track for the final stretch to the hall.

From the summit of The Cheviot to the col there is a good path alongside the fence, and only in the upper reaches of Lambden Burn does it virtually disappear; neither path from Lambden Burn or Hawsen Burn actually strikes the col, meeting instead a short way up the southern slopes of Broadhope Hill, at a gate. The line is correctly shown on the maps, but is far from obvious on the ground.

Walk 4 : Cushat Law and Bloodybush Edge

Maps: (1) OS Landranger 1:50,000 series: Sheet 80 – Cheviot Hills and Kielder Forest; (2) Harveys Walker's Map: Eastern Cheviots

Start: Alwinton. Car park in centre of village, near Hosedon Burn.

Distance: 23 kilometres (14 miles)

Ascent: 575 metres (1885 feet)

Type of walk: At least half of the walk follows good graded forestry tracks, and although the stretch between the two summits is wild and wet moorland, best tackled after dry weather, it is seldom a problem at any time of the year. In spite of its length and ascent, the walk is less arduous than might be supposed, and regular walkers should not be deterred from tackling this circuit of Kidland Forest.

Kidland round

Much of the native forest that once cloaked the rolling hills of Northumberland has gone, to be replaced eventually by Forestry Commission plantations of introduced conifers. In the intervening period, for a few centuries, there existed little more than a vast emptiness, desolate moorland, treeless sheep country stretching grimly from the Roman Wall to the border with Scotland and beyond. Most of the forest that exists now is of recent origin, but Kidland Forest, flanking the southern slopes of Cushat Law, Bloodybush Edge and Yarnspath Law, has existed for many centuries, being under the control of the monks of Newminster Abbey from 1181 until the Dissolution of the Monasteries.

Kidland is still wild country, close to the central massif of the Cheviot Hills, the summits visited on this walk having a grandstand view of much of the long ridge claimed by the Pennine Way and of the upper reaches of the delectable Breamish Valley.

The walk begins in the village of Alwinton where the River Alwin descends to join forces with the Coquet. A study of the map will reveal that north of Alwinton, into the heartlands of The Cheviot, the valleys are narrow and steep-sided, while to the south they relax, becoming broad and shallow. The distinction is due to a fundamental

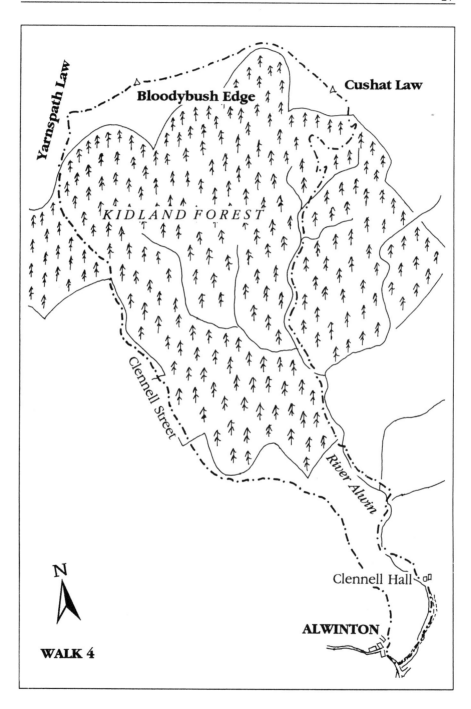

Yarnspath Law

Bloodybush Edge

Cushat Law

KIDLAND FOREST

Clennell Street

River Alwin

N

Clennell Hall

ALWINTON

WALK 4

change in the underlying rock structure; north of Alwinton the rocks are igneous and hard, yielding begrudgingly to the influence of water so that valleys are carved deeply with precipitous sides. At Alwinton, however, the rivers emerge into a region of sedimentary rocks, a strata more easily worn down.

Alwinton, during the Middle Ages was one of the most important junctions on the ancient cross-border highway, Clennell Street, from which radiated tracks across the hills towards the Tweed. Today, it provides the key to the exploration of Kidland and Upper Coquetdale. Nearby Clennell Hall (GR 929071) provides a superb base for visitors to the region, offering ample accommodation whether residential, camping, caravanning or in neat self-contained chalets.

Although cars may be driven a good way into the Alwin Valley, there is much more to be gained from starting at Alwinton and walking in. In any case, without proper authority cars should not venture beyond the forest boundary at GR 920092, below The Dodd.

Just before the bridge over the Alwin, south of the village, a minor road goes left (east), over another bridge and on towards Clennell Hall. Ahead we can already see how dramatically the valley narrows, and there is a keen air of expectancy. Continue ahead, alongside the river, crossing and recrossing until we reach the forest boundary at Kidlandlee Dean. Now follow the forest track along Yoke Burn, later taking the right branch (below Heigh—not named on the Harveys map), heading for Cushat Law. A Cushat is a dove, and the name of the hill is usually taken to mean 'the hill of the wood pigeons', of which Kidland Forest has many.

The onward track cavorts through the upper plantations, and a periodic check on the map at junctions will ensure we eventually emerge safely from the forest at a gate not far from the summit of Cushat Law. A short uphill pull across trackless ground is all that now remains, a matter of minutes to a summit marked by a large cairn, just north of a line of dilapidated fence posts. In a slight hollow, overlooking the upper Breamish valley, beyond which rises the impressive dome of Hedgehope Hill, stands a large circular mound within a ring of stone footings. This is a relaxing spot, and a great access of determination is needed to get going again.

The continuation to Bloodybush Edge has nothing complicated about it, though it tends to be rather wet underfoot. We set off downhill, along the line of redundant fence posts until a more substantial fence is reached, which may now be followed throughout its twists and turns to the summit of Bloodybush Edge.

Possessing neither an edge, as walkers reared on granite or gritstone might understand, nor much in the way of shrubbery, bloodstained or otherwise, Bloodybush Edge perches high above the lonely habitation of Uswayford (pronounced Oosyford) from where it may be ascended with ease.

In spite of the military presence to the south, usually proclaimed by the activities of aerial transport, this is unspoiled, untamed countryside at its best, providing a unique blend of flora and fauna. A springtime visit will find much of the moorland covered with the single white flowers of cloudberry, while autumn sees their transformation to bright orange berries. The forest, too, has its wealth of wildlife, supporting a large number of animal communities. Birds are by far the most obvious, with canopy-feeding insectivorous birds like goldcrest, coal tit and chaffinch forming the bulk of the population. In the less dense parts of the forest a quiet, and fortunate, visitor may startle a woodcock from its daytime camouflage, or spot some of the roe deer that sift softly through the shadows. The commonest bird of the moors is the meadow pipit, but the song of the skylark is never far away, nor the scolding calls of visiting whinchat, wheatear and ring ouzels.

To the southwest of Bloodybush Edge lies the large mound of Yarnspath Law, the col between the two hills being crossed by a track heading to Uswayford. It is by this route that we must now return, following a fenceline to the col, and from there locating the path flanking Yarnspath Law. Do not be tempted into the upper forest by a rather more conspicuous bridleway (which would nevertheless bring you to new forest trails that lead across the treeless top of Sneer Hill, and down to the confluence of White Burn and Lindhope Burn), but make instead for the path entering the forest at GR 891136. Soon this broadens and takes you around Mid Hill to join Clennell Street near the top of Hosden Hope. Now begins the long, but essentially downhill, return to Alwinton, always close by the forest edge and staying with the high ground until, near the remains of a hill fort, the Street finally leaves the hills behind and deposits us back in the valley.

The summit of Cushat Law

Walk 5 : Mozie Law, Beefstand Hill and Lamb Hill

Maps: (1) OS Landranger 1:50,000 series: Sheet 80 – Cheviot Hills and Kielder Forest; (2) Harveys Walker's Map: Western Cheviots

Start: The hamlet of Hownam along Kale Water. GR 779193. Room to park one or two cars only.

Distance: 19 kilometres (12 miles)

Ascent: 510 metres (1675 feet)

Type of walk: A delightful excursion into one of the Bowmont's side valleys, an area seldom visited by walkers. Mainly moorland wandering on generally good paths throughout, with a stretch along the Pennine Way. The views are magnificent.

An away day

The picturesque village of Hownam lies at the confluence of Heatherhope Burn and Kale Water, in a delightful and secluded side valley branching from the main Bowmont valley. This is a spot ideal for a day away from the more popular centres, and has a homely, relaxed air about it.

The three relatively minor summits we visit spread themselves across the Anglo-Scottish border, and though on the face of it superficially uninteresting and invariably hastened over in a state of tired oblivion by Pennine Wayfarers intent on making Kirk Yetholm by the end of the day, they form a fine objective for meandering excursions from both sides of the border. South of the border ridge the hills and moors sprawl massively, stretching out lazily to make room for themselves, and contrast sharply with the pattern of tight, narrow, steep-sided valleys and hummocky ridges that tumble and twist towards the Tweed. The key to the start of this ascent from the north (as indeed it is from the south) is The Street, an ancient drove road linking Upper Coquetdale and the Bowmont valley and at its busiest before the Border troubles which began about 700 years ago.

From Hownam we begin by ascending a prominent track opposite the last house on the right. The track climbs to a large white house (initially obscured) on the hillside, and there we turn right, through a gate to follow the line of The Street which for most of its length is easy to follow. A moment's doubt, however, occurs quite early on, as

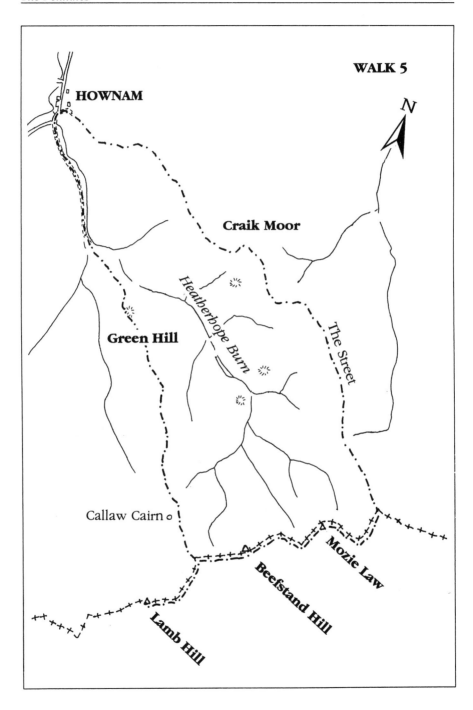

we cross Windy Law, for here greater prominence is given to a broad track used by farmers, but which does not serve our purpose. Keep your eyes open for a gate on the left, beyond which the correct route will be seen running alongside a wall and heading for Craik Moor, an obvious large lump on the left. Once this little test of navigation is passed, the rest is plain sailing, and extremely pleasant.

In springtime the valley slopes are a carpet of wild and mountain pansies, exquisite purple and yellow flowers growing in profusion. This already wild upland is popular with breeding wheatear, curlew, meadow pipit, skylark and lapwing, while overhead the occasional kestrel or cruising buzzard go about their predatory business. Understandably, birds often feature in the naming of places, though many derivations are obscure. 'Yearning', as in Yearning Law, a small hill we shall see later from Lamb Hill, is thought to derive from an Anglo-Saxon word ('erne') meaning 'soarer', in this case believed to apply to the white-tailed eagle, which became extinct in Britain over 60 years ago though now successfully if albeit tenuously reintroduced in remote parts of Scotland; a moving and imaginative tale of the white-tailed eagle's plight is recounted in William Horwood's book *The Stonor Eagles*. Golden eagles, too, occasionally patrol these border hills, harried by crows and other birds of massively inferior size. Other bird names crop up also, as in Gowkhope ('gowk' meaning a cuckoo), Cocklawfoot ('cock' referring to the woodcock) and Corbies Crag (a 'corbie' being a carrion crow, though before long their range overlaps with the hooded crow), and we encountered the woodpigeons of Cushat Law in Walk 4.

The approach to Mozie Law from Hownam; Windy Gyle is the summit on the left.

As we press on over Craik Moor the hillfort on Blackbrough Hill is quite conspicuous, and may be investigated by a short diversion. This whole area contains many similar hillforts built before, during and after the Roman presence. The Blackbrough

Hill fort is a particularly good example, and commands a fine view of the Heatherhope valley.

At the head of Singingside Burn the track bends left to pass through a pair of gates before resuming its upward march to the border. Prominent ahead is the flat pudding of Windy Gyle, sweeping round to the volcanic core that forms The Cheviot and The Schil. Within a kilometre of the ridge, a good path ascends from Heatherhope, and in an emergency this is a good way down; the fact that it, too, forms a pleasant way up is typical of these tight-packed hills, networked as they are by so many ancient trods and drove roads a determined walker could spend a week or more exploring them with little repetition.

Once we reach the border we cross into England to be greeted by the suddenness of the view over Coquetdale. For a moment follow the fence on your right which leads quickly to the top of Mozie Law, its summit marked by a tall post.

We continue now south and east along the fenceline to Beefstand Hill, and on and down to Lamb Hill, some of the more difficult terrain being avoided by granite slabs or strategically placed board-walks. Much of the vegetation along these hills is sparse, mainly mat grass and heather, comfortable to relax upon but otherwise unappealing. Yet for hundreds of years wild goats roamed these hillsides, surviving harsh and often bleak conditions, as far from human civilisation as possible.

To return to Hownam we must retreat from Lamb Hill (which could easily be omitted) towards Beefstand Hill. There is a gate in the border fence at GR 815141, and beyond it another fence and an indistinct path which may be followed to join a much better path on the east side of Thorny Hill. Callow Cairn, prominent on Thorny Hill, is a good target if you are in any way uncertain about the correct direction.

From Thorny Hill we head for a wall running towards Green Hill, and then amble easily downwards to another hillfort at GR 796169. This beautiful spot is a compulsory coffee stop whenever I make this walk, and more than once I have nodded off, exhausted by the effort of appreciating the serenity which surrounds me, the haunting bubbling of curlew filling the springtime air.

Finally, at Greenhill Farm we reach a metalled roadway that leads us quickly to Hownam.

Walk 6 : Windy Gyle via Upper Coquetdale

Maps: (1) OS Landranger 1:50,000 series: Sheet 80 – Cheviot Hills and Kielder Forest; (2) Harveys Walker's Map: Western Cheviots

Start: Confluence of the River Coquet and Rowhope Burn. GR 859114, where there is limited room to park cars.

Distance: 15 kilometres (9.4 miles)

Ascent: 385 metres (1260 feet)

Type of walk: A walk passing for a while along the Anglo-Scottish border, with wonderfully wide-ranging views. Pathways exist throughout the walk, mostly crossing grass- and heather-covered terrain. Even so, this would be an excellent walk on a clear winter's day with crisp snow underfoot. Such ascent as is required, is disposed of in a succession of relatively minor rises, the last of these leading to the summit of Windy Gyle.

Good country, wild country

Forming along their northwestern flank the border between England and Scotland, the Cheviot Hills contain some of the finest, if not *the* finest, walking country in the whole of the Pennine range. It is a region quite unlike any other part of the Pennines, where the hills possess a shapely countenance that is easy on the eye, and which bears an invigorating sense of distance and freedom.

The range is not particularly large, having about it rather more length than width, but as much as from the hills, the Cheviots draw their appeal from radiating valleys of remarkable beauty and tranquillity, in spite of the close presence of a military training area. Crossing the whole of the Cheviots from end to end, as one might if tackling a walk along the Scottish Border, should by rights consume little more than a couple of days; super-fit walkers could complete the whole lot in a single day, but what a waste that would be!

At the southern end around Kielder the landscape has undergone a major transformation; a good part of the North Tyne valley now lies beneath Kielder Water, and the once barren hills are again, as of old, swathed in forests where roe deer flit among serried ranks of spruce like shadows in spring: the trees are of different varieties, of course, but it is pleasing to see the countryside, in this corner of England at least, shaping up much as it might have done 2-3000 years ago. To the north hilltop after hilltop undulates ever higher to the broad flat mound that is The Cheviot itself. In *Walking the Scottish Border* Bob Langley refers to these benign giants as: "Good country, wild country, but with a subtle gentleness that makes it seem like home."

The hills are a relatively recent range formed during the Ice Age, and possess a mixture of volcanic rocks, glacial deposits and granite. For the most part they consist of uncluttered grassy slopes devoid of human habitation, except for the occasional hill farm or shepherd's hut.

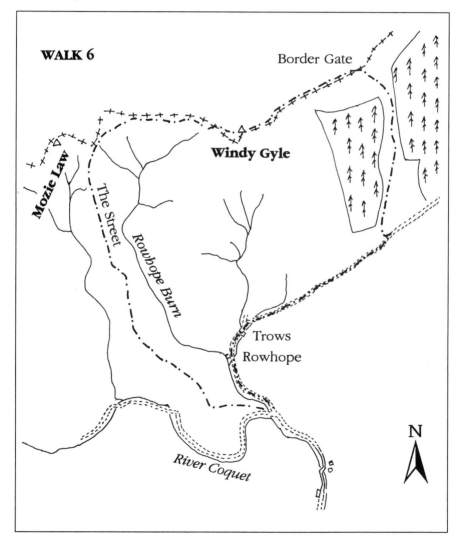

Yet in spite of all this outward calm, the Cheviots are a region that has seldom known peace. They were inhabited long ago by Neolithic man and the Beaker people, by the Romans, who built such outposts as the Chew Green camps, then by the Norse invaders. From the tenth century they were the battlegrounds of the long war of attrition between the Scots and the English, mostly made up of reiving forays when a quick advantage could be taken and long-standing feuds could be nurtured and celebrated in border ballads. Occasionally the hills were the crossroads for a military show of strength by rival monarchs. Now the battles here are the war games of military training, for a good chunk of the central Cheviots is an artillery range, not that this poses problems for walkers.

The Cheviots also comprise the highest ground in the Northumberland National Park, Britain's most northerly, and often neglected, national park, one with few orthodox beauty spots or craggy mountainsides, where virtue lies instead in a subtle and pervasive variety of form and colour, and in an immense richness of flora and fauna.

The long and winding trail to Uswayford

Viewed over the top of Bloodybush Edge from Cushat Law, Windy Gyle (GR 855152), the highest point on this walk, appears as a mere flattened mound of little significance. It is not the highest of the range, for that accolade goes to The Cheviot itself, but it is the focal point of a number of rewarding excursions, some beginning in England, others in Scotland. And, of course, it lies on the Pennine Way.

Essentially it is the approach to Windy Gyle that forms the attraction rather than the mountain itself, which is indeed a flattened mound. But seen from Hindside Knowe (GR 846120) above Rowhope Burn it has a bold, dominating profile, one that unquestionably pulls you on to seek out its summit.

The highest point of the mountain lies in Scotland, and for the single stretch of ground along the Windy Gyle ridge so, too, does the Pennine Way. At either end of the ridge the Way skips back into England. I must confess, however, to a lack of conviction on this point. Careful examination on the ground reveals telltale signs of an earlier fenceline, and these are in places some distance removed from the modern fence. The occasional collapsed fence-post on the old line prompts me to speculate that this marks the true border.

The ascent from Rowhope, on the English side of the border, begins where the River Coquet and Rowhope Burn meet (GR 859114). From here, The Street, an ancient highway and now a Land Rover track, provides a splendid and uncomplicated ascent to the border ridge. The route is never in doubt, ascending steadily over a succession of minor summits to join the Pennine Way a short way east of Mozie Law (GR 829150). As you walk, the view all around, hemmed in lower down by steep-sided hills, starts to open up, and gives a fine sense of careless freedom, an excellent weekend panacea for weekday ills.

Much of the ground to the south and west as you ascend falls within the Otterburn Artillery Ranges and Training Area, and sections of The Street cross uncleared ground. Warning flags are flown whenever there is activity on the ranges, and notices advise against picking up things "which may explode and kill you". The circumstances, however, are far less dire than the warnings, if they are obeyed, and no one should be deterred from visiting this exquisite corner of England.

From the junction with the Pennine Way a good track, the Way itself, continues across the intermediate bump of Windy Rig before tackling a short pull to the top of Windy Gyle.

Although the true position of the border may be in doubt, the highest point of Windy Gyle is anything but. An untidy cairn of monumental proportions and surmounted by a trig point is conspicuous for some distance. On most maps this is identified as Russell's Cairn, named, it is claimed, after Lord Francis Russell, though the claim may be false. It seems that in mid-1585, when the border troubles were at their height, Sir Thomas Kerr of Ferniehurst, Scotland, and Sir John Forster of England took their places at a Warden's Court somewhere high on the ridge to deal with complaints and offenders from both sides of the border. Lord Francis Russell, Forster's son-in-law, was also present though he was the object of a grudge nursed by Kerr over the matter of the interception of coded messages. During the meeting a disturbance broke out among some bystanders which Russell attempted to quell, and for his pains received a bullet in the chest from which he died. Whether the killing was accidental or contrived is not clear, though subsequently Kerr was removed from his wardenship. In commemoration of the incident some of Russell's soldiers are said to have built a cairn at the place where he died, hence Russell's Cairn. Dispute, however, a constant hallmark of the Border region, surrounds even this tantalising snippet of border history, for there is evidence to date the cairn to prehistoric, probably Bronze Age, times.

From the summit of Windy Gyle continue northeastwards, towards The Cheviot, which graces the skyline ahead, following the border fenceline to the Border Gate at GR 871160. Many times I have sat high along this stretch of the border gazing first this way into England, then that way into Scotland, each time overcome by a fine sense of relaxation and peace that more than once has had me whiling away the hours resting on a comfortable bed of heather with the call of the curlew and the buzzard's cry seeming like distant echoes from a long lost time.

At the Border Gate the ridge is crossed by another ancient highway, Clennel Street, which if followed southwards will bring you into the Usway valley, near Hepden Burn. Nearby stands Uswayford, a remote habitation in a wild cradle among the hills, passing time by in a most beautiful of inner sanctums, Upper Coquetdale, a valley to rival any in the Pennines and many in Lakeland or across the border in Scotland.

The return to Rowhope Burn is downhill and delightful, easily effected, and requires no more than to follow a good path, south, passing to the west of Hazely Law to join a more substantial track descending rather more steeply to meet the Uswayford track. This is a graded track, rough at first, but metalled once Trows (GR 855125) is reached, and allows an ambling end to a splendid circuit.

Just after the Border Gate a couple of tracks go east and southeast, initially rather less obvious than the main line. The second of these leads to Uswayford itself, and affords a slightly longer return for walkers with energy in reserve.

Variant: Along the ridge over Windy Gyle it is impossible not to feel drawn to the Bowmont valley and its tributaries beyond, the scene is one of pastoral loveliness. The upper reaches of the side valleys, Bowmont Water and Calroust Burn, are seldom visited by walkers, though two places, Calroust (GR 824192) and Cocklawfoot (GR 853186 — which lies on the continuation of Clennel Street, mentioned earlier) both provide the opportunity for varying this walk by an approach from the Scottish side.

Walkers seeking a longer day among these fine hills might like to consider starting at Rowhope Burn, ascending by The Street to Windy Gyle, then retracing their steps to descend Windy Rig to Cocklawfoot before returning uphill to the Border Gate and the Usway valley along Clennell Street. This would give a circuit of 22 kilometres (13.75 miles), with ascent of 765 metres (2510 feet).

Walk 7: Carter Bar via Peel Fell to Kielder Water

Maps: (1) OS Landranger 1:50,000 series: Sheet 80 – Cheviot Hills and Kielder Forest area; (2) OS Explorer 1:25,000 series: Sheet 1 – Kielder Water (covers this walk from Peel Fell)

Start: Carter Bar, on the A68 trunk road. Mobile refreshment bars often turn up here in summer.

Distance: 32.5 kilometres (20 miles)

Ascent: 470 metres (1540 feet)

Type of walk: A long linear walk happily combining high moorland and forest trails, and necessitating the solution of transport problems. The walk can be terminated satisfactorily at Kielder Castle, thereby reducing the distance to 21 kilometres (13 miles), but the trails on the north side of the Kielder Reservoir provide a more fitting, and historically interesting, conclusion to a walk of some substance. Most of the first part of the walk is to all intents and purposes trackless, and likely to be spent well away from the summer crowds that gather both at Carter Bar and around the Kielder Reservoirs. On the moors a surfeit of cotton grass betrays the generally wet conditions underfoot, though these often dry to a firm walking base in summer. The trails around Kielder are invariably well maintained.

Among the hungry hills . . .

The southernmost undulations of the Cheviot Hills cloak themselves in the massive shawl of spruce, Scots pine and larch that makes up Kielder Forest, claimed to be the largest man-made forest in Europe. The greater part lies just to the south of the border between Scotland and England, ringed by an orbit of old established villages, many of mid-18th century origin, set up as centres for local industry mainly due to the initiative of private landowners.

To the north, the Newcastle-Edinburgh road reaches its highest point at Carter Bar, a breathtaking spot, but sadly often cluttered with cars, caravans, motor coaches and querulous tourists. This ancient crossing frequently becomes blocked with snow in

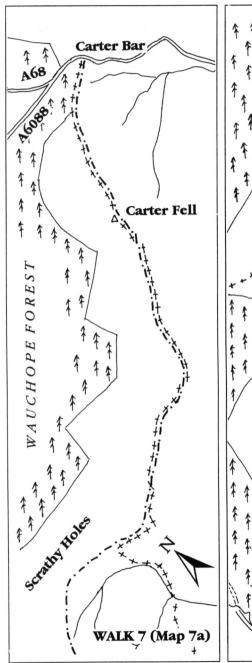

WALK 7 (Map 7a)

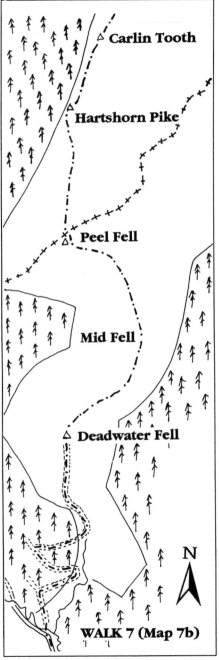

WALK 7 (Map 7b)

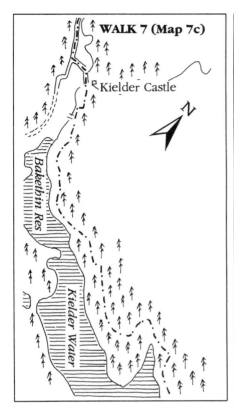

WALK 7 (Map 7c)

R Kielder Castle

N

Bakethin Res

Kielder Water

Plashetts

Kielder Water

P

Hawkhope

N

WALK 7 (Map 7d)

winter, though such an inconvenience was of little apparent consequence to the determined travellers of that famous coach, the Chevy Chase, which crossed the hills by this route in the early 1800s. In those days this was an isolated and desperate spot, and the horses that pulled the coach up a gradient which even now fazes some modern cars, must have possessed formidable strength, and their passengers far more tolerance than modern-day counterparts, judging by the impatience I have witnessed on the long ascent to the top of the pass. Sadly, by the mid-1840s, when the link between the English and Scottish railways was completed at Berwick, the coach service had declined to oblivion.

The traverse of the moorland hills lying to the south of Carter Bar begins abruptly. Carter Fell, a long, double-topped whaleback rises steeply from Carter Bar, a path of sorts setting off along the boundary of Wauchope Forest and following the fenceline that marks the national boundary. Catcleugh Shin, however, holds no fear that its initially steep beginning will continue, for soon the gradient lessens and easy ground crossed to the lonely trig pillar that marks the summit and provides the only shelter on a windy day. The view is expansive, but is restricted by the broad plateau of Carter Fell. Walkers with ample time should deviate to the large cairn at the head of Black Cleugh (not immediately visible from the summit) from where there is a good view of Catcleugh Reservoir and the long valley of Redesdale.

The continuation to Carlin Fell's lower summit and Carlin Tooth, fine moorland wandering if the conditions underfoot are dry, initially follows the border fence to the col at the head of Black Burn where, if we have not already done so, we cross into Scotland. From the col, ascend northwest to Scrathy Holes and then southwest, gazing steeply down on the Wauchope Forest, to Carlin Tooth. Due south, above the limb of Hartshorn Pike rises Peel Fell, the highest of the afforested summits south of Redesdale.

A short dip and a steady plod place us easily on Peel Fell from where we begin to gain a real impression of the massive forest called Kielder.

Since Norman times most of Britain has been continuously deforested, with the result that the country became one of the least wooded in Europe, and in consequence dangerously dependent on imported timber. Kielder Forest was planned and planted expressly to reverse this trend and hundreds of millions of trees, mainly sitka and Norway spruce, Scots pine and Japanese larch, have been planted in Kielder and its associate forests since the 1920s. In the space of but two generations one of the largest man-made forests in Europe was created, dramatically changing the landscape and the economy of the area. Whether Kielder is indeed the largest man-made forest in Europe is debatable, but it certainly represents one of the largest experiments in forestry and land management ever undertaken in Western Europe, one that is still on-going.

On Peel Fell we rejoin the Anglo-Scottish border, identified by a series of 'bounder' stones, with the letter N (for the Duke of Northumberland) on the southern side, and a reversed D (due to the stonemason holding the template the wrong way round) on the northern 'Douglas' face. From here, on a clear day, there is a splendid panorama, northwest to the Southern Uplands, northeast to the upper reaches of Jed Water and the red-tinged Border Lowlands.

We descend from Peel Fell to an intermediate top, Mid Fell, following the remains of a fenceline that may not see many more years. On Mid Fell there is a large cairn-shelter, a fine place to rest and take in the many minor Kielder summits and the distant swell of the higher Cheviot Hills.

A damp passage across Deadwater Moor takes us to Deadwater Fell, a summit cluttered with buildings and radio masts. Deadwater Fell is a watershed from where rain can run northwest to Solway Firth or southeast to Newcastle upon Tyne. Its name springs from the local view that because the stream at the foot of the fell is slow moving, as if undecided whether to opt for Scotland or England, and so contrasts with the numerous torrents that otherwise abound in these hills, it is called 'dead' water.

A broad path, servicing the summit buildings, now speeds us down from Deadwater Fell and into forest before emerging near Ravenshill, where a footpath, a little distorted by forestry work from that shown on the map, takes us down to Kielder. On the southern slopes of Ravenshill may be found all that remains of old Kielder, tradition-ally the home of the Cout of Kielder. The Cout or Colt of Kielder was Sir Richard Knout or Knut, who died on an uncertain date around 1290. Gone without trace is the former Kielder Castle in which Earl Thomas Percy and his wife took refuge in 1569 as they fled from Queen Elizabeth's fury after the Catholic 'Rising of the Northern Earls'. The present castle, which houses a visitor centre, is of no great antiquity, and was built in 1771/75 by William Newton for Earl Percy as a hunting lodge.

Before us now stand the waters of the massive Kielder Reservoir. A shortage of

Kielder Castle

water has never been one of Kielder's problems, and the hillsides flow with countless streams eventually to feed the North Tyne, the Rede, the Irthing and Liddel Water. Unlike many lowland waters, the streams and rivers of Kielder are 'spate' rivers, more responsive to fluctuations in rainfall, and within a matter of hours transforming innocent trickles into raging, peat-stained torrents. Work on the main reservoir, part of the Kielder Water Scheme, started in April, 1976, and the reservoir filled by the spring of 1982. Owners of the Ordnance Survey First or Second Series 1:50,000 map of this region, which pre-date the completion of the reservoir, can see how far the Scheme has affected this delightful valley by comparing it with the present day Landranger map. To avoid unsightly mud flats a second reservoir, Bakethin, was constructed at the upper end of Kielder Water, near the village, and this, together with the surrounding forest area, is now a nature conservation area.

The walk may be conveniently ended at Kielder, but, for strong walkers, just south of Kielder Castle a bridge spans the North Tyne river, and gives access to a forest trail that follows the line of Bakethin Reservoir, never straying far from the water until it reaches Plashetts Bay. Though difficult to believe now, there was a time when Plashetts and Bellingburn were the scene of much coal-mining activity. Coal had been known by the valley folk for centuries, and hacked from surface seams by the bucketful to enliven their smouldering peat fires. In 1851, permission was given to two gamekeepers to re-open a derelict drift mine near Plashetts on condition that they delivered coal for the fires of Kielder Castle. It soon became clear that the deposit was rich and extensive, but it was not until a company was formed in 1855 to build a railway to link Scotland with Newcastle that the possibilities for commercial exploitation became evident. The venture, however, was not successful, much of the coal turned out to be of poor quality and working conditions remote and difficult. As elsewhere, the General Strike of 1926 dealt an almost fatal blow to the industry, which by then had confined itself to the area around Plashetts: the workings were flooded and the mine never properly re-opened. More than forty years on the village exists as but a few foundations hidden amongst the grass, the railway has gone and the open moorland which then prevailed lies carpeted by spruce and pine. That there is a postscript is a tribute to the determination of the people of these parts, for in recent years a local family operating a small work force have sought out the old mines, and began once more digging in search of Plashett's black diamonds.

From Plashetts the main trial heads east across a broad promontory to Belling Burn and on through Hawkhope Forest to a parking place near the dam of Kielder Water. On Gilbert's *Iolanthan* principle: 'In for a penny, in for a pound', the shortcut between Plashett's Burn and Belling Burn can be given up in favour of a delightful but longer amble around the edge of Bellingburn promontory and Wind Hill, rejoining the original route where Belling Burn flows into Kielder Water.

Walk 8: A walk along Hadrian's Wall

Maps: (1) OS Landranger 1:50,000 series: Sheet 87 – Hexham and Haltwhistle; (2) OS 1:25,000 Historical Map: 'Hadrian's Wall'

Start: Steel Rigg. GR 751676. Car park.

Distance: 18 kilometres (11.25 miles)

Ascent: 570 metres (1870 feet)

Type of walk: An easy walk alongside the wall, followed by field paths that are in places muddy. **Note:** To fully appreciate this walk some fundamental knowledge is essential; an introduction follows, but this should be supplemented by a visit to the Museum at Vindolanda Fort (GR 771664), containing a full-size replica of a Wall section, and the Museum of the Roman Army (GR 667658) near Greenhead.

"... qui barbaros Romanosque divideret."

"To separate the Romans from the barbarians" is the only surviving Roman comment on the reason for building Hadrian's Wall. Inevitably, its mere presence poses many questions: Why, almost eighty years after the emperor Claudius invaded Britain in AD 43, should Hadrian, his tenth successor as emperor, decide in AD 122 that the Roman Empire should be given artificial boundaries where no natural ones existed; and why, in Britain, should that boundary take the form of a wall, effectively to separate the inhabitants, willing or unwilling, of the Empire, from the barbarians outside?

Why should the Wall, still in the process of modification, be abandoned for a new Wall in Scotland, the Antonine Wall; and why was that, too, later abandoned and a return made to Hadrian's Wall? Many answers to these and other questions are conjecture; other notions arise from a detailed study of the Roman occupation of Britain: a fascinating topic.

Throughout the Pennines, evidence of the Roman occupation is met with constantly – mine workings here, camps and forts there. Yet nowhere is the profile of their presence so raised, in this case quite literally, as along Hadrian's Wall. It is undeniably a massive monument, a testimony to the legionnaires who built it almost 2000 years ago, a commemoration of the soldiers who guarded it for two and a half centuries, and a salute (if you believe the Roman occupation was of no benefit to Britain) to the Pictish barbarians who finally overran it at the beginning of the Dark Ages.

The strength of the Roman Empire lay in the power and might of its Army, unparalleled in world history, an Army unbeatable on its chosen battle ground, the open field. This outstanding ability meant that Roman history essentially is a story of a nation trying to live with the incredible success of its Army. Even so, when Hadrian came to power in AD 117 he found trouble in Britain, his records revealing that "the Britons could not be kept under Roman control". Perhaps, then, it was in response to the disorders he found at the beginning of his reign that Hadrian elected to deal with the northern frontier in Britain. In the absence of a natural frontier, the sea, a river, the desert, as had been used in other parts of the world, Hadrian chose to build a massive barrier, supported by an existing network of roadways, in this case, the Stanegate, which would allow his Army to deal with small-scale movements of people, prevent raiding parties and large-scale attacks, and generally encourage the peaceful development of the province.

The resultant Wall spans England at its narrowest point, the neck of land between the North Sea at the Tyne to the Solway Firth at Carlisle. It was planned to be 76 Roman miles long (1481 metres/1620 yards: just over 113 kilometres, about 70 miles). Throughout much of its length the view to the north from the Wall is good, in other places expansive or restricted often according to the lie of the land.

Not all of the Wall remains in a good state of preservation, the western 31 Roman miles were in any case constructed from turf, not stone, more susceptible to collapse but less prone to the vandalism and stone-theft which occurred in later years when building materials were in demand to construct the walls and buildings of castles and farms. This walk, however, visits the best maintained section, lying within the Northumberland National Park, where the supporting roads, ditches and forts have been preserved from the march of progress and the mindless whims of vandals.

Often, throughout Britain, we recognise the handiwork of Roman engineers as much by the directness of their route lines as anything else. But here, on the northern frontier, they abandoned the most direct line and took advantage of a natural offering, an undulating ridge of quartz-dolerite called Whin Sill, which intruded into the surrounding sedimentary strata to form a craggy escarpment facing north, and of great military significance. The Cawfield – Steel Rigg – Housesteads section, with which we are primarily concerned, is typical of the way the Wall was constructed throughout most of its length, wherever possible running along the top of steep cliffs.

The Wall, whether built of stone or turf, was not a closed frontier as is sometimes supposed. At intervals of one Roman mile fortified gateways were built, and conventionally these have become known as milecastles, of which there are three – 39, 38 and 37 – between Steel Rigg and Housesteads, and the remains of one more, Milecastle 42, near Cawfields. Milecastles provided a way through the wall, having double gates at front and rear, and a few seem to have been surrounded by a ditch.

From the fir-lined Steel Rigg car park a path leads along the edge of a field to a gate giving direct access on to the Wall, continuing east above Peel Crags to Steel Rigg and the first milecastle, number 39. In Roman times the Wall was much higher,

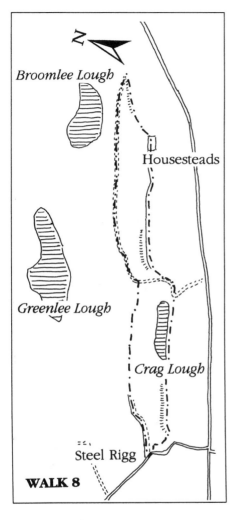

Broomlee Lough

Housesteads

Greenlee Lough

Crag Lough

Steel Rigg

WALK 8

and while we may not be walking exactly where Romans once trod, we may nevertheless experience a keen sense of history all around us. Gazing northwards, to the dark plantations of Henshaw Common and Wark Forest and the soft, moulded Cheviot foothills, we might with a little imagination begin to visualise the bleak sight which must have faced the Roman legions. Modern pasturelands and grassy fields now largely replace the heather, bracken and scrub that lay north of the Wall 2000 years ago, but little else will have changed. Southwards across the Tyne Gap, the Pennines rise to the hazy, purple heights of Cold Fell, Melmerby Fell and Cross Fell, and this cold, windswept, distant corner of the Roman Empire must have seemed like the last place on earth to soldiers of a warmer climate and far from home.

Just beyond Milecastle 39 is Crag Lough, one of the most beautiful of Northumberland lakes, lush and green, decorated by trees and backed by dramatic steep crags; this is a popular place with wildfowl, especially in winter when whooper swans and wild geese — pink-footed and greylag — visit here. The lough and surrounding farmland, as well as a good stretch of the Wall, including the Housesteads fort are owned by the National Trust.

Through the plantation of pine, wych elm and sycamore bordering Crag Lough we reach Hotbank Lane, followed by a short steep pull past the grass-covered ruins of Milecastle 38 to reach Hotbank Crags. From this splendid vantage point four lakes may be picked out. Immediately west lies Crag Lough; to the southeast Grindon Lough, one of the finest bird-watching sites in the area. North is Greenlee Lough, and northeast Broomlee. None of these loughs is deep, having been created during the Ice Age by scouring of the bedrock to form shallow basins. What will become of these charming lakes is uncertain; some old maps show Caw Lough (not named on the 1:50,000 map), near West Hotbank, as an area of open water. But there is nothing to see of it now, and it may be presumed both that many more similar loughs existed centuries ago, and that those that remain will share the same fate one day.

Beyond Hotbank Crags rise Cuddy's Crags, but between them a natural cleft in the Whin Sill, known as Rapishaw Gap, marks the spot where the Pennine Way, which has accompanied us from Steel Rigg, finally takes its leave and sets out northeast across marshy ground on the final leg of its journey northwards.

Cawfield Crags and quarry pond

Cuddy's Crags are named from St Cuthbert whose body is supposed to have been laid here en route from Lindisfarne to Durham. A short distance further and we find Milecastle 37, by far the best preserved of all the milecastles. It was excavated in 1853 by John Clayton, former Town Clerk of Newcastle, and a gifted amateur in matters of excavation. On clearing away much of the rubbish he discovered an inscribed stone set up by the second legion (Legion II) saying this section of the Wall had been built under the governorship of Aulus Platorius Nepos, a friend of Hadrian's and chosen by him to oversee the building of the Wall, a sort of early-day Clerk of Works.

Soon we will leave the Wall for a while, but first we unavoidably encounter the major fort, Vercovicium, at Housesteads, once a 1000-man garrison, and unquestionably the best Roman fort to be seen not only on the Wall, but almost certainly in

Europe. It is *the* most popular attraction along the Wall if the number of times it has been photographed is any indication.

Close by Housesteads is a wide saddle, Knag Burn, where a new gate was introduced into the Wall during the fourth century, and beyond this we climb again above Broomlee Lough to continue to a stile/gate at GR 798694.

Now we leave the Wall for a while, and pass north through it following yellow waymarkers, back below Hotbank Crags, Crag Lough and Steel Rigg. While the going underfoot is not as pleasant as it might be along this stretch, some idea may be gleaned of what the Wall must have looked like to anyone from the north contemplating an assault; it's quite daunting even now.

Once within the vicinity of Steel Rigg we can elect to finish the walk, having completed 10 kilometres (6.25 miles). With time and inclination on our side we can continue westwards, to visit Milecastle 42.

Follow the lane (right) around Melkridge Common and the subsequent footpath (indistinct) across fields to the farm track leading to Cawfields Farm and so on to the car park/picnic area at Cawfields (GR 713666) and its attendant quarry lake.

Pass north of the lake and head east again, once more on the Pennine Way, ascending easily back to the ridge crest and the skeletal remains of Milecastle 42). The ensuing walk along Cawfield Crags and Windshields Crag accompanies the best preserved section of the Wall, and rises to the highest point on the Whin Sill, marked by a trig pillar. From this high point with, on a good day, its wide-ranging views, a quick descent may be made to reach the lane near Steel Rigg car park.

Walk 9: Weardale: Burnhope Seat and Killhope Law

Maps: OS Landranger 1:50,000 series: Sheet 87 — Hexham and Haltwhistle
and Sheet 91 — Appleby-in-Westmorland

Start: Ireshopeburn, upper Weardale. GR 865387.

Distance: 32 kilometres (20 miles)

Ascent: 605 metres (1985 feet)

Type of walk: A long and challenging walk over undulating, heather-clad
moorlands around the upper Weardale watershed. The stretch between
Scaud Hill and Burnhope Seat is especially boggy in wet conditions, and in
poor visibility potentially confusing, though for most of the route
navigation is not a problem.

A boundary walk

Travellers passing through Weardale bound for Alston might well wonder if there is
a way out through the dark, brooding ring of moorland hills that hems in the dale
beyond Wearhead, for it seems not. The heather-clad hills extend in a massive arc
around the dale head, forming the boundary between Durham and Cumbria or
Northumberland. This is barren, open country, a place where strong walkers will find
their Mecca, while lesser mortals, like me, have to worry at chunks of it over a number
of repeat visits. Like a magnet the bleakness of the hills draws those who love solitude
and a bit of rough going, repelling walkers whose tread seeks only well-ordered
pathways: no noisome crowds here, unless you come in winter when many of the
hillsides resound to the excitement of skiers.

We begin from the village of Ireshopeburn, like others in the dale a straggling
collection of buildings dotted where purpose decreed along the banks of the River
Wear, and take a minor road leading to High Rigg and the Burnhope Reservoir. Not
far beyond the turning to the reservoir the road degenerates to a narrow track, easing
upwards uneventfully, but with improving retrospective views of the reservoir. Our
first objective is Great Stony Hill, its summit a great rash of stones rising from the
middle of wild moorland carpeted with heather, bilberry and cloudberry, all seeming
constant companions wherever we may be in the Pennines. To reach Great Stony Hill

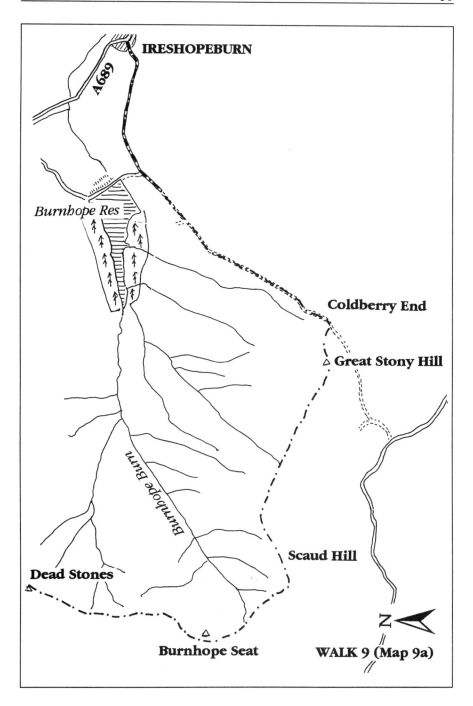

WALK 9 (Map 9a)

we must follow the track as far as Coldberry End, leaving it at its highest point to head for the trig across predominantly grassy terrain punctuated by islands of stones.

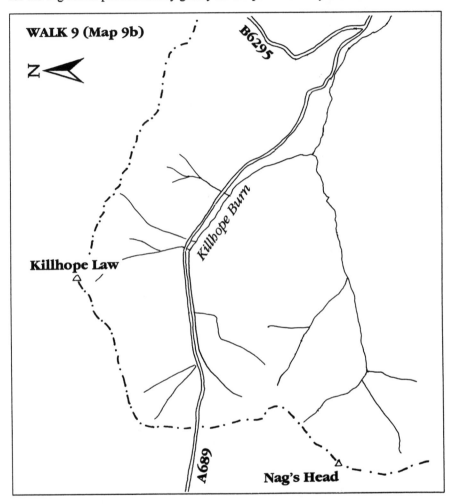

The stretch between Great Stony Hill and Burnhope Seat is the worst and most trying part of the whole walk, and not an undertaking to be considered in poor visibility even with a dilapidated fenceline as a guide. The going becomes progressively more difficult, calling for frequent deviations to negotiate the worst groughs and bogs. The summit of Scaud Hill is marked by a small cairn, at an elevation of 718 metres (GR 795363), and not where the 1:50,000 map locates it. From the cairn on Scaud Hill we basically head northwest, fairly secure in the knowledge that we will intersect the fence on the Cumbria-Durham boundary at some stage; ideally we want the dog-leg

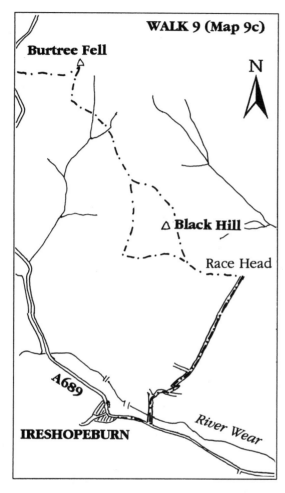

WALK 9 (Map 9c)

Burtree Fell

N

△ **Black Hill**

Race Head

A689

River Wear

IRESHOPEBURN

at GR 791369, from there to trudge upwards to the top of Burnhope Seat. The highest point (spot height 747) is marked by a small cairn, due west of the trig pillar, and lies in Cumbria. The trig, however, complete with a neat flight of steps, marks the highest point in Durham.

Northwards our route lies to Dead Stones, to which we are guided by the boundary fence. Conditions underfoot, while still damp, will have improved immensely since our slitherings on Scaud Hill. The summit is marked by a tall thin cairn on the Durham side of the fence, with a roofed stone shelter nearby looking down on Burnhope Moor to Wearhead and St John's Chapel.

Still with the fence, and wide, sweeping views to occupy the mind, we continue ever northwards to Nag's Head, where, a few hundred metres off the boundary line we can locate a small cluster of medieval crosses, similar to Killhope Cross, which we will encounter shortly. Fences and walls alternate as we head for Knoutberry Hill and Killhope Cross at the summit of the A689, at 627 metres (2057 feet) the highest A-road in England.

Continuing northwards we soon meet the boundary of Northumberland, and here sweep northeastwards to Killhope Law, and its unmistakable summit. Though far from obvious to the undiscerning eye these hills, on the frontier of three counties, are the scene of man's greatest endeavour to win lead from the landscape. Everywhere remains of industry abound, in the villages, dotted across the hillsides, high in the radiating dales. Mine shafts are encountered all over the place, and from time to time our sweeping eye alights on ruined smelt mills, some with tall chimneys designed to carry the poisonous fumes away from the smelters; a tired, lifeless testimony to an energetic era of man's industrious past, now like so many things consigned to the useless by the force we call progress.

Killhope Cross now marks the summit of the highest A-road in England

From Killhope Law it is in a sense, if not quite literally, all downhill. We continue along the broad ridge heading towards the B6295, from where, in but a few minutes, we can reach the top of Burtree Fell. The highest point lies on the county boundary, and anyone attempting to reach the nearby trig point will wallow in marshy ground. Since our final target is Black Hill, we can fortunately make use of a path (shown on the map) running southeast beneath the summit plateau. This intersects with a green bridleway leading to Race Head, where we can return to Ireshopeburn on the minor road linking Lintzgarth and St John's Chapel.

Walk 10: Cross Fell from Kirkland

Map: OS Landranger 1:50,000 series: Sheet 91 – Appleby-in-Westmorland

Start: Kirkland Church. GR 646325. There is a limited amount of parking adjoining the church.

Distance: 14 kilometres (9 miles)

Ascent: 690 metres (2265 feet)

Type of walk: The first half of the route follows the line of an old corpse road on which the gradients are gentle enough. Once across the summit plateau of Cross Fell the line of return, across open hillside, is not always evident on the ground, but presents no difficulty of route-finding in good weather.

A Wall of Brass

Better known perhaps for his *Robinson Crusoe* and *Moll Flanders*, Daniel Defoe was equally at home exploring the length and breadth of Britain, though his accounts were often idiosyncratically naive and not always accurate. Of the Pennines, lying "like a wall of brass" along the eastern edge of Westmorland, he had little to say, and from that one might suppose they were not worth bothering with. Nothing, thankfully, could be further from the truth.

Drawing to their greatest height at the very spot where the River Tees begins its long journey to the North Sea, and overlooking the massively broad Eden valley, the Pennines form a seemingly impenetrable barrier between the Land of the Lakes, which had commanded rather more of Mr Defoe's attention, and the moorlands of Cumberland and Westmorland and what was the North Riding of Yorkshire.

A casual study of the map suggests that Cross Fell, indisputably the highest of the Pennines and once thought to boast an even greater height than its 893 metres (2930 feet), promises only long and tedious walks. But only the flat, bleak and windswept summit plateau itself disappoints, and the arrival here of walkers who have trudged from Edale or Kirk Yetholm along the Pennine Way must evince an awful anti-climax. The rest is sheer delight, however; Cross Fell is an imposing mountain, simple of line and structure, and offering the walker a splendid selection of ascents, well worthy of its status.

In fine weather, the mountain has an avuncular appearance, and seems a calm, endearing place to visit. Alas, all is not as it seems, for its repertoire of dirty tricks includes sub-zero temperatures on at least a third of the days of the year, rain on two-thirds, and snow often well into summer. If that isn't enough, its *pièce de résistance* is a phenomenon known as the Helm Wind, a remarkably ferocious and localised gusting of the wind.

Two large cairns on the edge of Cross Fell's summit plateau mark the descent to Tees Head

The precise nature of the Helm Wind is neatly summarised in *Legends and Historical Notes of North Westmoreland* by Thomas Gibson (1887): "the air or wind from the east, ascends the gradual slope of the western (sic) side of the Pennine chain ... to the summit of Cross Fell, where it enters the helm or cap, and is cooled to a less temperature; it then rushes forcibly down the abrupt declivity of the western side of the mountain into the valley beneath, in consequence of the valley being of a warmer temperature, and this constitutes the Helm-Wind. The sudden and violent rushing of the wind down the ravines and crevices of the mountain, occasions the loud noise that is heard." As for its force, Thomas Wilkinson of Yanwath, a Quaker friend of Wordsworth, describes in his *Tour to the British Mountains* (1824), how "if I advanced it was with my head inclined to the ground, and at a slow pace; it I retreated and leaned against it with all my might, I could hardly keep erect; if I did not resist it, I was blown over."

With such a pedigree it is small wonder that Cross Fell's original name was Fiends'

Fell, before St Augustine (it is claimed) erected a cross on its summit, and built an altar to celebrate the Holy Eucharist in order to scatter the resident devils. Camden thought this "an extraordinary piece of devotion . . . to erect Crosses and build Chapels in the most eminent places, as being both nearer Heaven and more conspicuous." It any demons had the strength of purpose to remain in the face of such overwhelming Christianity there is every likelihood they finally packed their bags and left when, in days when political fervour was greater than it is today, some fifty brass bands gathered on the summit to celebrate the passing of the Reform Act in 1832.

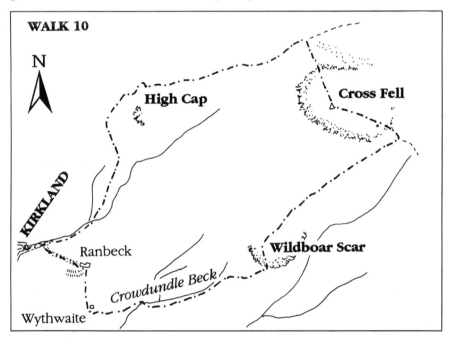

In spite of its unappealing summit and the high incidence of clouds which bedevil the mountain, Cross Fell is a superb viewpoint, taking in the fells of Lakeland, dotting the horizon beyond the Eden valley, and extending far across the northern countryside into Scotland.

Daniel Defoe's observation likening the Pennines to a wall of brass was innocently close to the mark for they formed for a long time the mainstay of a substantial industry in the extraction of lead ore. The mountain may look solid enough, but it is honey-combed by shafts and levels that contributed to a total yield, primarily during the eighteenth and nineteenth centuries, of over 3 million tons from the North Pennine fields alone. Nor was lead ore the only mineral to be won. From 1725 to 1870 the amount of silver refined from lead was approximately 5.5 million ounces.

Walkers tackling the Pennine Way will find the day which includes Cross Fell a long one, extending from Dufton to Garrigill, or Alston, and taking on board three other summits before even reaching Cross Fell. Less demanding walks however await the visitor with only a day to spare, or the need to return to a car at the starting point. And perhaps the finest of these, largely avoiding the Pennine Way, begins from the village of Kirkland, where there is parking to be found near the church (GR 646325).

This route, often used by hang-gliders who power their heavily laden four-wheel drives up it to gain the heights of High Cap, is an old corpse road linking the church and graveyard at Kirkland with the distant community of Garrigill. In the seventeenth century one funeral party, caught in a blizzard high on the mountainside, abandoned its burden, scurrying back to Garrigill, and returning only two weeks later for the coffin when it was finally considered safe to recover it. The mourners then brought the coffin back to Garrigill where it was buried in a piece of glebe land, subsequently consecrated by the Bishop of Durham as a burial ground in an act terminating future need for the corpse road, at least so far as the dead were concerned.

From the church, return to the nearby road junction and turn left to follow a road and later a good track along Kirkland Beck, taking you out on to the moors and curving north to skirt High Cap, a prominent bump due west of Cross Fell's summit. The gradient, nowhere unduly steep, is eased by a few bends, and on reaching gentler ground a few old pits might be found. Within sight of the summit plateau the corpse road bears sharply left, and here we can leave it to head eastwards on a cairned and grassy path, passing ultimately around the northern scree slopes of Cross Fell to locate the Pennine way on its hurried descent to Garrigill. On a clear day you could make for the summit as soon as you feel happy about it, although this entails negotiating a broad stretch of loose scree and some wet ground. But the line taken by the Pennine Way is clear enough, though initially also wet underfoot as it climbs away from the descent to Garrigill. It soon dries out, and a line of cairns steers us uneventfully to the summit shelter-cairn and trig point.

Having ascended to the highest point of the Pennines a return by the same route doesn't want for a lack of imagination: surely there is a better option than simply retreating the way we have come. Well, we can press on across the summit plateau, aiming towards the summit of Great Dun Fell and its conspicuous masts and globular radar station, and near the edge of the plateau a number of large cairns mark the way down to Tees Head. This proves to be the key to the completion of quite a pleasant round trip.

From Tees Head a cairned path, not immediately obvious and narrow in places, heads southwest across what is initially bouldery terrain to another cairn on the edge of Wildboar Scar (GR 679326). If you can't locate the line of cairns leaving Tees Head simply drop beneath the downfall of scree and boulders and skirt along its lower edge until cairns appear in the far distance, for which you can make. This stretch is open moorland, and there is an invigorating sense of freedom, with, more than likely, the whole place to yourselves, the Eden valley rolling away ahead of us, and the Lakeland fells sitting like a frieze on the skyline.

Wildboar Scar is nothing more than an abrupt escarpment, grassy, rounded and sporting a much clearer path. Ahead lies the dome of Grumply Hill, with the path keeping north of it (right) to join one of the tributaries of Crowdundle Beck, a place well suited to long rests on sunny afternoons.

Onwards the path descends easily through a sheep-fold and across a tract of ground scented in spring and early summer with gorse, to a large ruined barn at Wythwaite (GR 654317), with a fine retrospective view of Great Dun Fell in particular. At the right time of year this enchanting section of moorland resounds to the eerie call of the golden plover, as white-rumped wheatears dart about and chatter busily, and curlew bubble a constant accompaniment.

Once at Wythwaite we turn right, through a dilapidated gate, and follow a good track to a curious feature marked on the map as the Hanging Walls of Mark Antony. Precisely what they are, or were, is open to question, and other than a series of mounds, claimed by some to be natural, there is little to see. Certainly local inhabitants seem unimpressed, questioning whether Mark Antony even ventured to Britain, and suggesting that the only thing Roman about the mounds is the name.

From this strange place it is only a short walk along a good track back to the church at Kirkland.

Walk 11: Cross Fell and the Dun Fells from Garrigill

Maps: OS Landranger 1:50,000 series: Sheet 86 – Haltwhistle, Bewcastle
and Alston – and Sheet 91 – Appleby-in-Westmorland

Start: Garrigill. GR 745416.

Distance: 29.5 kilometres (18.5 miles)

Ascent: 695 metres (2280 feet)

Type of walk: A long and energetic walk, climbing to the highest summit
in the Pennines, and returning over wild, remote and very bleak moorland.
A considerable amount of time is spent far away from civilisation, and it is
best not to tackle this walk alone without some bivouac equipment and
supplies, and a fair amount of experience of wilderness wandering. Set
against these considerations, you will encounter possibly the wildest terrain
in the Pennines, and on a good day, love every minute of it.

Far from the madd(en)ing crowds

The verdant loveliness of the tiny village of Garrigill stands as a stark contrast to a
good chunk of what follows. Not that the village is outstandingly attractive, few of
these northern villages truly are, seeming to be rather more preoccupied with the
struggle to hold themselves intact against the elements than in catering for idle fancies
or the pampered preferences of in-comers and occasional visitors. No, not pretty; but
certainly with attraction in its own way; a homely place; a few cottages framing a
village green, a shop, an hotel, and a twelfth-century church with a bell reputed to
have served as a dinner bell at Dilston Hall, the Northumberland seat of the third and
last Earl of Derwentwater, who in 1716 was executed as a Jacobite. For many years,
centuries perhaps, Garrigill church, and others like it, will have served as the most
important feature along the route we now call the Pennine Way, for then men believed
with a fervour that Heaven and Hell were far more lasting than Earth. What then do
we make of the fact, everywhere evident, that across the length and breadth of the
Pennines the priests who called the faithful to their places of worship have been
replaced by publicans, and those who engaged in corporate worship by people who
commune alone with the mountains and wild places?

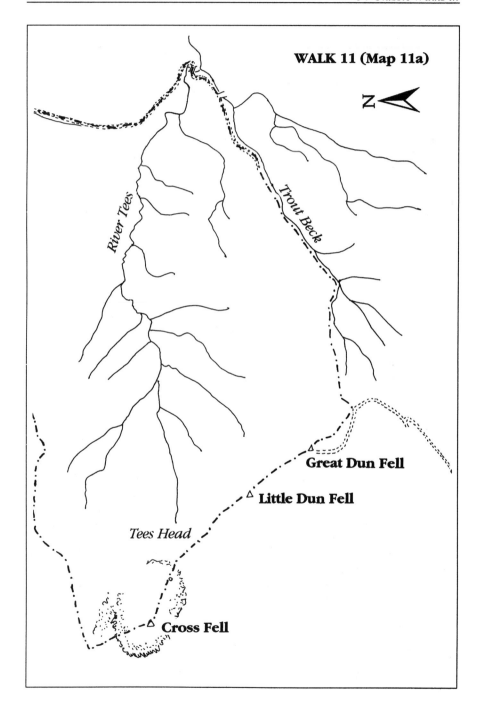

WALK 11 (Map 11a)

N

River Tees

Trout Beck

△ **Great Dun Fell**

△ **Little Dun Fell**

Tees Head

△ **Cross Fell**

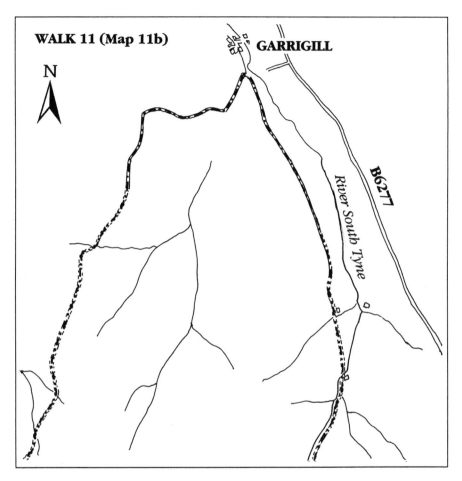

WALK 11 (Map 11b)

N

GARRIGILL

River South Tyne

B6277

A short distance south of the village a walled lane (signposted "Pennine Way") sets off up the hillside, twisting this way and that, losing first one of its walls and then the other as it flanks Pikeman Hill and contours around Long Man Hill. Now we have a landscape of moorland, as far as the eye can see. From time to time we encounter old mine workings, relics of a former time. This is what remains of the Cashwell Mine, one of the most productive in the Northern Pennines. These abandoned mines and their ruins are of great interest to the industrial archaeologist, but they are potentially dangerous and best avoided. If we cannot resist some exploration, at least search above ground for fragments of the lead ore (galena) that was mined here, lumps of barytes, and the yellow and blue fluorspar which in Derbyshire is known as Blue John Stone, and claimed only to be found there!

Eventually we reach the edge of the Cross Fell screes, a collar of bouldery debris, beyond which easy slopes rise to the highest point of the Pennines, a bare stony plateau sporting a trig point, cairns and a cross shelter. Very little grows up here, but the short turf somehow provides shelter and sustenance enough to attract small annual contingents of that rare mountain bird, the dotterel, on migration.

The summit shelter on Cross Fell

A broad path now heads southeast, aiming for a tall cairn, and ahead rise the two mounds of, first, Little Dun Fell and, beyond, Great Dun Fell hopelessly ensnared in the man-made paraphernalia of a radar station.

The crossing to Little Dun Fell brings us very close to the source of the River Tees, indeed the col is called Tees Head. Waterlogged peat and dark pools make Tees Head an unattractive place, but with a short, sharp pull, we can soon be up and over Little Dun Fell, and squelching across another marshy saddle to reach the northern slopes of Great Dun Fell. The gigantic golf ball on top of Great Dun Fell is a conspicuous feature from far afield; its accompanying mast and buildings are unsightly, but their service road from Knock Fell means that walkers wanting to reach the high ground without too much effort may drive almost to the top of Great Dun Fell – of course, no self-respecting walker would dream of such a thing!

Walking down is another matter, and for a short distance we follow the service road to its col with Knock Fell. Now we prepare for a truly wild moorland crossing, for to the east of the col an old stony track, overgrown in places strikes down to Trout Beck and to the head of Teesdale. This is what remains of an old mine road constructed by the London Lead Mining Company, and it takes us not only to a crossing of the Tees, but on, across a minor watershed, into the valley of the South Tyne, the source of the river being indicated by a small sign on the right of the track.

Lead mining in this area has a long history, and there is evidence to support the claim that Romans worked lead ore alongside the South Tyne, at a place known as Chesters, though it is not named on maps. The great period of expansion came after 1706 when the London Lead Mining Company, a Quaker organisation founded by Royal Charter in 1692, acquired a number of mines and, later, the estate of the luckless Earl of Derwentwater.

Before the arrival of the London Lead Mining Company, no one paid particular heed to the welfare of miners; many lived in Alston, and walked to work each day, while others fashioned crude, turf-built, thatched huts close by the mine entrances. Such a situation did not please the Company and in 1753 they began construction of a mining village at Nenthead, and encouraged the miners to develop an interest in farming, as a hedge against lean times. Such foresight proved beneficial, and brought immense prosperity to one of the most remote and inhospitable regions of the country; in 1767 the income from 121 mines amounted to more than £77,000, a King's ransom, and at a time when the highest paid worker would command less than £100 per year.

There is little evidence of all this activity as now we descend the old track alongside the South Tyne, but the hills are riddled with mines, betrayed only by the occasional spoil heap or smelt chimney.

For the final stage of this walk, the South Tyne is an amiable companion. There is still some way to go before returning to Garrigill, but the track is firm underfoot, and near Hill House we rejoin the metalled roadway which services the upper valley for the final 3 kilometres (2 miles).

Walk 12: High Cup Nick and Backstone Edge

Map: OS Landranger 1:50,000 series: Sheet 91 – Appleby in Westmorland

Start: Dufton village (Town Head). GR 694248. There is no car park as such in Dufton though limited parking is possible near the village green. A few cars may also be parked off the road in Bow Hall Lane (GR 695249). Wherever you park, please take care not to inconvenience residents.

Distance: 15.5 kilometres (9.75 miles)

Ascent: 510 metres (1675 feet)

Type of walk: Mainly easy walking on good paths as far as High Cup Nick. From there to the summit of Backstone Edge involves some rough going across peaty undulations and tussock grass, followed by a longish descent of a mine track down Rundale to Dufton Pike. The stretch across Backstone Edge is without rights of way, though it has been regularly walked without hindrance for a good many years. Considerate walkers are unlikely to encounter any opposition to their presence.

High moorland amphitheatre

Unlike many mountain ranges, the Pennines, being soft, moulded hills, own few dramatic, sharp-edged profiles certain to catch the eye and lodge in the mind. Instead, the impact of this wild landscape springs from a subtleness of light and shade, the broad sweep of heather-purpled slopes, the glint of sunlight on water, the whole ensemble orchestrated by the ever changing moods of the weather, moods which prompted one cynic to bemoan the Pennine climate as one of nine months winter followed by three months of rain. One of the few exceptions to this Pennine generality is the impressive sculpted escarpment of High Cup Nick, object of this walk, and formed by forces cold, wet and windy where outcrops of igneous Whin Sill dolerite have intruded into the thick layers of mountain limestone and gritstone.

The walk starts from the rural cluster of cottages that forms Dufton, a charming, friendly oasis, contrasting sharply with the mountain wilderness high above it, and owing its notoriety to an idiosyncratic kink in the Pennine Way, which here quits the high ground for an overnight halt before pressing on to the highest Pennine summit,

Cross Fell. Ironically, the day which transports walkers heading north from Teesdale to Dufton lands them further removed from their destination, Kirk Yetholm, than when they began the day. But, quite reasonably, the designers of the Way considered the long haul from Teesdale, along Maize Beck, and up by Knock Fell to the Dun Fells and Cross Fell, more than a body could stand in one day – though bionic walkers will manage the 56 kilometres (35 miles) of such an undertaking in around 12 hours – and good luck to them!

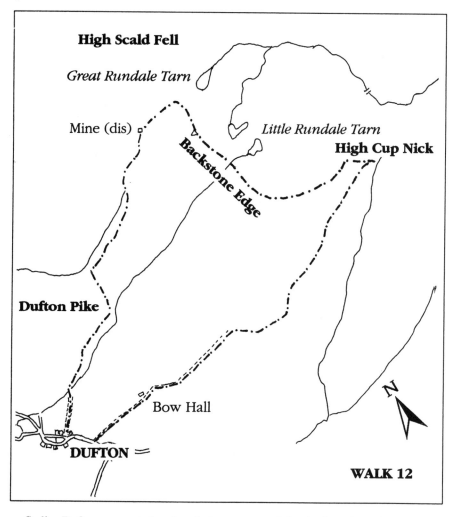

Sadly, Dufton seems to be singularly unprepared for the invasion of Wayfarers, offering limited accommodation possibilities, a feature which disposed Wainwright, author of *The Pennine Way Companion*, to opine: "Wise virgins book their beds in advance." Perhaps there's a dissertation in there struggling to get out . . . *The incidence of wise virgins undertaking the Pennine Way, their motives, hopes and desires.*

At the southern end of the village the Pennine Way is signposted, and leads you along the road to Bow Hall Farm, set on gently sloping pastures and offering teas and accommodation. Beyond the farm, the route lies along a walled green lane, and beyond climbs high onto the hillside. There is invariably a red flag mounted at the entrance to Bow Hall Lane, and this signifies activity on the Warcop Artillery Range, part of the Warcop Principal Training Area. Firing on the range is unlikely to affect anyone ascending to High Cup Nick, but walkers tempted to stray on to Murton Fell could be walking into trouble. Activity, with no concession to walkers, occurs on every day except Mondays.

As you climb the hillside, and so come to pass through the intake wall, the views open up across the Eden valley to the fells of Lakeland and southwards to the Howgill Fells. Just as you pass the intake wall, a small shelter, up on the left of the path used to be in regular use when there was a lime kiln nearby.

Continue easily now along the edge of the escarpment which drops in precipitous green slopes to unseen High Cup Gill. As the gill narrows, so the scenery assumes a more inspiring and dramatic aspect, and the Pennine Way, crossing a couple of cascading streams, then relaxes to form a gentle greenway around the craggy amphitheatre to the Pennine watershed ahead. The path, as if possessing no head for heights, maintains a respectable distance from the escarpment, but as the crags become more evident a cautious diversion will reveal an architecture of shattered pinnacles and precarious columns of basalt. The most notable of these, Nichol's Chair, is named after a cobbler who used to live in Dufton, and who not only climbed the pillar but is reputed to have repaired a pair of boots while on its top. Any ascent now is likely to precipitate the collapse of the whole column, so unstable does its structure seem.

For all its comparative lack of stature the stream flowing lemming-like over High Cup Nick, when caught by a westerly wind, often plumes high into the air, reminiscent of Kinder Downfall in the Peak District, and nearby folds in the grassy shoulder of the escarpment offer lunch-time shelter. Here the Pennine Way presses on eastwards to Teesdale, while for Backstone Edge you must now about face to ascend the easy slopes northeast of Narrowgate Beacon, which has overlooked much of the route thus far.

From the Beacon there are two choices: one to pursue an intermittent gritstone edge around the lip of these high moors, the other to tackle a trying section of bogs, giving way eventually to heather and tussock grass. A clear day in winter, when the ground underfoot is frozen in its grip, may well be the best time to tackle these featureless moors. Your immediate objective is the trig pillar, a lonely sentinel in a severe landscape made auspicious by its position on the watershed of Britain, for here the waters of Little Rundale Tarn gush westwards to the Eden and on to the Solway, while those of nearby Seamore and Great Rundale Tarn empty to the North Sea. The highest point of Backstone Edge lies a short way northeast of the trig, marked by a cairn of large boulders.

Hidden from the summit, the deep valley of Rundale, sports a broad track, descending from the col with High Scald Fell along the line of Great Rundale Beck

The vertical rocks of the Whin Sill make a fine display at High Cup Nick

to Dufton. Quarry workings are shortly encountered, relics of the search for barytes, a dormant place, still in use from time to time as market forces create and determine the demand for minerals.

Wild and rugged, and despoiled by man, Great Rundale is less open than High Cup Gill, the view westwards restricted by the pyramid of Dufton Pike. But for all the damage that has been done it in its upper reaches, the lower valley is quite a charming end to the day. As you approach Dufton Pike, pass south of it, finally to regain the village not far from your starting point.

Walk 13: Upper Teesdale: High Force and Cauldron Snout

Maps: OS Landranger 1:50,000 series: Sheet 91 –
Appleby-in-Westmorland or Sheet 92 – Barnard Castle.

Start: Bowlees in Teesdale. GR 907282. Car park.

Distance: 19.5 kilometres (12 miles)

Ascent: 275 metres (900 feet)

Type of walk: A splendid riverside walk visiting two of the highlights of
the Pennine Way in this region, High Force and Cauldron Snout. The whole
of the walk is in the Teesdale National Nature Reserve, and
less-than-considerate walkers are likely to find themselves invited to go
elsewhere. This is a unique habitat, and the Nature Conservancy Council go
to great lengths to protect this exquisite environment.

An introduction to Teesdale

For much of its great journey the Pennine Way is charted over desolate and potentially
dangerous ground, the preserve of well-equipped and experienced walkers. But for a
while, as it progresses northwards from Middleton-in-Teesdale, it relaxes its challenge
and injects a soft, pastoral interlude of riverside meadows, before heading for the
highest ground of all. And what better companion for this refreshing chapter than the
River Tees, here but a few miles from its source, in places meandering smoothly over
a wide bed of rock, in other places cascading forcefully with all the might of a major
river over rocky downfalls. For any walker, whether they come on foot, on two wheels
or four, there can be no better introduction to Teesdale.

Once a remote corner of the North Riding of Yorkshire and part of the ancient
Forest of Teesdale in which many deer roamed free, the walk now lies entirely within
the County of Durham. Middleton-in-Teesdale is the largest town hereabouts, formerly a local centre of lead-mining activities, and for a while sustained by the building
of nearby reservoirs, it now appears to be without visible means of support beyond its
role as an agricultural market and tourist centre for Upper Teesdale.

From a long trail of boulders it is possible to chart the course of the massive glacier
which fashioned this region, sweeping over gaps from the Eden Valley, the Lake

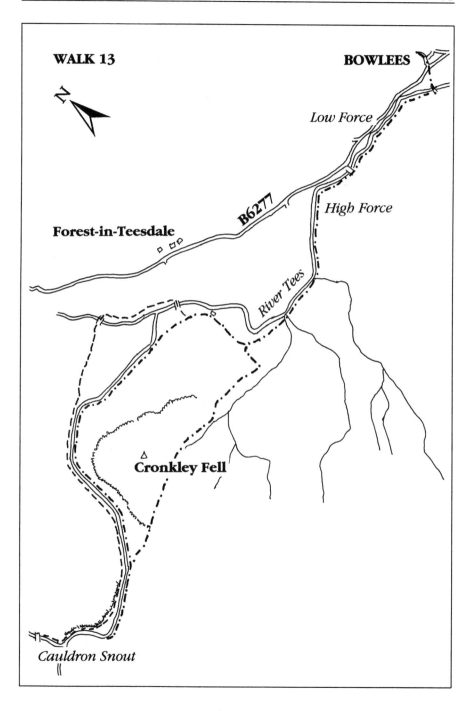

WALK 13

BOWLEES

N

Low Force

B6277

Forest-in-Teesdale

High Force

River Tees

Cronkley Fell

Cauldron Snout

District and even the south of Scotland, carrying Shap granite and Borrowdale lava as far as the mouth of the Tees where an off-shore accumulation of granite pin-points what must have been the terminal moraine of the Tees glacier.

The walk begins from a parking and tourist information area at Bowlees, and from the main road descends to cross the Tees by Wynch Bridge. The original Wynch Bridge was built in 1704 for miners, but it collapsed in 1820 and had to be rebuilt ten years later. Now it serves a local beauty spot.

Within a matter of minutes we encounter the first hint (if we didn't already know it) that the river has something spectacular to reveal, for we come upon Low Force, a place where the river bed is wide and punctuated by islands of dolerite. Set against a backdrop of dark woodlands this is the Tees at its most beautiful.

Our way continues beside the Tees, and, at the right time of year, we may begin to notice the array of plants which have given Teesdale an international reputation among botanists, who at times outnumber the plants about five to one. Globe flower seems to grow everywhere, while among the rocks shrubby and alpine cinquefoil have found root. The number of visitors to this spot, with or without the help of guidebooks, is considerable, and has prompted the Nature Conservancy Council to introduce board-walks to minimise the risk of damage to this unique habitat. Anyone with a modicum of knowledge of the wild flowers of Britain will know of Upper Teesdale. Plans to flood parts of the valley to form the Cow Green Reservoir, in the 1960s led to a public inquiry. The inquiry rejected appeals from botanists and the valley was flooded in 1971-72, leaving Teesdale's rarities to flourish high on adjacent fells.

The most famous of Teesdale's plants is the spring gentian, making its home here among other rarities, the alpine forget-me-not, bitter milkwort, bog sandwort and others. To the uninitiated (and that includes me) it is a puzzle that such a wide variety of rare plants should survive here and in few other localities. I have marvelled at the sheer beauty of these plants in the Pyrenees and the Alps, where they grow in profusion, but to find them popping up on British ground is quite remarkable.

The answer, as ever, lies in the study of geology and early land formations. Teesdale, and parts of Scotland, were grassy islands in a sea of forest, fragments of the carpet of tundra which covered Britain after the Ice Age, and later, when the climate improved, shaded out by trees. Carbon dating of pollen remains in the underlying peat reveals a history going back some 10,000 years. It would be a pity if something which had survived for so long was trampled fatally by a misplaced boot, and so the rangers of Upper Teesdale are constantly vigilant, and know how to distinguish real botanists from fibbers.

As we press on beside the Tees we may notice the juniper bushes cloaking the slopes above Keedholm Scar. Juniper wood, now more often encountered in garden centres, was once gathered to make high quality charcoal, and the berries to flavour London gin.

The river bends sharply just past Keedholm Scar, and suddenly we are aware of a distant rumbling, the sound of thunder perhaps, but in reality the most famous of Pennine waterfalls, High Force. Soon we see it, framed by trees, our attention most likely drawn to it by the trail of tourists on the opposite bank who, unlike those who pursue the route described here, will have paid for the privilege of entering private

High Force

grounds for a view of the falls. The Force is a dramatic plunge over a shelf of dolerite and shale of some 21 metres (70 feet), dark brown and peaty, often lost in a fine mist of spray. This is not the highest waterfall in the country by any means, but it is the biggest, and a sight everyone should see.

Up stream the sound of the falls quickly dies away and the Tees resumes its docile air, rising in restless moorland wandering to its source high on the southern flanks of Cross Fell. The double falls of Bleabeck Force are nothing by comparison, a mere ripple. Ahead we ascend brackenless Bracken Rigg before reaching Cronkley Farm. Now continue north along the Pennine Way to the farm access bridge, but remain on the south bank of the river following a good path which circumnavigates Cronkley Scar, and connects with our return track just opposite Falcon Clints. From this position we gain little real impression of the Tees' other showpiece, Cauldron Snout. A short extension along the path will bring us to the confluence of the Tees and Maize Beck, the former boundary between Yorkshire, Durham and Westmorland, and from the south side of the river we must satisfy ourselves with that. But we can modify the route by crossing the Tees using the Cronkley Farm access bridge and then pursuing the Pennine Way over Saur Hill Bridge and on to Widdybank Farm before squeezing through Falcon Clints, across an awkward passage of scree and boulders, for a closer inspection of Cauldron Snout. The harsh facade of whinstone which comprises Falcon Clints is often relieved by bright green ferns and lichens, the darting of dippers and grey wagtails along the river or the occasional ring ouzel or falcon among the crags.

Use of this diversion involves a simple retracing of our outward steps, but among such diversity of flora and fauna this is no hardship, while Maize Beck below Cauldron Snout is a mesmeric spot from which, perhaps some hours later, to retreat.

If we elected to remain on the south side of the Tees, we must now turn around and ascend steeply on a good path across Cronkley Fell, finally to descend once more to the Tees which is then followed back to Wynch Bridge.

So much will have been encountered on this delightful walk that, I suspect, a return visit will be necessary before we can appreciate all we are being allowed to see. For this reason I conclude the walk with a reminder that here especially, from among all the special places along the Pennines, we have a most unique and precious environment that as conscientious walkers and country-lovers we must do everything to preserve and protect. Such a plea is appropriate anywhere in the Pennines, but especially appropriate here.

Walk 14: The Calf from Sedbergh

Maps: (1) OS Landranger 1:50,000 series: Sheet 98 – Wensleydale and Upper Wharfedale, with a small amount on Sheet 97 – Kendal and Morecambe; (2) Harveys Walker's Maps 1:40,000 series – Howgill Fells

Start: Loftus Hill Car Park, Sedbergh. GR 658920. Toilets.

Distance: 17 kilometres (10.5 miles)

Ascent: 625 metres (2050 feet)

Type of walk: In spite of very easy going underfoot this is a strenuous walk, the height gain making it feel longer than it is. Virtually the whole of the ascent to The Calf, just under 7 kilometres (about 4 miles) is uphill. For all that it is a splendid outing, and returns via Cautley Spout and by a long pastureland traverse above the River Rawthey. Not recommended for a misty day; although there is a path almost the whole way, there are few identifiable features, and it would be easy to go astray.

"... that makes the Sedbergh man"

According to a Sedbergh School Song: "It is Cautley, Calf and Winder, that makes the Sedbergh man", and it is by these three features, and more, that this route goes. The town itself is an ancient market town, mentioned in the Domesday Book as being among the numerous manors held by Earl Tostig, one of the sons of Earl Godwin of Wessex and brother of King Harold. But its fame today rests very much on the laurels of its school which began in 1525 and grew steadily to become a place with a national reputation.

Sedbergh is the largest town within the Yorkshire Dales National Park, and is the main western gateway to the Dales. Its market charter dates from 1251. Towards the end of the eighteenth century the Turnpike Acts of 1761 brought improvements to the Askrigg-Kendal and Lancaster-Kirkby Stephen roads, both of which pass through Sedbergh. This, coupled with a period of industrial growth as the local domestic knitting trade was augmented by a cotton industry based on mills at Birks, Howgill and Millthrop, meant that Sedbergh grew at the expense of Dent (known originally as Dent Town), until then the more important township.

The walk begins from the Loftus Hill Car Park from where we stroll up past (or round the back of) the church to the main street. Here turn left for a short distance, and then right along a minor road (signposted 'Howgill'), following this as it ascends

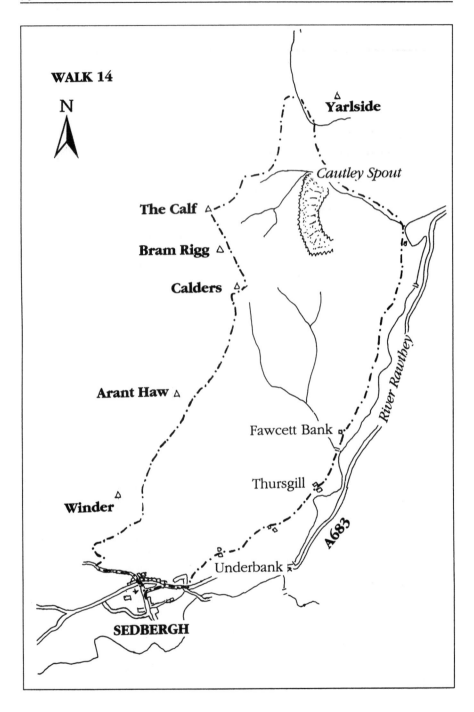

WALK 14

N

Yarlside

Cautley Spout

The Calf

Bram Rigg

Calders

River Rawthey

Arant Haw

Fawcett Bank

Thursgill

Winder

A683

Underbank

SEDBERGH

easily to the access road to Lockbank Farm. There is a permissive route through the farm by which we gain the open fellside, though here the fell is anything but open and rears in front of us, marking the start of an ascent which will impress itself on your legs if nothing else.

A slanting green rake leads up and across the lower slopes of Winder (the 'i' pronounced as in 'win'), and soon changes from a northwest direction to northeast. At this point we can divert to take in Winder, either by tackling the slope ahead straight on, or by going left and still up, until an easier gradient is reached, and there heading east to the summit. From the top, a good path leads northeast to meet the original path at a small cairn (GR 658937), continuing easily to an unmarked (but obvious) grassy path heading north to the summit of Arant Haw. As with Winder, a good path heads northeast from the summit of Arant Haw to rejoin the main path at a small collapsed cairn (GR 667950), and we can take a direct line should we want to bypass Arant Haw, a summit included (along with the next section of the route to The Calf) in the Fairmile Circuit (see Walk 17).

Calders and Bram Rigg Top from Arant Haw

The path now drops across a narrow neck of land (Rowantree Grains), as a fence appears on the right. This fence will guide us to within a few paces of the summit of

Calders, though the path is clear enough. Nearing the top of Calders the path bends through 90°, and shortly passes close by the summit cairn.

In poor visibility, take care not to continue along the path beside the fence, for this does not take you to The Calf. A compass bearing will put you on the right line, and soon leads you on to the right path for the highest of these fine hills.

The quickest way back to Sedbergh is to return by the onward route just described, and if time is short this is the best option. Otherwise locate and follow a path, running northeast to a small tarn (GR 671975 – and sometimes dried up), where the path forks. The left branch takes you down over Hazelgill Knott to Bowderdale village but follow instead the right fork. It, too, leads into Bowderdale, this time the valley of that name.

The watershed in Bowderdale marks the boundary of the national park, and this broad, flat col is our objective. By staying on the path descending from The Calf, we needlessly go too far north into Bowderdale. Instead, when you feel you can cope with the untracked ground on the right, descend across it to reach the valley bottom near a makeshift sheep-fold (GR 681981). Cross the stream, and follow a narrow path leading south to the steep descent east of Cautley Spout. In good conditions you will have fine views of this magnificent fall, which may be approached more closely by ascending the prominent Cautley Spout Tongue.

Down into the broad valley of Cautley Holme Beck, the path heads for the prominent temperance inn, the Cross Keys, but as we reach valley bottom, leave this and bear right (south) to cross the beck by a footbridge. At a subsequent barn, take the right fork and ascend slightly behind it to follow a good path leading to a gate in the intake wall. The path continues easily through fields, passing through a number of gates and over stiles until eventually Fawcett Bank farm is reached, at the entrance to Hobdale. Here the track improves dramatically, and leads across Hobdale Beck by a bridge (gate), and on to Thursgill, Ellerthwaite and Buckbank, by a delightful and now motorable road to reach the A683 1.5 kilometres (one mile) from the starting point.

Walk 15: The Eastern Howgills

Maps: (1) OS Pathfinder 1:25,000 series: Sheet 607: NY 60/70 – Tebay and Kirkby Stephen and Sheet 617: SD 69/79 – Sedbergh and Baugh Fell; (2) Harveys Walker's Maps 1 : 40,000 series – Howgill Fells

Start: The Cross Keys Inn: parking alongside road, near footbridge. GR 698969.

Distance: 15 kilometres (9 miles)

Ascent: 1010 metres (3310 feet)

Type of walk: An energetic walk with a lot of up and down and some steep slopes. The first half contains most of the collar-work, while the second section is by comparison a gentle reward for all the effort – which is unquestionably worthwhile, for this is classic Howgill country.

Nothing to jar

"Wherever you look in the Howgills," commented Sir Clement Jones, youngest son of the sometime Vicar of Burneside, "everything is composed and in the right spot and there is nothing to jar." This axiom is nowhere better exemplified than among the fells that rise to the east of the great Bowderdale valley. Set aside from the highest fells of the range they form a unique, virtually untramped wilderness of considerable charm and beauty.

In *The Old Hand-Knitters of the Dales*, Marie Hartley and Joan Ingilby describe the fells as "hump-backed hills as sleak as seal skin, (that) reflect the sunlight like shot-silk". Come upon them from the confines of Garsdale on a fine autumnal day, and you will see just what these writers mean, for the hillsides do indeed seem to have a painstakingly-designed architecture, here a gentle fold, here a sharp-edged valley to catch the eye, here a dash of sparkling water cascading down a rocky gully that someone thought appropriate, to balance the picture. Add a ray of burnishing sunlight or the hoary frost of a winter's day, and the scene is complete, everything in its place, nothing that jars.

Unlike the fells west across Bowderdale, the summits tackled on this walk stand rather more independently of each other and call for a fair amount of descent and re-ascent. But don't let that deter you, for all the real effort comes early in the day, and the rewards are quite breathtaking (in more ways than one!).

The walk commences at the Cross Keys Temperance Hotel on the Sedbergh-Kirkby

Stephen road. The hotel is now a National Trust property, described as: "A small whitewashed inn, built circa 1600 and altered in the early eighteenth and late nineteenth centuries. Acquired in 1949 with 17 acres of land, under the Will of Mrs E. A. Bunney, to be held as an unlicensed inn in memory of her sister Miss M. B. Hewetson." During summer months excellent ham and egg teas may be obtained here between 12 and 6, and at other times preferably by arrangement, though the hotel is closed from early January until Easter. 'Temperance' here embraces a prohibition on smoking, but, having reserved yourself a table, you may circumvent the prohibition on the sale of alcohol simply by taking your own!

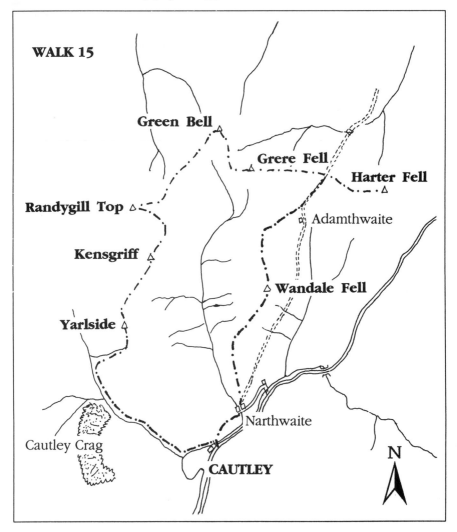

Close by the hotel a footbridge eases us across the River Rawthey, when we bear left on a good path into a pleasant flat-bottomed valley. Ahead, the falls of Cautley Spout are prominent against the broken cliffs of Cautley Crag, the only significant expanse of rock in the Howgills, but of little interest to the rock climbing fraternity. For us the way lies by a steeply ascending path far to the right of the falls by which we can reach the broad col of Bowderdale Head.

But if you have the time it is worth diverting to clamber up Cautley Spout Tongue to gain a better view of the falls. Your efforts won't be wasted; the falls are among the highest in the country, having a vertical height of more than 200 metres (about 700 feet). When you approach the top of the falls you can safety cross right (north) and so gain Bowderdale Head.

Bowderdale Beck finds its source high on the southern slopes of Yarlside, and we must now follow it and ascend to the shallow col south of the summit. There is no especially prominent path here, and the line you take will depend very much on how fit you are feeling. Once at the col it is an easy matter to ascend the last few metres to the summit.

The view from Yarlside is quite remarkable in spite of the restriction southwest which the slightly higher ground of The Calf plateau imposes. The Lakeland fells range across the distant skyline from the heights of the Coniston massif to the lonely fells of Mungrisdale, around Carrock Fell. The highest summit of the Pennines, Cross Fell and its two acolytes, the Dun Fells, rise high above the Eden valley, while nearer at hand, and closer to the source of the Eden, Wild Boar Fell, Swarth Fell and Baugh Fell frame a tantalising glimpse of the Wensleydale hills. The panorama, inspiring enough, is completed by the unmistakable limestone summits of Whernside, Ingleborough and Pen y Ghent.

The continuation to the minor intermediate summit, Kensgriff, involves the descent of a very steep grassy slope to the Saddle, demanding great care and only to be undertaken in winter conditions by experienced walkers properly equipped. Beyond Kensgriff all that lost height has to be regained on the ascent, easy but steep, to the top of Randygill Top; a tiring proposition, but well worth it. Surely these two summits can claim to be the most impressive of all the Howgill fells, and it is from here that the appeal of this fine range of fells will most impress itself upon our hearts and minds. And if you've reached this far, you will be relieved to know that the hard part is now over.

Northeast now a faint path leads down to and over a minor bump, Stockless, before rising gently to the trig on Green Bell. This northerly summit looks down on the Lune valley, towards Weasdale and Newbiggin, with some significance, for only a few hundred metres down its northeast slope a few bubbling springs well up, the birthplace of the Lune, and worth a diversion on that count alone.

By retreating slightly, south from Green Bell, we can cross pathless ground over Grere Fell and Adamthwaite Bank, not without a few marshy stretches, to the minor road linking the farm at Adamthwaite with Ravenstonedale. It is only a short excursion across the road to visit the summit of Harter Fell and to return to the road, and on a fine day the extra distance will tax no one.

Having regained the road turn left until a distinct green track branches right near a small plantation, passing the farm at Adamthwaite. Lying south of the watershed, Adamthwaite nevertheless is served by an access road from Ravenstonedale, over the hill to the north. This is a delightful spot, deep set among trees, remote, unsuspected, rarely visited by walkers.

Continue through a gate in a cross-wall, and on past a barn to another gate in the wall on the left. From here it is a gentle climb to the top of Wandale Fell, followed by an equally easy descent southwest to reach a path dropping down to Narthwaite, a cluster of buildings perched on the crest of a hill. A footbridge spans Backside Beck, and by using the bridleway it carries an easy return may be made to the Rawthey footbridge.

Randygill Top, Kensgriff and Yarlside

Walk 16: Carlin Gill and Blease Fell

Maps: (1) OS Pathfinder 1:25,000 series: Sheet 607: NY 60/70 – Tebay
and Kirkby Stephen and Sheet 617: SD 69/79 – Sedbergh and Baugh Fell;
(2) Harveys Walker's Maps 1:40,000 series – Howgill Fells

Start: Salterwath Bridge, near which there is parking for one or two cars.
GR 612009.

Distance: 12 kilometres (7.5 miles)

Ascent: 460 metres (1510 feet)

Type of walk: An exciting expedition plunging deep into the folds of the
western Howgills, potentially difficult after prolonged wet weather, but
otherwise the gem of these rounded hills, and one of the highlights of the
whole Pennine range. Above Carlin Gill the walk takes in some of the
lower fells overlooking the Lune gorge.

So buxom, blithe and debonair

Milton may not have been thinking of the Howgills when he penned *L'Allegro*, nor
could he have realised how apt his words, applied as I have made them, to describe
these 'buxom, blithe and debonair' fells. Nor, surely, is terminal curiosity needed to
excite passers-by, whether on the Roman Road from where this walk begins, or the
A685 turnpike road, the railway or the motorway, to wonder what lies within the
deeply-folded gash that strikes east from the constriction of the Lune gorge into the
heart of the Howgills. And if too often such dramatic invitations flatter only to deceive,
rest assured: only a moribund soul would judge Carlin Gill a pretence, and only then
because it didn't lead to Heaven.

The walk begins at Salterwath Bridge, on an old salt packhorse train route, near
Low Borrow Bridge, where the Romans positioned a fort. There used to be an inn at
Low Borrow Bridge, meeting place of the local manorial court, and where, in 1831,
one Gideon Maude stayed and described the location as "a place of delightful retreat
for the summer months, yet must be very dreary and desolate of comfort in the winter
season." It certainly is delightful, but seldom dreary for there is an energy about the

Howgills that sparks the flame to the candle of our rambling desires even amidst the worst of winter's gloom.

The start of the walk: in this early stage there is no hint of the narrow wonderland that lies in the valley to the right.

The road from Salterwath, once a Roman road, leads us easily to Carlin Gill bridge, on the boundary between Cumbria and North Yorkshire. Here we gain access to the north (true right) bank of Carlingill Beck, to be followed until Weasel Gill descends to join it from the slopes of Uldale Head. Now we cross the beck to reach a well-trodden sheep track on the opposite bank that takes us into a quite different world. Ahead the gill cuts sharply into the hillsides, and has created a steep-sided ravine with a bed so narrow that progress is only possible by constant hopping from bank to bank, grappling with collapsed and recumbent trees, and performing balancing acts on boulders that in times of spate would be well and truly submerged.

Within minutes we have moved from gentle grazing lands, easy on the eye, to a wild and chaotic rudeness, that could be miles from anywhere. A short distance further and the transformation is complete. Like a vice the gill closes in remorselessly, groups of birch and alder cling to the banks, forcing us to dodge and weave about to make progress. Suddenly a broad gash opens up on the right, and we find ourselves at the foot of an enormous chasm, Black Force, a rocky gorge of unimagined severity in such otherwise gentle surroundings, down which plunges a series of waterfalls. To ascend Black Force, should the spirit move you to such recklessness, requires an aptitude for scrambling, and should not be countenanced by anyone less skilled.

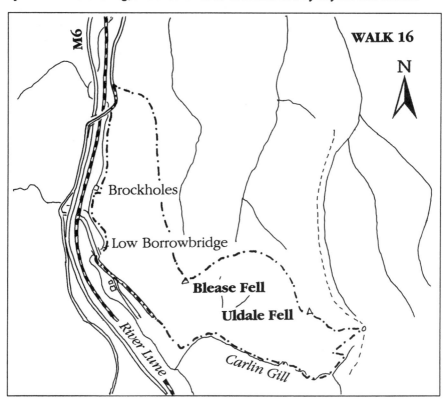

Beyond the entrance to Black Force, after more cavorting with the beck, we are faced by yet another waterfall, The Spout, one that very efficiently restricts forward progress. Two escapes present themselves. The simplest is to tackle the steep (and I mean steep) grassy fellside on the right (south), until you reach a horizontal path which will lead you left into the upper reaches of the gill. More adventurous individuals will tackle the narrow rib which contains The Spout in a small amphitheatre. A sequence of footsteps takes you up to meet a slabby section of friable rock, which must be negotiated with care before the security of firmer ground above is reached.

When above The Spout we can gaze down on its puny efforts to hold us up, but not before! Once nerves have settled and legs regained their composure we can continue by following the beck until finally we emerge on a broad grassy plateau, Blakethwaite Bottom, in the middle of which stands an isolated boulder, Blakethwaite Stone. This once marked the boundary between Yorkshire and the former county of Westmorland, before Cumbria got its greedy hands on its treasures.

From Blakethwaite Bottom ascend west up the grassy slopes of Uldale Head to a large cairn before pressing on a short way further to its summit. What follows is a purely delightful stroll across Howgill fells that are as typical as any. Largely trackless, though paths come and go, the going is nowhere difficult. Our immediate objective is the flat col north east of Blease Fell, between the heads of Ellergill Beck and Grains Gills. From here a short ascent takes us to the top of Blease Fell where more than once I have reclined among the tussock tufts and fallen soundly asleep, lulled by the gentlest of breezes laden with the calls of skylarks, curlew and golden plover.

By descending the broad north ridge of Blease Fell to a shallow col due east of Lune's Bridge we can then descend to a disused quarry (GR 614030) to meet the old turnpike road.

A few minutes south along the road brings us to the access road to Brockholes Farm. Follow this to the farm, and keep ahead on entering the farmyard. The map shows a right of way passing north of the farm buildings, but I have never been able to get through this way, and the occupants themselves have directed me through the farmyard, immediately then to turn right to head for the banks of the Lune. All that now remains is a pleasant amble alongside the river, the meadows lush in springtime with wild flowers and reeking of wild garlic. A path through a final section of woodland returns you abruptly to Salterwath Bridge.

Walk 17: The Fairmile Circuit

Maps: (1) OS Landranger 1:50,000 series: Sheet 98 – Wensleydale and Upper Wharfedale, with a small amount on Sheet 97 – Kendal and Morecambe; (2) OS Pathfinder 1:25,000 series: Sheet 617: SD 69/79 – Sedbergh and Baugh Fell; (3) Harveys Walker's Maps 1:40,000 series – Howgill Fells

Start: Area of level ground, north of Fairmile Gate. GR 629979.

Distance: 13 kilometres (8 miles)

Ascent: 845 metres (2770 feet)

Type of walk: This concoction is an unashamed attempt to maximise the pleasures of the Howgills, by cramming as much as possible into the shortest distance. Inevitably, that means a considerable amount of ascent, which hits you from the very start, and virtually all of it being concentrated in the first four kilometres (2.5 miles). So, be prepared for a strenuous start, but one followed by some of the most pleasant high level wandering the Howgills have to offer. The going underfoot is easy throughout.

The Howgills: A western approach

As it is today, so was the Lune valley a key access route in days gone by. For the Romans in particular, who had a fort not far away at Low Borrow Bridge, it was of strategic importance, their western way northwards, eventually linking with the Eden Valley at Kirkby Thore. Between Sedbergh and Fairmile Gate the ancient road is these days known as Howgill Lane. But on reaching Fairmile Beck, where the enclosed fields and pastures of this rich and fertile neck of land finally recede, in the far north west corner of the Yorkshire Dales National Park, it becomes Fairmile Road (sometimes Fair Mile Lane). Here, little more than half a kilometre distant, modern man's access routes, the M6 motorway and the Glasgow-London railway line, squeeze through a narrow gap carved thousands of years ago by glaciers and the infant River Lune.

Just north of Fairmile Gate, a flat stretch of open ground provides ample parking, and from the car an abrupt and direct ascent is made of the adjacent minor top, Linghaw. We begin by following the obvious grassy path, roughly on the line of Dry Gill, and steeply, until as the gradient eases we can move right to the tussocky summit, marked by a small pile of stones. Beyond we continue on a narrow path and descend to the col, crossed by a good path ascending from Beck Houses, and climb again to the summit of Fell Head.

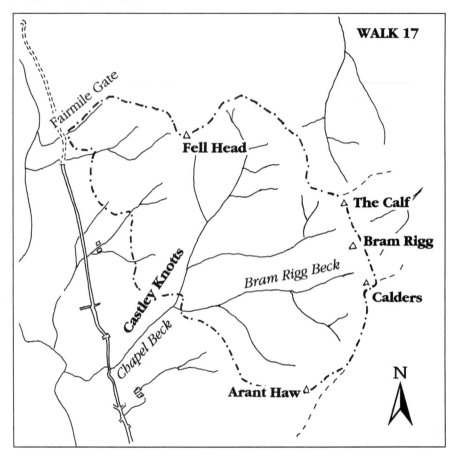

A simple ridge follows, curving lazily round the head of Long Rigg Gill and Long Rigg Beck, to a descent to a neat col, Windscarth Wyke. Yet another ascent follows, this time steadily to the top of Bush Howe, where we gain our first real view of The Calf. As we head for the highest point, the path improves, now demanding very little ascent. There are tremendous views along this broad and lofty ridge, west to the Lakeland fells, southwest to the Kent estuary, and southeast into Dales country.

From The Calf a broad path presses on east of south to Calders, though on a clear day a diversion to take in Bram Rigg Top will reward you with a splendid vantage point to stop for lunch, gazing down on Chapel Beck and the distant Crook of Lune.

Once across the summit of Calders we encounter a fenceline which we can follow, on a good path, to the narrow col, Rowantree Grains. As we start climbing again, more or less for the last time, a collapsed cairn marks the diversion (right) of a grassy track leading to the summit of Arant Haw – the left fork will eventually descend to Lockbank Farm on the outskirts of Sedbergh, so ignore it.

Continue across the summit of Arant Haw, and descend at first west then, no longer on a path, northwest, aiming for the confluence of Bram Rigg Beck and Chapel Beck, below the minor top of Castley Knots. In times of spate conditions the becks may look impassable, but Bram Rigg Beck may usually be forded near its confluence with Swarth Greaves Beck (GR 650958), and Chapel Beck at GR 646963.

From here the return to Fairmile Gate is a delightful stroll, initially ascending above the intake wall around Castley Knotts, and then following the intake wall back to Fairmile Beck.

Fell Head summit

Walk 18: The Langdale Round

Maps: (1) OS Pathfinder 1:25,000 series: Sheet 607: NY 60/70 – Tebay and Kirkby Stephen and Sheet 617: SD 69/79 – Sedbergh and BaughFell. (2) Harveys Walker's Maps 1:40,000 series – Howgill Fells

Start: Brow Foot, near the hamlet of Bowderdale. It is possible to park cars, off the road and without hindering farm vehicles, on open pastureland at approximately GR 682047.

Distance: 23 kilometres (14 miles)

Ascent: 700 metres (2295 feet)

Type of walk: A long, lofty walk, tackling the Howgills from the north, though most of the walking is easy, and the last 6 kilometres (4 miles) connecting the point at which the Lune valley is regained with the starting point. Transport at both ends would save this distance, although the link is pleasant and without difficulty. Hardly any of this walk travels rights of way, and once above the intake fields you will encounter few of the trappings with which man likes to surround himself – no fences, walls, or trees for that matter, no quarries or mines to mar the landscape, no unnatural intrusions, save the odd sheep-fold. There is as a result a tremendous feeling of openness, of nature as nature intended, and our freedom to roam is a privilege retained very much on the consideration and respect we show for the land and property of the farming communities.

Free as a bird

Bowderdale is a small hamlet of three farms, and Brow Foot an isolated farm nearby. This tiny community gathers at the northern end of a long valley, also Bowderdale, that slices through the Howgills to Cautley on the Sedbergh-Kirkby Stephen road and has the bleak, "miles from anywhere", feel of a remote Scottish glen. On the east of the valley rise the summits of Randygill Top, Kensgriff and Yarlside, while on the west a long, gradually ascending grassy ridge plods easily to the highest point of the Howgills, The Calf. Cross this ridge laterally and you come into a truly remote and tranquil valley, Langdale, and it is around this valley, keeping very much to its watershed, that this walk goes, before finally dropping in to it at the end of the day.

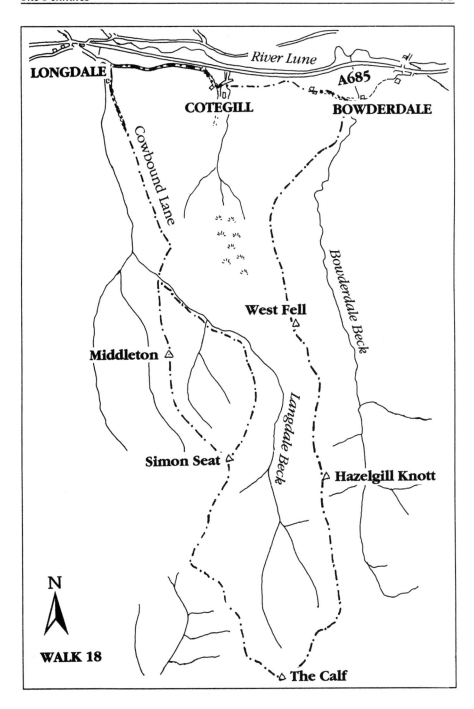

Having left the car on pastureland just off the access road to Scar Sikes Farm we can cross due west to gain the road to the Bowderdale farms, over the bridge spanning Bowderdale Beck and on to a rutted farm track leading left (south) along a wall just before a cattle grid on the access road to Long Gill. Continue south along this track, through two gates, until the open fellside is reached.

As we now move ahead, parallel with a wall, the prospect into Bowderdale opens up. Not surprisingly, the valley is a long established right of way through the Howgills, and ranks as a fine expedition in itself, if transport can be arranged at either end (Walk 19). As for our journey, we continue ascending on a grassy vehicle track, past the entrance to Bowderdale, and up the slopes of West Fell which seem longer than they are. The ridge continues, and as it climbs again to another minor top, Hazelgill Knott, the view into Langdale grows as all the while the distant domes of other Howgill summits increase in stature.

In the distance now you will see The Calf, and off to the right the mound of Simon's Seat, our final summit. You feel as free as a bird up here, the path drawing you ever onward, around, rather than over, Hazelgill Knott, and again climbing to the summit plateau of The Calf which we reach near a small tarn before strolling across to the trig. Suddenly the view across the Lune valley to the near Lakeland Fells and the Kent Estuary appears dramatically, virtually held at bay by the broad shoulders of The Calf until the very last moment.

From the summit, which apart from the trig is quite bare, we head northwest, following the boundary of the Yorkshire Dales National Park, across Bush Howe and the subsequent col, Windscarth Wyke, followed by a short pull to Breaks Head, the easterly point of Fell Head. Now we descend slightly east of north, across Bleagill Head and Wethercalf Moss to the narrow col just south of Simon's Seat. Another ascent follows, some 80 metres (260 feet), to the top of Simon's Seat, indeed a pleasant place to sit, especially if you do so gazing back to The Calf, though 'seat' in this context refers to an area of land belonging to Simon.

North from the top of Simon's Seat the ground drops gently to the valley of Langdale, and presents us with a choice. Either we can descend directly to Langdale, reaching it at a triple sheep-fold where Nevy Gill joins Langdale Beck, and then following the path which there appears out of the valley. Or we can stay high for a while longer, and head for the trig (GR 653013 – 486 metres) on Middleton before finally being forced to come down. Whichever line we take our objective is the ford at GR 651022, where we cross the beck and take a slanting path on the final ascent of the walk to reach the intake wall.

Follow the intake wall until a gate on the left gives access to a long, walled track, known as Cowbound Lane. This leads directly to Town Head at Longdale. Curiously, although lying at the mouth of a valley called Langdale, the village is known as Longdale, though signposts, writers and cartographers all dispute the name. It does seem rather odd. Langdale, or is it Longdale? was once a manor in its own right, granted by Henry II to the Priory of Watton in Yorkshire, and like nearby Ravenstonedale, sold to the Wharton family after the Dissolution of the Monasteries. Later still it became Lowther property.

From Longdale a minor road continues eastwards to Cotegill, from where a track takes us on to the next farm, Flakebridge, which takes its name from its ancient bridge, made of *flaki* (Old Norse), meaning 'hurdles' or, I suppose in this sense, anything wooden. From Flakebridge, another track leads on to Long Gill, and so back to Bowderdale, rejoining our outward route at the cattle grid just west of the hamlet.

Looking back to the broad ridge of West Fell

Walk 19: Cautley Spout and Bowderdale

Map: Harveys Walker's Map 1:40,000 series: Howgill Fells

Start: Loftus Hill Car Park, Sedbergh, GR 658920. Toilets.

Finish: Brow Foot, near the hamlet of Bowderdale.

Distance: 15 kilometres (9.4 miles)

Ascent: 315 metres (1035 feet)

Type of walk: This linear walk will need transport problems sorting out, but presents no other significant difficulties: the return, other than by private car, from Bowderdale to Sedbergh, is not easy. The ascent beside Cautley Spout, though steep, is not unduly arduous, and the long valley walk that follows, sheer delight.

From Sedbergh to Bowderdale

Perfectly capable of being undertaken in the opposite direction, this walk, I feel, benefits from starting in Sedbergh because it allows a gradual approach to the splendour of Cautley Spout from below, rather than coming upon it from above. The walk may be abridged by starting near the Cross Keys Hotel at GR 698969.

From the car park in Sedbergh, turn immediately right to follow a one way street (in the wrong direction) until you leave the eastern end of the town. Stay on the main road (A683) until, just after the road to Garsdale, you can take a track on the left leading up to Buckbank Farm. This access track continues to Ellerthwaite and Thursgill before crossing Hobdale Beck by a bridge (gate).

At this point the track deteriorates to a path, at Fawcett Bank Farm, and sets off across a number of fields, always ahead, using gates and stiles, and in spring alive with the bleating cacophony of new born lambs. With little opportunity for confusion the path arrives at a barn at the point where the valley widens on the left.

Descend to cross Cautley Holme Beck by a footbridge, directly below the dark cliffs of Cautley Crag, and take a prominent and broad path heading for the conspicuous white dash of Cautley Spout. A deviation to inspect the Spout is always worthwhile, and a way out above the falls is feasible, but it can be slippery and dangerous in wet and windy conditions. For this reason, I recommend an inspection of the falls

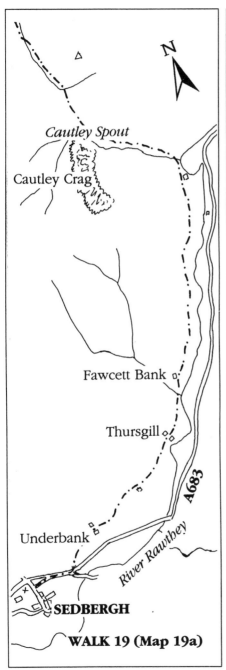

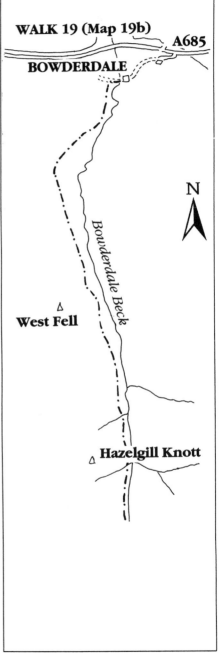

from near their base, after which return to the main path that climbs up into Bowder-dale. The gradient for a while is quite steep, eased by zigzags, but once the marshy expanse below Yarlside is reached, the going becomes a little easier.

The further you progress into Bowderdale, the less distinct does the path become, until finally it peters out altogether. When this happens, cross Bowderdale Beck (though there is no bridge – so do it sooner rather than later) and gain a well-trodden path that now runs all the way out of the valley. This long valley walk is exquisite, if taken at a leisurely pace, and the grassy fellsides often grazed by semi-wild fell ponies.

As the route finally leaves the valley behind, so the broad expanse of the Lune valley opens before you. The path approaches an intake wall, but keeps above it to join a vehicle track which is easily followed down to Brow Foot, near the tiny collection of farm buildings that comprises Bowderdale.

The main road linking Tebay and Kirkby Stephen is only a short distance away, and carries an infrequent bus service into Kendal. Cars brought to Brow Foot awaiting completion of the walk should be parked off the farm roads on a stretch of level ground just above the last farm (GR 682047).

Walk 20: Along the River Lune

Map: OS Landranger 1:50,000 series: Sheet 97- Kendal and Morecambe

Start: Loftus Hill Car Park, Sedbergh. GR 658920. Toilets.

Finish: Crook of Lune Bridge. GR 620963

Distance: 11 kilometres (7 miles)

Ascent: Nominal, mainly undulating ground

Type of walk: An outstandingly pleasant walk across riparian and agricultural pastureland, making use of one of the finest sections of the Dales Way. If transport can be arranged at either end, then this linear walk is one to be lingered over, savouring the easiest of walking in one of the most attractive fringes of the Pennines. By means of leafy back roads, however, the walk may be turned into a circular tour, returning pleasantly to Sedbergh.

Riparian Ramble

On its journey from Ilkley to Windermere, the Dales Way passes through some of Britain's most attractive landscapes, none more so than its woefully brief acquaintance with the River Lune. Rising on the northeastern shoulders of the Howgills, the River Lune makes a long loop around the northern flank of the fells before heading southwards en route to Lancaster and the sea. This walk makes its acquaintance not far from Sedbergh where it is joined in force by the River Rawthey and the River Dee.

From the Loftus Hill Car Park turn left, heading away from Sedbergh centre, and continue down the road to the tiny suburb of Millthrop. Just north of Millthrop Bridge a path (signposted: 'Birks') sets off through a kissing gate (on the right). Follow this across the ensuing field to a squeeze stile that gives access to a small copse. Trend to the right in the copse at a walled trench, and head for another kissing gate where we leave this small, pleasant woodland.

Turn left with the fence and climb a small hill to pass by a curious ruined structure, that seems to date from the Second World War. Go ahead down the field to a stile close by the riverbank, and follow the edge of Sedbergh School rugby grounds to a stile in a small hollow. Continue with the path beyond past a house, to reach a minor road between Birks and Sedbergh.

Go left along the road, through Birks, and on as far as Birks Mill, a former cotton mill, where a footbridge spans the River Rawthey. Ignore the bridge, and keep left of the mill to a stile that leads back to the riverbank. Keep on, through another small copse, finally to reach the embankment of the former Ingleton-Tebay branch railway. Go across the embankment and drop on a narrow path along the edge of a field to a stile. The on-going path remains in the company of the River Rawthey for a while longer, as far as Brigflatts, beyond which it follows a path sandwiched between the

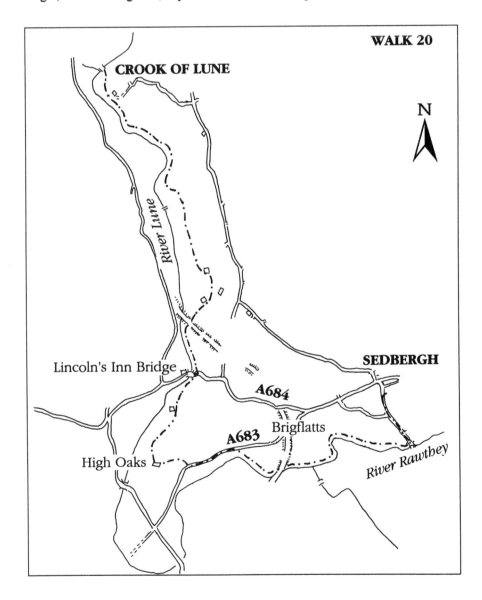

river and a barbed wire fence. Shortly, the Rawthey takes it leave and sets off to meet the Lune, while we continue to the A683.

Brigflatts was once a flax-weavers' settlement, and, in its Friends' Meeting House, hosts an historically important building, built in 1675. Access to the house is not possible directly from the walk, but involves a detour around country lanes. If time is not of the essence, such a detour is well worthwhile.

Keep along the A683 for just under half a mile to a double stile through a hedgerow on the right (signposted: 'High Oaks'). Follow the ensuing fence to a concrete bridge spanning diminutive Haverah Beck. Pass around a small hillock, and cross a meadow, aiming for a gap in a hedgerow. On reaching the gap, following the hedge to a gate giving on to an attractive green lane, by means of which we reach the hamlet of High Oaks. On reaching the hamlet, look for a footpath (signposted) on the right, along a farm cart track, and follow this until confronted by a gate and stile. Cross the ensuing field, keeping to its right edge, and, ignoring a step stile on the right, continue across the field to a farm gate. A broad path ensues, flanked on the left by a tall hedgerow, that leads to Luneside Farm: the path is often muddy (and well-fertilised).

Pass the farm, using its access track, for a short distance to a gate on the left. Go across the next field to a tree and then keep along the fence as far as a low step stile on the left. A good path now runs on towards the River Lune (signposted: 'Lincoln's Inn Bridge'), and should be followed to the bridge.

Lincoln's Inn is now a farm, but used to serve drovers waiting to ford the river in the days before the distinctive double-arched bridge was built. 'Lincoln' was a former landlord of the inn, and no doubt a wealthy man.

Between Lincoln's Inn Bridge and the Crook of Lune Bridge we finally come on face to face terms with the River Lune, but for a very brief period.

Turn right, away from the bridge, along the A684, but leave the road almost immediately at a gate on the left (signposted: 'Low Branthwaite'). Go across the field, by its left edge, close by the busy river, and towards the prominent Lune viaduct ahead.

When in-flowing Crosdale Beck is reached, just below the viaduct, go right, along a wall, ultimately to reach an underpass. On the other side you reach a gate, go left after the gate, as the Howgills come into view once more, and continue to another gate. Now turn right to cross the top edge of a sloping field, and as the field narrows, so we reach a meeting of pathways.

Here descend left to a step stile in a corner, giving access to Low Branthwaite Farm. Keep ahead for a short distance to a signpost pointing out a ladder stile on the right. Now we are heading for Bramaskew Farm, along a pleasant path that leads to an iron gate. Just before the gate cross a low fence on the right, and follow a hawthorn hedgerow until it becomes enclosed by a wall. The wall is short-lived, but as the path continues, it becomes enclosed once more and arrives at a gate. Go through the gate and press on between walls.

At a gate look for a sign ('Dales Way') fixed to a tree, beside which there is a narrow gap stile. Keep Bramaskew Farm to the right, and follow a fence to another stile. Make use of an electricity supply line to guide you to a barn, concealed in a dip. Keep left at the barn and ahead to a double gate. Cross a small stream and enter another enclosed path leading to Nether Bainbridge Farm.

As Nether Bainbridge Farm is approached, pass a storage shed and barn, and look for a stone squeeze stile. Go right, around the barn, to a wall with a signpost ('Hole House'). Ignore the nearby gate, but continue left, moving along the wall, keeping it on the right, to reach another gate with a footpath sign. A slight brow ahead gives a particularly fine view of the Howgills, and is a good spot to pause for a moment.

From this modest rise, head directly for Hole House Farm, which lies in a hollow, by the Lune. At the farm gate, go ahead into the farmyard, turning right as barns are reached. A short way on, keep left, passing between the residential buildings of the farm, with yellow waymarkers as confirmation that we are on the correct route. At the ensuing gate, descend into a wooded gully to a footbridge spanning Smithy Beck. Now follow the signposted path to Crook of Lune Bridge, the lower of two paths. Having left the river for a short while, in the next meadow return to it, ignoring the green path swinging away to the right. At a collapsed wall, continue ahead, once more in company with the Lune. An undulating path follows, always staying with the river, and in and out of woodland, until we reach a track leading to a gate below Crook of Lune Farm.

Follow the track beyond the gate to meet a wall, and press on ahead, keeping the wall on the right. Now the Lune Viaduct starts to come into view, signifying the end of the journey. At a gate we reach a minor road, where a left turn leads down to the bridge, crossing the Lune in one of its loveliest reaches.

For those who have been able to leave transport at this spot, the Crook of Lune Bridge marks the end of the walk. But the return to Sedbergh, should you elect to make it, is not difficult, and returns up the minor road to a road junction. Here turn right, on a narrow road with high hedgerows, taking care to watch (and listen) for approaching traffic, and follow the road back to Sedbergh, bearing left at the first main junction. This return will add about six kilometres (3 miles) to the distance, but in springtime especially is a fascination: the hedgerows are alive with wildlife and flowers, the pastures filled with lambs, and the skies echoing to the mewing of circling buzzards on the make. This return route brings you back into Sedbergh only a short distance (left and right) from the car park.

Walk 21: Janet's Foss, Gordale Scar and Malham Cove

Maps: (1) OS Landranger 1:50,000 series: Sheet 98 – Wensleydale and Upper Wharfedale; (2) OS 1:25,000 Outdoor Leisure Map: Sheet 10 – Yorkshire Dales – Southern area

Start: National Park car park and information centre, Malham. GR 900627. Charge for car parking. Toilets. Refreshments in Malham.

Distance: 11 kilometres (7 miles)

Ascent: 195 metres (640 feet)

Type of walk: An easy walk through spectacular limestone scenery. A little scrambling is called for in Gordale, made intimidating by the cascading falls, but not as difficult as it looks. Above the falls a wide limestone plateau opens up to Malham Tarn, followed by a delightful amble back to the top of Malham Cove. But the true splendour of this walk derives from its wealth of geological and botanical interest.

A botanist's paradise

Not surprisingly this walk is immensely popular, not only with walkers, but with geography students, for whom this represents one of their most important field trips. As a result, whichever day of the week you choose for your visit it is unlikely you will have it all to yourself. Suffice to say that here is a walk which in terms of peace and quiet better rewards a visit during the week, if you can contrive such an arrangement. Hopefully then you can wander round in relative tranquillity, without (at least) the hordes of Wally Arnold's Tours that invariably accompany a weekend trip.

My personal preference, as to time of year, is undoubtedly spring and early summer, for then it is that the sublime contrast between the white limestone, the expansive green swards, and the rich blue sky is at its most vibrant. And then, too, the immense richness of the floral landscape for which this region is renowned is at its best.

By no means a lengthy walk, the full round is however best allocated a complete day, so captivating is the scenery and the way its changes unfold, so compelling the grandeur, so relaxing the air, that you will not want to hurry by.

Like a well-stocked staging post, the village of Malham, one of the main tourist centres of the Yorkshire Dales, offers the walker everything he or she needs, from a capacious car park (though in summer it is never enough) with attendant toilets and information centre, to plenteous opportunity for post-perambulatory refreshment, wet or dry. Tiny shops, which seem to increase annually, sprout from odd corners to furnish you with maps, guide books, foodstuffs, ice cream, sweets and chocolate, and a veritable cornucopia of trinkets and souvenirs. While to the northern end of the village, you can acquire anything in the way of equipment you may have forgotten or want to replace.

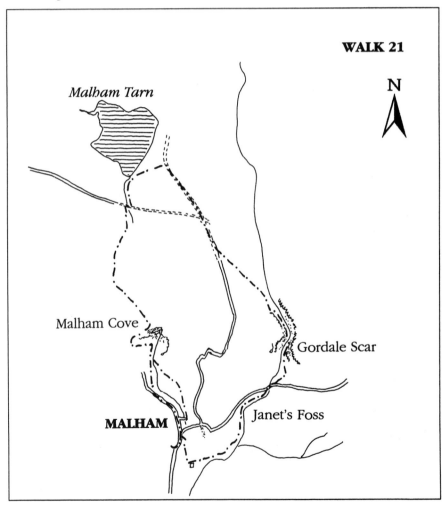

The origins of Malham go back to 700 AD, to a simple settlement centred on the present village green. Around 1100 AD, the village was cut in two when the beck became the boundary of lands owned by Fountains Abbey and Bolton Priory. Henry VIII's dissolution of the monasteries, however, brought new prosperity, replacing old wooden houses by stone buildings that still form the core of the village today. Also surviving to present times is the humped packhorse bridge, built across the beck in 1636.

Leave the car park and follow the road for a short distance towards the village centre. Keep an eye open for a small footbridge across the beck on your right, and use it to gain and follow downstream a broad path on the opposite side (signposted: Janet's Foss). A stile gives access to a meadow, the path keeping to its edge, beside the stream. Shortly, we pass through a gate not far from an old stone barn, and here change direction. The onward route passing the barn is never in doubt, and leads to a small woodland flanking Gordale Beck, in spring permeated by the strong and garlicky smell of wild ramsons which flower from April to June and especially like damp woodlands. The woodlands are a favoured haunt, too, of green woodpecker, while the beck is invariably patrolled by dippers and the occasional kingfisher.

The head of this shallow gorge is taken by a waterfall, Janet's Foss. Here, you may perch comfortably on rocks before the falls, watching white water tumble five metres into a crystal plunge pool, or walk around and above it to approach the very lip of the falls, formed by a bank of tufa about four metres wide. Tufa is similar to stalagmite in that it too is calcium carbonate precipitated from lime-saturated water. Unlike stalagmite, tufa is formed in a surface stream where algae grow and cause the precipitation by altering the chemistry of the water. Along Gordale Beck there are many spots where you will find tufa, some inactive, but some, as at Janet's Foss, still forming. It is most evident at the Foss in the way it projects over a rock ledge to create the cave behind the falls where a legendary fairy queen, Janet, once lived.

There is something mesmeric about this idyllic spot, as if indeed the fairies have cast a spell to charm all who pass by; or perhaps it is simply the fascination of water in motion.

Near the falls a narrow gully leads to a path and a metalled road. Turn right along the road and follow it for a short distance, the towering cliffs of Gordale Scar now in evidence before you. At a gate we enter beckside pastureland (often used as a camp site) and can take a path into the very jaws of the chasm. Arguments still rumble quietly as to how this unique rock architecture came into being, some propounding the view that it once formed an enormous cavern which in later times collapsed, leaving only its walls standing, but there is little real doubt that it was cut by retreating meltwater flowing from Ice Age glaciers.

The path into the gorge gives no indication of what awaits around a sharp corner, for here the walls close in dramatically, 50 metres high and barely 15 metres separating them at one point, severely overhanging at their base, and vertical at their easiest angle. Higher still more crags and scars continue upwards to the plateau surface almost 100 metres above the beck. Hidden from external view, a fine waterfall gushes through an eyehole in a thin wall of limestone, pauses in its downward flight in a natural amphitheatre, and spills splendidly to the broad base of the chasm floor. Close by the eyehole falls, which are actively depositing tufa on a bank below, a larger bank of inactive tufa, to the left, marks the site of an earlier waterfall. This was active until

250 – 300 years ago when the beck suddenly discovered its new route through the eyehole.

Many walkers elect to retreat from this point to find an alternative route to Malham Cove, but by splashing through the shallows you can reach the base of a prominent (in all but spate conditions) buttress of banded and inactive tufa dividing the falls, which, improbable though it may seem, offers an entertaining scramble to the sanctuary of the upper gorge, safely reached damp of foot but not of spirit. Plans were once afoot to construct a staircase up the falls, and this would have denied many a memorable experience. Even so, a flight of steps leading out of the gorge above indicates how close man came yet again to interfering needlessly with Nature's own way of doing things.

A good path climbs easily away from the gorge, which from above can clearly be recognised as a meltwater channel with rocky walls, and across a wide plateau of limestone, the limestone pavement for which this region is so well renowned. The path, absorbed now by a rich green fescue turf, broadens and presses on to reach another metalled road (it would take you back to Malham should the need arise). But it is the limestone pavement, both here and on the section leading to Malham Cove, to which the botanist will be attracted, for the range of plant life is immense, and quite remarkable. The fissures between the blocks (clints) of limestone are called grykes, and in them, protected from sun and the attentions of sheep, a rich variety of woodland and cliff-face species of plant exists. Hart's Tongue Fern is but one of a dozen ferns growing side by side with herb robert, wood sorrel, dog's mercury and, in a few secluded spots, baneberry. The turfed areas too have a wealth of flora: violets, fairy flax, bedstraws and birdsfoot-trefoil.

Follow the road for a short distance and continue to a minor crossroad (GR 904657). Just before the junction you will have traversed the North Craven Fault which marks the end of limestone pavements, for the rock ahead, supporting Malham Tarn, is impermeable slate. By keeping ahead, you will follow a graded track towards Lings Plantation, where a left turn, leaving the main track, brings you shortly to the outflow of the tarn, a natural lake.

A small dam, constructed in 1791, stabilises the level of the lake, the overflow of which, Malham Water, flows south under the road and across the North Craven Fault where it encounters limestone and promptly disappears underground at a spot labelled, unimaginatively, Water Sinks.

The scenery around Malham and its tarn has been the inspiration of many, including John Ruskin, and Charles Kingsley, who wrote part of *The Water Babies* whilst at Malham Tarn House as a guest of millionaire Walter Morrison. Charles Darwin, too, found the unrivalled setting conducive to his studies.

By following the line of the stream issuing from Malham Tarn you soon regain the road which should be used to cross the stream and reach a gate and a path on the opposite bank. Logic suggests that the waters from Malham Tarn are those which emerge in due course at the foot of Malham Cove, but this is not so. Tests were first carried out in the 1870s, and again a hundred years later, which demonstrate that the waters of Malham Tarn issue at Aire Head Springs, 700 metres south of Malham village. For this reason Malham became famous as one of the places where it was shown that underground streams are capable of crossing over one another independently in a complex system of limestone hydrology.

The water from Malham Tarn disappears sullenly into stream-bed debris, and from the spot we follow a path into a deepening dry valley, though the limestone underfoot can be slippery, until it curves sharply to avoid a dry waterfall, Comb Scar. Here the path doubles about to gain a stile at the head of a tributary gully which gives easy access to the floor of Watlowes, which about 14,000 years ago carried a powerful meltwater river. In those distant times the limestone was still frozen, of course, and prevented the water sinking underground as it does today.

The cliffs of Malham Cove

Ahead now we come to the very lip of Malham Cove, and this unsuspecting approach is infinitely more dramatic and awe-inspiring than the easy walk from the village. No one can fail to be impressed by the landscape, which is nothing short of spectacular, and justifies its popularity on that score along. The last few strides to the lip of the cove are over limestone pavement once more, with only the distant views to suggest there might be an abrupt drop ahead. Walkers with a good head for heights can approach the very edge for an aerial perspective of the people some 80 metres below.

Across to the right, the limestone pavement may easily be followed to a couple of stiles at the top of a staircase forced on the national park authority by the sheer weight of numbers that pass this way every week. Only a few minutes are needed to descend to the valley floor, where a left turn will lead you to the base of the cliff. In the centre, where a small dry valley cuts in, the height of the wall is 70 metres, topped on either side by another 10 metres of outcropping. The span of the cove is some 200 metres, with grassy ledges reaching in from the edges, but never quite meeting in the middle. Malham Beck, the infant River Aire, here issues from a small pool at the foot of the cliff, and in spite of cave-diving efforts, limited by a low underground passage, the caves behind the cove remain a mystery.

So rich is this region in its diverse interests that even the short distance back to the village holds your attention. Across the scree slopes on the east side of the cove are to be found the tall blue flowers of Jacob's ladder, here abundant, but nationally rare and not to be picked or trampled. Also rare, is a small tree, almost wholly confined to limestone crags, the rock whitebeam, whose delicate silvery leaves catch the eye.

As you follow the path away from the cove you pass through an open museum of farming history, if you know what you are looking for! The dry stone walls across the valley date from the Enclosure Acts, about 200 years ago. Above the beck may be observed a series of horizontal ledges, linches, or lynchets, built almost 1000 years ago to improve the land, while low grass ridges across the valley floor, better picked out in late evening sunlight from above the cove, are now all that remain of Celtic field boundaries from about 2000 years ago.

In a short while you reach the road back into Malham, passing en route Calamine House (the first on the right) where quantities of zinc mined early in the nineteenth century were stored before shipment to the brass foundries of the Midlands.

With such a wealth of interest, it is small wonder that such a comparatively short walk demands so much of your time. But it is unquestionably worth it.

Variant finish: After leaving the cliffs of Malham Cove, watch for a clapper bridge on the left crossing the stream to a gate. From the gate climb diagonally right to a small plateau of fescue turf and continue ascending gently to a prominent stile beyond which a good path works its way back to Malham by a succession of narrow walled lanes, reaching the village close by the humped packhorse bridge and the village green. Even here you can delay a moment longer returning to the main roadway (which is invariably heavily trafficked especially in summer), by continuing along the true left bank of the beck until you reach the narrow bridge across which you began this walk.

Walk 22: Whernside

Maps: (1) OS Landranger 1:50,000 series: Sheet 98 – Wensleydale and Upper Wharfedale; (2) OS Outdoor Leisure Map 1:25,000 series : Sheet 2 – Yorkshire Dales – Western Area

Start: Chapel-le-Dale, near Old Inn. GR 743776.

Distance: 13 kilometres (8 miles)

Ascent: 445 metres (1460 feet)

Type of walk: Lofty walk across elongated ridge with good views. The route descends to the Ribblehead Viaduct before returning easily through pastureland to the start.

Chapel-le-Dale to Ribblehead

Owing its fame rather to an association with its siblings, Ingleborough and Pen y Ghent, which together form the famous and popular Three Peaks Walk, than to the distinction of being the highest mountain in the Yorkshire Dales, Whernside boasts a variety of ascents, two of which are used in the route that follows. It is an elongated ridge (few people realise just how elongated), narrow and undulating, rising from the distant village gardens of Ingleton and descending gently northwards into Dentdale some 14 kilometres (9 miles) away. On a clear winter's day, suitably equipped walkers will find the traverse from Chapel-le-Dale to Ribblehead one of the most entertaining in the Dales; in summer you'll just have to pick your way through the crowds.

The walk begins near the Old Inn on the ancient Lancaster to Richmond road, now the B6255. There is a camp-site near the inn, and room to park a few cars; higher up the road, near the track which leads to the Great Douk Cave, a slight deviation in the wall has created room for yet more cars.

We start along a farm access road (Philpin Lane) which leaves the B6255 at GR 742776 and leads pleasantly and easily to Bruntscar Farm (GR 739791). At Bruntscar the access road forms a T-junction, and here we turn right and walk a short distance to a stile giving access to wide grassy pastureland. [Note at this point a gate, just before the stile. This leads on to a bridleway to Winterscales Farm near the viaduct, and is the route by which we will return.]

Crossing the lower part of the pasture is easy enough, and brings us to a couple of stiles, one on either side of a gate, beyond which the going becomes steeper and muddier until we reach two more stiles at the intake wall. A pause for breath will allow you to take in the Ribblehead Viaduct, and the long wall on the south side of the dale, reaching from the distinctive top of Ingleborough, across Simon Fell to Park Fell overlooking the Ribble valley.

Over the intake wall a flight of steps awaits; these can only have been constructed with long-legged giants in mind, and more diminutive travellers may be suitably impressed with their fitness if they can make it to the top without stopping or dying. Thankfully, the end of this leg-wearying wonder brings the end of all significant ascent: only minor ups remain, and these follow the ridge wall all the way to the summit. A stretch of about one kilometre along the ridge has undergone some footpath repair work as part of the Three Peaks Project; how successful it will be remains to be seen, but Heaven knows it was badly needed.

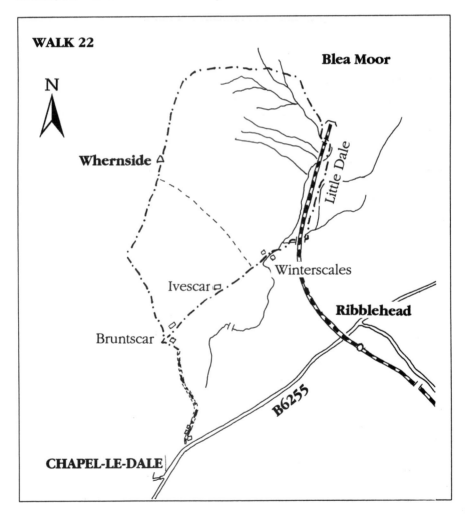

Shortly before the summit we encounter at a stile the direct ascent, used by the Three Peaks route, from Batty Green and Winterscales, and a signpost here tells you that it is 4 miles to Ribblehead. The summit, when finally we arrive, is marked by a trig on the other side of the wall in Cumbria, so you will have to change counties if you want to tick this one off. Personally, I have a suspicion that a few metres further on along the wall you will find marginally higher ground, the true summit, unmarked, and in Yorkshire!

Whernside and the Ribblehead viaduct

The continuation to Ribblehead is easy to follow, setting off along the wall which, in varying states of disrepair, keeps us company across Whernside's highest ground for just under 1.5 kilometres (about 1 mile) and as far as a large cairn. Here the route drops sharply at first towards Little Dale, later easing with predictable bog-trotting and some more erosion control trials to join an ancient track, the Craven Way, at a stile. More attempts to minimise the damage to the path are met with on the long descent to Little Dale.

The valley bottom is reached near the entrance to Blea Moor tunnel, a remarkable feat of engineering on the Settle-Carlisle line, for many years threatened with closure. The tunnel burrows for 2 kilometres (almost 1½ miles) under the moors, and was constructed in the 1870s.

At the same point stands another remarkable feat of ingenuity, for the bridge spanning the railway line is also an aqueduct carrying the waters of Force Gill. The crossing of Little Dale Beck can sometimes be a problem after prolonged wet weather, but in normal conditions should present no difficulty.

The hard work is over now and all that remains is a gentle amble back to the starting point. A broad path continues from the bridge, past Blea Moor Sidings, and passes beneath the railway line to make for Winterscales Farm. It would, however, be a pity to have come this far and not carry on (rather than pass under the line) as far as the Ribblehead Viaduct. This is one place where I suspect everyone will stand in wonder at the skills of those hardy engineers who in the early 1870s constructed this giant monument.

The railway, a stark reminder of the Midland Railway's determination to construct its own route to Scotland, was built at enormous cost both in terms of finance and of human life. In recent years, affected by the ravages of time and the sheer inhospitality of the climate, the future of the railway was called very much into question as the old spectre of financial viability once more reared its ugly head. During this time a vigorous campaign was waged to keep the line open, and all the effort which went into the campaign was at last vindicated in April, 1989, when the Government announced that the line was to remain open. It will long remain as a proud testament to Victorian endeavour and achievement. From 1989 into the early 1990s, the viaduct saw massive repair work, funded by a consortium comprising British Rail, English Heritage, local authorities and other interested bodies, and designed to resolve a problem of water seepage and falling masonry.

We can now pass quickly under the bridge and follow an access road to Gunnerfleet Farm. Cross Winterscales Beck, and in a short while turn left to pursue the bridleway past Ivescar Farm and on to rejoin our outward route at Bruntscar.

Walk 23: Ingleborough from Clapham

Maps: (1) OS Landranger 1:50,000 series: Sheet 98 – Wensleydale and Upper Wharfedale; (2) OS Outdoor Leisure Map 1:25,000 series: Sheet 2 – Yorkshire Dales – Western area

Start: National Park car park and information centre, Clapham. GR 746692. Charge for car parking. Toilets.

Distance: 17 kilometres (10.5 miles)

Ascent: 560 metres (1840 feet)

Type of walk: A fine walk of no great difficulty (unless you fall into Gaping Gill) beginning in a charming village, and taking in meltwater ravines, pot-holes, wild, moorland wandering, a high mountain summit, and dramatic limestone scenery. There are other ascents of Ingleborough, but this is undoubtedly the best.

Karst away

Clapham is a village of rare delight, captivating at every turn of the road, tastefully decorated with old bridges and waterfalls, white cottages, old stone houses and stands of ancient trees. It is a place of which 'rural charm' is not so much a cliché as a way of life, one now thankfully restored with the building of a bypass to divert the ever-increasing volume of through traffic, and allowing the return of the comfortable atmosphere of peace and tranquillity. Weekends, as happens throughout the Yorkshire Dales, inject an element of fretting and fraying as visitors trip in to revitalise their jaded weekday spirits.

Viewed from the southwest, Ingleborough rises as an isolated summit from an extensive plateau of limestone culminating in a fine series of scars overlooking Chapel-le-Dale. Once thought to have been the highest summit in England, the mountain has a unique appeal, its great sprawl dominating the countryside of west Craven, its distinctive flat-topped summit a feature easily identifiable from as far away as the western fells of Lakeland. Unspectacular in mountaineering terms, the vast Ingleborough landscape is nonetheless remarkable, its diverse nooks and crannies an immense store of botanical and archæological goodies, its geological infrastructure a honeycomb of delight.

Based on a thick layer of limestone, the mountain and its moorland surrounds are a repeated succession of shales, limestones and sandstones – the Yoredale Facies – capped by a resilient layer of millstone grit. Twenty thousand years ago a deep covering of glacial ice gouged out the features we see today, while meltwater rivers carved valleys and gorges in the still frozen landscape. Then, as the climate changed, and the caves became unblocked, rivers sank underground into the heart of classic karst country. It is this treasury of geological history that gives Ingleborough its distinctive profile and its claim to fame.

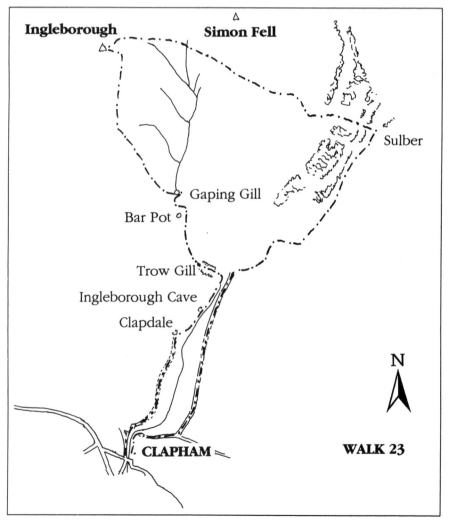

Ascents, none of them difficult or demanding, may be made from virtually all directions, but that from the village of Clapham, is unequivocally the most popular, and facilitates a grand tour of all Ingleborough's finer points.

We begin with a pleasant walk along Clapham Beck, having left the car park (GR 746692) near the National Park Information Centre (the old manor house), and moving right to cross the beck by an old stone bridge. A variety of cottages accompany our way and lead quickly to the fine church of St James, substantially rebuilt in 1814, though its tower dates from the fourteenth century. Along this stretch the beck is a favourite haunt of dippers and grey wagtails.

Along Clapham Beck

There is an option, soon encountered, of visiting the landscaped grounds of Ingleborough Hall Estate (an attractive proposition, for which there is a small fee), or you can continue past the entrance to the grounds to follow Clapdale Lane (signposted: 'Ingleborough; Gaping Gill: Ingleborough Cave') and amble lazily as far as Clapdale Farm where a sharp descent, right, back towards the beck will reunite you with the path through the estate grounds.

Ingleborough Hall, now an outdoor centre, was formerly the home of Reginald Farrer (1880-1920), a renowned botanist who during the second half of his brief life made repeated journeys to far corners of the world in pursuit of his passion, and brought many foreign plant specimens to Clapham to decorate the grounds of their home. A visit to the grounds is always a delight.

Further along Clapham Beck there are guided tours into Ingleborough Cave, and these too will waylay your intentions. In the early years of the nineteenth century the underground network of caverns between Gaping Gill and Clapham Beck Head remained a source of mystery and wonder. Ingleborough Cave, the obvious entrance, was blocked after only a few metres by a wall of stalagmite beyond which a tiny space of air stretched above a pool of water into the darkness. Occasional floods suggested that this cave might be connected to the underground river of Gaping Gill, and so in 1837 the landowner ordered the stalagmite barrier to be broken down, to drain away the lake it held back, and to allow exploration of the interior. A fine cavern was found part of the way to Gaping Gill, but it took almost another 150 years of spasmodic exploration before the final link was made.

If you can resist the temptations of Ingleborough Cave, continue along the path through a sheltered glen between low scars of limestone. Ahead the main valley curves to the left and a stile helps you into the rocky maw of Trow Gill.

Rising steadily the gorge is overlooked by slopes becoming higher and steeper, until it narrows between vertical rock more than 25 metres high on each side. The gorge narrows dramatically to a spill of boulders over which you must clamber to reach the dry, grassy valley beyond. Trow Gill is a classic example of a limestone gorge, built by a surface stream of meltwater flowing off the limestone plateau above as the glaciers retreated at the end of the last Ice Age.

The path here follows the line of a wall to a couple of adjacent stiles, beyond which lies the broad limestone plinth of Ingleborough. Only a few metres ahead, on the left, a sizeable pot-hole, Bar Pot, provides the easiest access for cavers into the Gaping Gill system whose network of caverns underlies all this stretch of moorland. Bar Pot is not a place for walkers; the entrance is obvious enough, but the deep shaft immediately inside isn't.

Ahead rises the broad slope of Little Ingleborough (not named on the 1:50,000 map), with the main summit overtopping that. The onward route is now obvious, picking a way around the worst stretches of bog to begin the ascent to the first minor summit. Away to the right, however, surrounded by a fence lies the most famous of all pot-holes, Gaping Gill. The pot takes its name from its great entrance, which swallows with ease the waters of Fell Beck as they gather from the high grounds of Ingleborough. This wide open hole, of obviously great depth, was an irresistible challenge to the explorers of the nineteenth century, but it was not until the last decade of the century that a Frenchman, Edouard Martel, in August 1895, finally reached the floor of the shaft, more than 100 metres down. The main chamber of Gaping Gill is the largest cavern in Britain, 140 metres long and almost 30 metres high and wide.

Because of the alternative entrances into the Gaping Gill system, a descent of the main shaft is now rarely undertaken. But on certain bank holiday weekends local caving clubs divert the flow of Fell Beck and rig up a bosun's chair so that visitors may descend in comfort (!). The clubs treat this as a much-needed fund-raising exercise, but to intrepid walkers it represents an opportunity to glimpse a totally different and fascinating world beneath our feet.

From Gaping Gill the path heads northwest for the base of Little Ingleborough which is gained by a steepish pull to a bevy of shelter-cairns on its upper edge from where there is a fine prospect across Ribblesdale to Pen y Ghent and Fountains Fell. A dry path, one of the many stretches of experimental restabilising work undertaken by the national park authority, leads onwards across marshy ground to begin a slanting ascent to the rim of Ingleborough's main summit.

As you reach the rim you pass through the remains of a hillfort wall, a massive encircling wall, now collapsed, around the edge of a summit plateau which also contains the foundations, still traceable in the peaty summit, of nineteen circular huts believed to be a settlement of the first Iron Age man in this district. It was from this elevated vantage point, named Rigodunum, that the Brigantian leader, Venutius, led a revolt against the Romans which was not finally quelled until AD 74, by Julius Agricola.

The continuation to the summit follows a line of small cairns to a massive cairn beside a trig point and a crossed-wall shelter surmounted by a view indicator and erected by the Ingleton Fell and Rescue Team to commemorate the Coronation of Queen Elizabeth in 1953. The highest point, the true summit, is marked by another cairn on a rocky plinth a few metres northwest of the trig, and overlooks the Doe valley and the long descent to Crina Bottom and Ingleton. This has a history of its own, being the site of a round tower (a hospice) built in 1830, but substantially destroyed on the day of its opening by participants rather the worse for drink: the curved stones which formed its base are still clearly seen.

The onward descent leaves the northeast corner of the summit plateau to gain a reconstructed path along the southern flank of Simon Fell to a derelict shooting hut. Beyond lies a weird landscape known as Sulber Scars, a massive desert of fissured white limestone through which a path picks its way to a lonely signpost at GR 778735. Horton-in-Ribblesdale lies not far ahead, but here we must turn right on a grassy path to reach a stile at Sulber Gate.

Continue ahead, keeping the wall on your left and when the path forks at a cairn a short distance further on, keep right, making for the conspicuous cairn atop Long Scar. Later, before reaching Long Scar, another cairn marks a change of direction, again right, to enter a wide grassy amphitheatre known as Clapham Bottoms. The path is clear enough and brings you via one gate to another at the head of Long Lane, an old bridleway connecting Clapham and Selside in Ribblesdale.

A short way down Long Lane there is a fine view of Trow Gill, its naked limestone walls contrasting with the moulded grassy slopes of glacial moraine to its right. There are splendid views, too, across woodlands below in which shelters the village of Clapham, while a conspicuous dip in the lane marks the line of the North Craven Fault. Long Lane in due course meets Thwaites Lane at a T-junction; this ancient route is a continuation of Mastiles Lane above Kilnsey, a monastic highway that crossed the southern Dales to link the lands of Fountains Abbey.

Turn right into Thwaite Lane and descend towards Clapham, passing through two tunnels built by the Farrers to protect the privacy of their estate. This tunnelled lane ends near Clapham church at the top end of the village, from where, left, you will find the car park only a short distance away.

Walkers wanting to add a little extra to their day can pursue an alternative finish from Sulber Gate. Here, on crossing the stile, turn immediately left, through a wicket gate beyond which an outstanding rocky amphitheatre opens up. A faint path leads via strangely-named Thieves Moss through the rocky pavement to Beggar's Stile in the escarpment at the very head of Crummack Dale. Cross the stile and descent to grassy terraces traversing the west side of Crummack Dale to Crummack farm. Follow the ensuing track either to gain Thwaite Lane direct, or earlier, at a bend, bear right through a stile to the crags of Nappa Scars and the famous Norber Erratics, a fine display of slaty boulders deposited here from an outcrop higher up the valley, by a retreating glacier. This diversion will bring you beneath Robin Proctor's Scar to meet Thwaite Lane about a kilometre east of Long Lane; and that kilometre is about the only significant addition to the length of this fine circuit of classic karst country.

Walk 24: Pen y Ghent from Horton-in-Ribblesdale

Maps: (1) OS Landranger 1:50,000 series: Sheet 98 – Wensleydale and Upper Wharfedale; (2) OS Outdoor Leisure Map 1:25,000 series: Sheet 2 – Yorkshire Dales – Western area

Start: National Park car park, Horton-in-Ribblesdale. GR 808726. Toilets. Charge for parking.

Distance: 7.25 kilometres (4.5 miles)

Ascent: 460 metres (1510 feet)

Type of walk: Once a substantial quagmire, the ascent has been vastly improved in recent years making what was tedious almost enjoyable, with the result that you can now concentrate rather more on the scenery than where you put your feet.

A little of what you fancy

Pen y Ghent is the lowest of the Yorkshire 'Three Peaks', but makes up for it by being the only one to entertain the Pennine Way. It lies barely three kilometres (2 miles) by crow from the valley of the Ribble which it overlooks, and its ascent need occupy little more than half a day. Like an ancient galleon, its two-tiered prow sails purposefully across the surrounding countryside, drawing thousands to its summit each year in an endless tread which has stamped the life out of its pathways and necessitated urgent cosmetic surgery.

Opinions differ as to the meaning and origin of its name, which in spite of a once strong Norman influence in the valley below, must derive from the Celtic, from the Kingdom of Brigantia and the tribes forced into what were then remote regions by Roman and Teutonic settlers. Generally thought to mean "Hill of the Winds", but believed by others (not without equal validity) to mean "Hill of the Border Country", its name unquestionably comes from the Welsh language, rendered *Pen y Gwynt* and *Pen y Cant* respectively, – *cant* meaning a rim.

The walk begins in the straggling village of Horton, mentioned as a farming community in the Domesday Book (1086-87), and to which King Henry VI came during the Wars of the Roses (1455-85) to hide from his enemies.

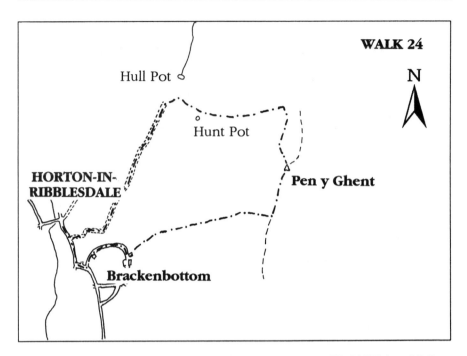

WALK 24

Hull Pot

Hunt Pot

HORTON-IN-RIBBLESDALE

Pen y Ghent

Brackenbottom

From the car park turn right to a track leaving the road at GR 809724, and follow the Pennine Way, which in spite of heading northeast is in fact the southbound route. A steady amble along the walled path brings you easily to the fell gate, with Pen y Ghent looming large on your right. This route, Horton Scar Lane, is part of an ancient packhorse road once used to cross to Littondale. Retrospectively, the view of Ingleborough is marred by the ugly scars of the Beecroft limestone quarry, where at the beginning of the second World War quarrying activities attained then new heights of landscape devastation as some 43,000 tons were blown from the cliff face.

Horton Scar Lane is easy walking, gaining height almost imperceptibly. On the right a dry valley is a reminder of the underground drainage system which permeates these hills. Above all this, at the fell gate our path turns sharply right, but another prominent track continues ahead to Hull Pot, a great square-cut hole which looks almost as if it is man-made. The pot is only 300 metres beyond the gate, so it is worth a few minutes of your time. In dry weather no water enters the pot, but when it is wet, with upstream sinks constricted, the resultant waterfall in Hull Pot is a splendid sight. In spite of its massive size, 90 metres long and nearly 20 metres deep and wide, there are times, perhaps only once or so each year, when the pot fills up completely. Normally all the water sinks beneath the boulders, but this route, too, is constricted so that in times of full flood the water overflows down the dry valley. As a source of attraction to cavers, however, Hull Pot is a disappointment.

By way of contrast, return to the fell gate and pursue the new path which now leads ultimately to the rim of Pen y Ghent. On the way, but off route to the right, lies Hunt

Pot, a classic pot-hole with a dramatic entrance to the underground world beneath our feet. Here a small stream cascades down a staircase of ledges before it disappears into a vertical rift. You can, with care, reach the northern end of the rift and peer down into the eerie depths, which though apparently bottomless in fact descends only about 30 metres before plunging unseen into another deep waterfall shaft.

Return to the path and follow its direct and conspicuous route to the edge of the escarpment, where it turns abruptly right, and eases along the edge before a final short scamper to the summit. The view is now quite expansive, typical of the fine airy panoramas for which the Pennines are justly famous.

Pen y Ghent from Dale Head

A wall crosses the summit of Pen y Ghent, and just over it a trig and a large cairn mark the highest ground. Immediately in front of them a path seems to leap out into the space between Pen y Ghent and distant Fountains Fell, but it turns quickly right and pursues a drier line to the prominent tiered southern end of the mountain than of old. A few board-walks are met a short distance before the start of the descent, and then it is hands, feet and bottoms to the rescue as we begin the rocky drop to the first platform. Ahead stretches the line of ascent from Dale Head, the on-going (or on-coming) Pennine Way, it, too, having undergone a measure of repair work.

The descent of the second rock step has a narrow path running along the edge, and this in spite of its proximity to the rolling hillside has a more secure feel about it than nearby rocks, which are quite slippery when wet. In a matter of minutes a couple of stiles are encountered on the right, beyond which the long descent to Brackenbottom undulates easily to the valley bottom.

By turning right on reaching the minor road at Brackenbottom, we arrive in a short while back on the main road, near St Oswald's church. The church dates from about 1100, but has seen restoration work in 1400, when the tower was added, 1823 and 1879, as well as in modern times.

The car park is now only a few minutes away along the road.

Walk 25: Gragareth and Great Coum

Maps: (1) OS Landranger 1:50,000 series: Sheet 98 – Wensleydale and Upper Wharfedale; (2) OS Outdoor Leisure Map 1:25,000: Sheet 2 – Yorkshire Dales – Western area

Start: Near Leck Fell House. GR 674791. There is ample room on the left of the road to park cars without causing obstruction.

Distance: 11.5 kilometres (7.2 miles)

Ascent: 360 metres (1180 feet)

Type of walk: The walk is almost entirely on grass, with very little bog, and although there are no rights of way along the summit ridge, a path exists which suggests that considerate walkers are tolerated. The panorama is vast, indeed it is one of the finest in the whole of the Pennines. The return journey involves descending a wild and tussocky fellside until a farm track is reached.

A walk on the wild side

Tucked away, definitely out of sight and for many walkers most certainly out of mind, in the top right hand corner of Lancashire lies a wild stretch of moorland Lancashire that I'll bet no one knows about. It is a stubby finger of ground poking into Cumbria and North Yorkshire, but once flanked by Westmorland and the West Riding of Yorkshire. It rises easily to a moorland fell with a strange name, Gragareth. At 627 metres (2058 feet), and after the wanton and disgraceful transfer in the reorganisation of local government boundaries in 1974 of the Old Man of Coniston from Lancashire-beyond-the-Sands, as it was known, to Cumbria, Gragareth is now the highest summit in Lancashire, a loss of altitude of some 176 metres (577 feet).

Gragareth forms part of a ridge culminating at its northernmost end with an even higher summit, Great Coum, in Cumbria and overlooking Dentdale. The whole ridge is an excellent vantage point with splendid views over the Yorkshire Dales, the coastal plain of Lancashire, and as far as Lakeland. Yet it is an area seldom visited, except by that species of humanity which pursues its pleasure under the hilltops rather than on them. It is truly wild, a massive, sprawling amphitheatre of burbling becks, dry stone walls, and some of the finest pot-holes in the Pennines. Few trees grow here, the tussock grass bends low cowering from the prevailing winds, and the few birds you see pass swiftly by in search of more rewarding fare.

The easiest approach is from Leck, and this also facilitates a pleasing circuit equally suitable for occasional walkers and the more regular frequenters of our hills. Leck is a small and quiet village, lying just off the A65, a short distance southeast of Kirkby Lonsdale, and close by Cowan Bridge.

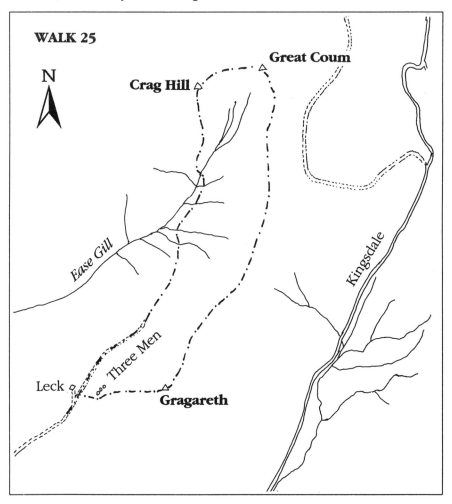

Cowan Bridge itself owns a certain notoriety, for here you will find the school for clergymen's daughters attended by the Brontë sisters. The original school, immortalised in Mrs Gaskell's biography of Charlotte and as Lowood in *Jane Eyre*, though altered and now a row of terraced cottages, is still there, a plaque commemorating its place in history. The school was moved to Casterton, three miles away, in 1833. In its present day setting, with the main road and the constant drive of holiday traffic hurrying by, it is difficult to imagine how harsh and isolated a place the school could have seemed in the 1820s.

Cowan Bridge, and Ireby a short way further south, both afford access to Leck, and from there to a metalled roadway running into the great hollow of the hills as far as Leck Fell House, surely the most isolated inhabited dwelling in Lancashire.

There are two ample parking areas near Leck Fell House – still an active farm – and you should begin from there. There are no legitimate access routes on to the hills, but well behaved walkers have enjoyed unrestricted use for years. Don't be alarmed then if you are approached by a local farmer enquiring whether you have a permit; it's the pot-holers he is concerned about, especially those without proper authority to enter the many systems that honeycomb the landscape.

The Three Men of Gragareth

Begin along the road to a gate on the right, just before Leck Fell House, beyond which a broad track heads out across the lower slopes of Gragareth. You can follow this track for a short distance if you wish, or take immediately to the hillside. Either way your immediate objective is the stand of three stone pillars, the Three Men of Gragareth, prominent from your starting point, but not from the track below them. It is presumed the pillars were constructed by the men who built the stone wall you will find along the summit ridge.

From the Three Men head east over easily sloping ground until you either hit the trig point marking the highest point, or the wall beyond, which marks the county boundary: the trig stands about 200 metres from the wall, as if declaring itself to be firmly in Lancashire, and could be missed in poor visibility. On a good, clear day the view is superb! Barbondale and the Howgills are close to hand, Kirkby Lonsdale and the winding River Lune, Lancaster, the great mud flats of Morecambe Bay glinting in the sun, the high fells of Lakeland, the Forest of Bowland, and the broad sweep of the Yorkshire fells and dales. Quite one of the best.

To continue to Great Coum simply follow the wall, a remarkably well-constructed and unusually high affair that might have been intended to keep Lancastrians and Yorkshiremen apart in days gone by. On the eastern side of the wall many more walls ascend from Kingsdale, but the western side is free of these impediments to progress. As a result you can stroll easily over the intermediate top, Green Hill, all the way to Great Coum, having to negotiate only one wall, and that by a convenient gate.

Just beyond the gate, where its wall and the ridge wall meet, you will find the County Stone, a large, primeval boulder where the old counties of Lancashire, Westmorland and West Riding met.

Further on, up a slight rise, the top of Great Coum is adorned by an impressive and large cairn. It stands on the north side of the ridge wall, and there is no easy way to it now that once-convenient gaps in the wall have been repaired. The cairn does not mark the highest point of the hill, though it is commonly regarded as such. The true summit is a vague spot height, 687 metres, at GR 701836, impossible to reach without climbing walls, and not worth the dilemma – should we, or shouldn't we?

To return to Leck Fell House, continue along the wall to Crag Hill, and from there descend untracked ground to the confluence of Long Gill and Ease Gill. Ascend gradually from the becks, aiming for the intake wall above Ease Gill where you will pick up a narrow path leading in due course to the broad track on which you started this round. The rest of the journey is a simple stroll, for the most part gently inclined downwards.

Walk 26: Dodd Fell Hill and Drumaldrace

Maps: (1) OS Landranger 1:50,000 series: Sheet 98 – Wensleydale and Upper Wharfedale; (2) OS Outdoor Leisure Maps 1:25,000 series: Sheet 2 – Yorkshire Dales – Western Area and Sheet 30 – Yorkshire Dales – Northern and Central areas. These two maps overlap to cover this walk; if you only want to take one map use Sheet 30

Start: Hawes: Car Park adjoining National Park Information Centre in the old station yard. GR 876899. Toilets.

Distance: 20.5 kilometres (12.75 miles)

Ascent: 510 metres (1670 feet)

Type of walk: Good walking initially along the Pennine Way ascending to Kidhow Gate. The diversion to take in the summit of Dodd Fell Hill is boggy, but not desperate. A metalled roadway leads from Kidhow Gate to a broad track heading for Drumaldrace, from where the long descent to Burtersett starts by following a vague path through a stretch of wet ground, loses it, then finds it again by a gate giving on to a long and enjoyable descent to the village. The final section is along the main road, though there are less fume-laden alternatives.

Slumbering sentinels

One might be forgiven for supposing that neither of these summits could inspire the mind to romantic lyricism. Like a pair of slumbering sentinels they rise protectively above the ancient market town of Hawes, waiting, it seems, to trap the unsuspecting visitor beguiled by the subtle attractiveness of this part of upper Wensleydale.

On second thoughts, an unsuspecting visitor more accustomed to the extravagant beauty that is in the valleys below would probably fail to see the subtlety and restrained charm of the hills, for these rewards await the walker with time to take it all in, time to observe these grand and bleak, brooding landscapes.

The walk begins in the town of Hawes, a quaint arrangement of alleyways and cottages, concealed nooks and crannies, that give the impression of mellowed old age,

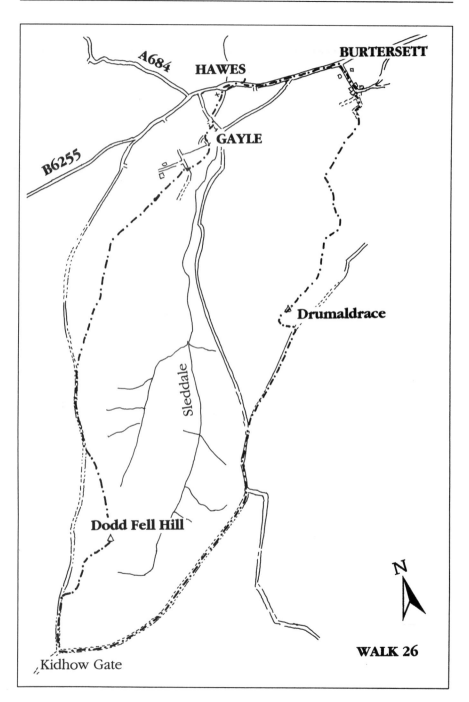

A684

HAWES

BURTERSETT

B6255

GAYLE

Drumaldrace

Sleddale

Dodd Fell Hill

Kidhow Gate

N

WALK 26

a veteran whose credentials must at least extend back to the Domesday Book. If it were so, you could forgive the town its eccentricity, its indifference to law and order as if its blocks of buildings had tumbled haphazardly from a toy box. Then you find it's nothing of the sort, that the town is a mere youngster unable to trace its pedigree beyond the fourteenth century. In fact, when the Domesday Book was compiled, Hawes and the countryside about was forest land, and, as Camden saw it, "such a dreary waste and horrid silent wilderness among the mountains . . .". The region, above and around the town, is still wild, but perceptions change and the conditioned opinions of ancient chroniclers drift lazily into the pages of history to serve only as peepholes into the past, to be drawn into modern books like this, as old wine in new bottles.

Leave Hawes on the Pennine Way, which cuts behind the church to the village of Gayle, and by a narrow path through a housing estate, across fields by a paved pathway, to West End, where by a stile you enter a field. Continue ahead a short distance to another stile at which a change of direction is called for to head for Gaudy Lane (not named on the 1:50,000 map). The lane leads to Gaudy House, but before this the path branches left, through a gate and up an incline to begin the long, but gradual ascent to Kidhow Gate at GR 829834. This stretch is little more than pleasant strolling along an old packhorse route, named West Cam Road. Away to the right the profiles of Swarth Fell and Wild Boar Fell rise above the hollow of Mallerstang, while to the left the bulk of Drumaldrace blocks all views in that direction, for the moment.

Walkers making for the summit of Dodd Fell Hill (tautology gone mad!) should leave West Cam Road after the last intake wall ascending from the left, at about GR 840857, and head across rough ground to the summit, marked by a trig. On leaving the summit, aim for a gate at GR 832841, near a ruined cottage, Rock Edge Cottage (shown, but not named on the 1:50,000 map), where you rejoin the Pennine Way for the final section to Kidhow Gate.

At Kidhow Gate the track meets the Roman road from Ribblehead to Bainbridge (Virosidum), and this is our direction. But Kidhow Gate is a convenient place to halt for a while, and to reflect how the ill-defined slope to the southeast separates the waters ultimately destined for the Wharfe and the Ribble, a distinction more apparent on the map than on the ground. Northwest the streams feed Snaizeholme Beck and in due course the Ure.

The long stroll from Kidhow Gate to Drumaldrace (also known as Wether Fell), along the Roman road, is an easy and tranquil traverse high above Langstrothdale. At the start of the deep descent into Sleddale the Roman road branches right, initially as an enclosed track. Stay with this track until the wall on the left ends, and from here an easy jaunt brings you to the large cairn which marks the summit of the fell.

The quickest way back to Hawes is to return to the road and descend into Sleddale. But good navigators should aim for a gate in a wall at GR 880874, beyond which a green path winds downwards to the hamlet of Burtersett. Both before and after Burtersett there are short-cuts back to Hawes if time is pressing, but once through the hamlet the quickest return is along the main road (A684).

The complete round trip involves a modest amount of ascent, all of which is accommodated gradually, and most of that on the ascent of Dodd Fell Hill. Tackling this walk in poor visibility may well deny you the vistas which so characterise the

Pennines and are the main reason for doing this walk, but the walk has considerable merit in its own right and there are no navigational difficulties of any note other than on the short stretch from the summit of Drumaldrace.

On the summit of Dodd Fell Hill

Walk 27: Across the Watershed: Buckden to Dent

Maps: (1) OS Landranger 1:50,000 series: Sheet 98 – Wensleydale and Upper Wharfedale; (2) OS 1:25,000 Outdoor Leisure Maps: Sheet 2 – Yorkshire Dales – Western area and Sheet 30 – Northern and Central areas

Start: Buckden village, Wharfedale. GR 942772.

Distance: 39 kilometres (24 miles)

Ascent: 530 metres (1740 feet)

Type of walk: A long linear link between the River Wharfe and the River Dee, and pursuing a mild flirtation with the Ribble en route. The walk substantially follows the Dales Way, and is best reserved for a long summer or late spring day. Much of the route is signposted and on good footpaths, and may be conveniently broken at Ribblehead if necessary.

The tang of wild places

There is a quiet lustre about the village of Buckden, like an unpolished gem it lies on a green and bracken-coloured cushion in a trough of high hills, hemmed in by a beauty that makes the heart ache and the spirit rejoice. Buckden is the "valley of the bucks", the home of deer as far as records take us, to the days when knights rode north from Skipton Castle in pursuit of sport, and the hillsides echoed to the huntsman's horn; indeed deer roamed the wooded slopes of Birks Fell until as recently as the early 1950s, but, alas, there are none there now.

The first objective of this walk is the hamlet of Hubberholme, barely two kilometres down the road to Langstrothdale, and walkers wanting to make progress in the early moments of what is a long walk should press on along the road while the rest of us pursue a more adventurous route.

At the northern end of Buckden village a broad track leaves the National Park car park rising easily through Rakes Wood on the first stage of the ascent to Buckden Pike. When the track deviates uphill towards higher ground, continue ahead contouring along the green lane of Buckden Rake until by an indistinct footpath we can descend to the hamlet of Cray. Buckden Rake is a continuation of Gilbert Lane further

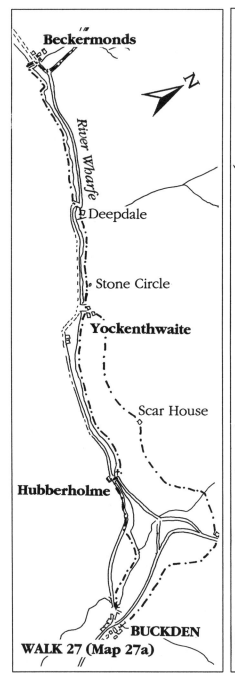

WALK 27 (Map 27a)

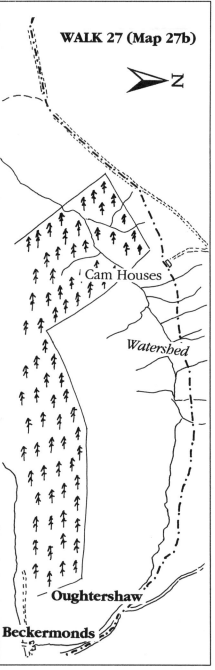

WALK 27 (Map 27b)

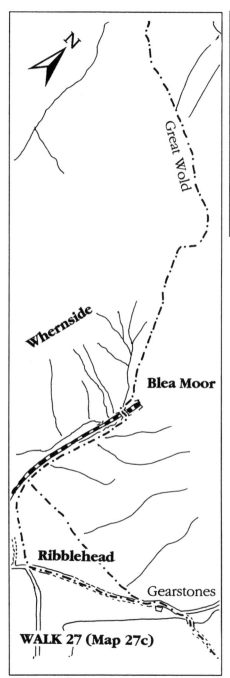

WALK 27 (Map 27c)

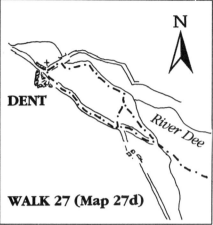

WALK 27 (Map 27d)

north, which goes over the Stake Pass into Raydale, on the line of the Roman road from Bainbridge to Ilkley.

Opposite the White Lion pub at Cray the route goes through a ford, and climbs by a farm to begin a looping traverse above Todd's Wood and Hubberholme Wood to Scar House, half concealed by trees. Scar House is an early Quaker meeting place, where, in 1652 and 1677, George Fox, founder of the Society of Friends, came a-preaching the perfectibility of all men through inward personal experiences. It is not recorded what he thought of the outward personal experiences that must have impressed themselves upon him in this secluded corner of beauty. Here, the limestone bed and the trees serve to enhance the superb view down the length of Wharfedale, which below us changes course abruptly, having issued from the narrower confines of Langstrothdale.

The looping path, less obvious now, continues along the southern fringes of Yockenthwaite Moor, to the hamlet of the same name. En route it passes, not that you would notice it, the fissured entrance to Strans Gill Pot, a cave system totally unknown until 1967, and possessing for many pot-holers in its 'Passage of Time' one of the best decorated cave passages in the Pennines. Fortunately, (for the sake of its preservation) the Passage of Time is way beyond the reach of we mortal travellers, and accessible only to the most experienced, and by all accounts the slimmest, of pot-holers.

A descent from Scar House to Hubberholme is an alternative to continuing directly to Yockenthwaite, and one that will bring us back to the company of the Wharfe. Though barely a hamlet (a 'humlet', perhaps), Hubberholme possesses two fine buildings both worthy of our attention. In the Domesday survey, Hubberholme, then recorded as 'Huburgham', is noted as part of the manor of Kettlewell, though there is evidence further up the valley of an Iron or Bronze Age presence here, and in many ways it is easier to visualise Neolithic man stalking the wooded slopes than the hunting nobility of medieval times.

Like a caring shepherd keeping watch over his scattered flocks, the venerable church of St Michael is a real attraction, set among hills dressed in larch and fir, a timeworn place of worship still very much as its architect intended. It possesses two altars, one originally at University College, Oxford, but its best feature is undoubtedly its 500-year old oaken rood loft, one of only two remaining in Yorkshire. Outside the River Wharfe flows swiftly by, and once overflowed, carrying live fish into the nave of the church.

Across Hubberholme bridge stands the George Inn, a former landlord of which, being also the Parish Clerk, coveted the oldest altar and had it removed to the inn as an ale bench, claiming, as Parish Clerk, an entitlement to put the altar where he wanted. Such secular misappropriation was inevitably frowned upon, and the landlord ordered to return the altar to its rightful place.

The George Inn, however, is still the venue for an annual "land-letting" ceremony, an auction timed by candlelight, at which bids are made for a year's use of a pasture owned by the church, the last bid before the flame flickers out being the rent payable. The bids, made by the "Commons" in the bar, were considered by the "Lords" (the Vicar and his Churchwardens) in the parlour, and the rent of the successful bidder distributed to the parish poor. At least that was how it used to be until 1971, when a Skipton auctioneer took over the letting . . . how mundane is progress!

But now Langstrothdale awaits, a name that holds a tang of wild places about it. We pass through a gate near the church, and beyond the churchyard wall abandon the wide access track by which we descended from Scar House, to pursue a lower path (signposted) across meadowland and so regain the river. Up-dale lie Yockenthwaite and Deepdale, similar farming hamlets, that probably have altered little over the centuries since the Forest of Langstrothdale Chase was a jealously-guarded hunting haunt. As elsewhere, the Wharfe is a popular restaurant for feeding dippers, pied and grey wagtails, while the flanking trees and mossy walls offer an appetising à la carte menu for tree creepers, nuthatches, wheatears, pipits and the various members of the tit family.

The riverside path is nowhere in doubt, never straying from the river bank by more than a few metres, and soon we pass through Yockenthwaite, where the path goes through a narrow gap in the wall just before the first gate giving access to muddy sheep enclosures, and on to Deepdale. Yockenthwaite Bridge is worth a moment's attention, but do not cross it; keep instead to a signposted path passing along the northern bank of the river. Between the two communities, beside the path, a prehistoric stone circle is found, a compact arrangement of some 30 stones in a delightful riparian setting.

And so on to Deepdale and Beckermonds, at Deepdale crossing the Wharfe by a bridge where a wide path, well-defined between wall and water, courts the river as it fusses and gurgles over its smooth bed of limestone; this long stretch of river scenery, from Buckden to Beckermonds, is unsurpassed in all the Dales, and no one would criticise if you turned tail and walked all the way back to Buckden, this time going with the flow, as indeed many do.

Beckermonds, or Beggarmans, as some call it, is an oasis on the edge of Greenfield Forest, and presides over the confluence of Oughtershaw and Greenfield Becks, where the Wharfe can with certainty be said to begin, though its waters derive from much higher and more distant sources we have yet to meet. Just south of Beckermonds a footbridge spans Greenfield Beck, and a short, walled way takes us up to the Beckermonds access road.

From Beckermonds a stretch of road-walking ensues, steeply at first, and then more easily to Oughtershaw, the first or last community of any size in the valley, and one surprisingly well sheltered for its altitude, being located at a spot where surrounding hummocks protect it from all but the worst assaults of the weather.

As the roadway bends away to climb over Fleet Moss en route for Hawes, we must abandon it for a wide access track to and beyond Nethergill Farm, a track which finally ends at Swarthgill Farm. Here we pass left around the farm buildings to cross a small meadow to a gate where we pick up an indistinct path, with a wall on the left. Up here we are in the heart of Dales country, a wild, remote expanse of open moorland, where infant streams are raised and grow speedily in stature to feed the mighty rivers, while all around a sense of spaciousness permeates our thoughts and the skies press down on far and empty horizons.

A succession of stiles leads us to Breadpiece Barn where the short pull, climbing half right across two fields, to Cam Houses begins. Here there is a distinct sense of remoteness, though Cam Houses are not so isolated as might be supposed, for a good road runs north to Cam High Road and on to Hawes. Between Swarthgill and Cam Houses we will have crossed the watershed of England, separating the waters of Oughtershaw Beck, which flow to the Wharfe and the Ouse, and those of Cam Beck, which join forces with the Ribble.

Where the access road to Cam Houses sets off uphill we continue ahead, left of the last barn, to a gate, later to rise diagonally across a field to the top corner of Cam Woodlands. A stile allows access to the plantation wherein we climb to meet a wide forestry track. We soon quit the woodland and follow a fence to a stile and a rising track to a cairn and signpost on Cam High Road. Here we encounter the Pennine Way, on an ancient and well-worn thoroughfare across Cam Fell. There is some suggestion that this route is prehistoric; certainly it was used by the Romans, and by wool traders who gave it its name. The partnership with the Pennine Way is, however, short-lived, for at Cam End we leave it for a rough descent to meet the B6255, near Far Gearstones, where we also take our leave of the Dales Way, not to rejoin it until Mill Bridge across Deepdale Beck.

A short way along the B-road and we find Gearstones Inn, now readily accessible, but once a remote drovers' inn and site of a weekly corn market until the 1870s. Gearstones finally ended its service as an inn in 1911, but it would be nice if it opened up again.

The next stretch of the walk follows the road to Ribblehead, neither far nor unpleasant. But across from Gearstones the agreeable landscape of limestone scars may tempt a shortcut, heading in the general direction of the Ribblehead viaduct. Walk 22 gives a few details of the significance of this massive monument to Victorian engineering talent, and of the successful struggle which has ensued to keep its railway line open. On the ground before the viaduct a community of some 2000 workers sprang up, serving the construction work, complete with its own school, post office, hospital and even a library.

On a clear day it requires little navigational competence to contrive a route across the limestone scars from Gearstones to Ribblehead and Little Dale, and to do so will direct you away from the hordes of visitors that settle around Ribblehead and the mobile refreshment bar which turns up most weekends throughout the year.

Beyond the viaduct a path follows the railway until we can cross it not far from the entrance to Bleamoor tunnel by a curious double bridge carrying both the footpath and the waters of Force Gill. Once across the aqueduct we begin the final stage of our journey, a long traverse across the moors to Dent. A path, supported from time to time by board-walks, struggles upwards out of marshy ground, with the massive sprawl of Whernside frowning down on the little ways of men. A diversion at a sign (to Whernside) is ignored, and we continue climbing. This is the Craven Way, or Great Wold, an ancient packhorse route from Dent to Ingleton. Eventually it becomes a green lane, racing steeply to Deepdale near Whernside Manor, the national caving centre.

From bleak moors we pass finally to a landscape of lush green meadows. By following the road for a few minutes, Mill Bridge is reached and the Dales Way rejoined. Here we go right into trees, along a path beside Deepdale Beck to its confluence with the River Dee, which now escorts us the final steps of the way, until just prior to Church Bridge we are deflected left to cross a minor tributary and gain a roadway but a few minutes walk from Dent centre.

But a village in size, Dent, properly (or formerly) know as Dent Town, used to be of more importance than Sedbergh. Today it is an unhurried backwater, a place of cobbled streets, quiet cafés, shops and a fifteenth-century church. In its main street stands a block of Shap granite bearing the name of Adam Sedgwick. Born in Dent in 1785, he later became and served for over 50 years as Professor of Geology at Cambridge; it is hard to imagine that even in those bygone years he never ventured across the threshold from Dentdale to Ribblehead and far off Wharfedale as we have done.

Walk 28: Wild Boar Fell and Swarth Fell

Maps: (1) OS Landranger 1:50,000 series: Sheet 98 – Wensleydale and Upper Wharfedale; (2) OS Pathfinder 1:25,000 series: Sheet 617: SD 69/79 – Sedbergh and Baugh Fell

Start: Cotegill Bridge, Vale of Eden. GR 774969. Room to park a few cars.

Distance: 11 kilometres (7 miles)

Ascent: 470 metres (1540 feet)

Type of walk: A short and comparatively gentle walk, fine and varied, and the going is good throughout.

Of infamous distinction

Owing its name to the infamous distinction of being the place where, in the fifteenth century, Sir Richard Musgrave chased and killed the last wild boar in England, Wild Boar Fell rises majestically from the beautiful Vale of Eden, a perfect counterpart to the long escarpment of Mallerstang Edge across the valley.

Whether the last wild boar really was killed here is debatable. Certainly there is credence in Sir Richard's claim, for when the chancel and side chapels of Kirkby Stephen Parish Church were restored in 1847-51, Sir Richard was found to have been buried with his lovely lady together with the tusk of a wild boar. Which of the two he valued more is not recorded. This, then, is the generally accepted view, but the presence of a Wild Boar Inn at Crook, near Windermere, suggests other possibilities.

In *Legends and Historical Notes of North Westmoreland* by Thomas Gibson of Orton (1887), however, there is a story in verse penned by a Mr Joseph Steel of the legend of the death of a wild boar at the hands of a giant:

The giant with one stroke on loins
Deprived the boar of life,
Which gave a title to the hill
That ne'er will pass away,
For it is called Wild Boar Fell
E'en to this very day.

Joseph Steel was a working stonemason, chiefly employed at Stobars Hall, but later he was engaged "in a confidential capacity" as land steward until his death in 1882.

Whatever the derivation of its name, Wild Boar Fell is a fine lofty mountain, having a large and fairly level summit on which in former times there used to be horse-racing, wrestling and other athletic sports, just as on High Street above Kentmere in the Lake District.

Our walk starts near the head of the Vale of Eden, at Cotegill Bridge, on the ancient thoroughfare linking Kirkby Stephen with Hawes. This charming valley has long offered a gateway into the very heart of Dales country, and was used from the eleventh century onwards by Scottish raiders. Beside the bridge there is a small disused quarry where Near Cote Gill and Far Cote Gill meet in a small, but picturesque waterfall.

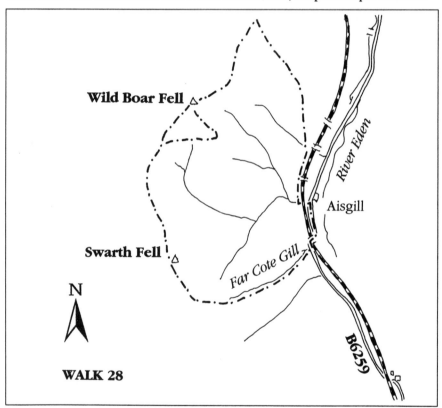

We begin by going down the road until we reach Aisgill Farm and there ascend left on a track beneath the railway viaduct, with its fascinating ceiling of miniature stalactites. Once through the viaduct, turn right, to follow a path accompanying the intake wall. In a little over a kilometre the wall bends sharply right, and we can continue, half left, along a line of pot-holes, Angerholme Pots, aiming for the ridge at the northern end of the escarpment.

There is no clear path along this stretch of ground, but a safe and fairly dry course

Stone men on Wild Boar Fell

may be taken along the edge of the limestone pavement which shortly appears. Above us the stone pillars of Wild Boar Fell are prominent on the skyline a little to the south, with the sharp, rocky silhouette of The Nab almost opposite. Across the valley, east of Eden, the long escarpment of Mallerstang Edge sweeps impressively upwards from the banks of the river.

A slanting path climbs easily to meet the Wild Boar Fell ridge, and here we turn left to follow the escarpment back towards The Nab. Strong walkers can consider a direct ascent from Angerholme Pots to The Nab, leaving the moorland as you draw level with it and simply going straight up. A short section of marshy ground needs negotiating first, but as you climb aim to the left of The Nab to reach a small shelf supporting an infant tarn surrounded by outcrops of gritstone. A short, sharp pull to The Nab, a little loose in places, presents no real difficulty.

The generally favoured summit of Wild Boar Fell is marked by a trig point surrounded by a shelter, reached by a good path from The Nab. But Wild Boar Fell infuriates, for there are two more spots of equal height, each with equal claim to the summit crown. One, barely discernible, lies due east of the trig at GR 761988, on the edge of the escarpment, while the third is among the conspicuous stone pillars a short distance further south, also overlooking the sharp drop to Mallerstang Common. A diversion to inspect these pillars, which seem to increase in number each year, hardly demands any additional expenditure of energy, and provides a convenient and sheltered spot for a short halt.

To continue from the pillars to Swarth Fell we need to circle around Aisgill Head on a narrow path. The path descends to the broad col between the two mountains on which nestles a shallow tarn. Nearby a fenceline would in poor visibility lead you to a wall, ascending from Uldale, that could be followed to the top of Swarth Fell. On a clear day no such aid is needed, and the summit, marked by a large cairn, is easily located.

All along this stretch from Wild Boar Fell to Swarth Fell the sprawling mass of Baugh Fell is a dominant feature to the south, with the top of Whernside beyond, while to the west rise the inviting domes of the Howgills.

There is a good path between Swarth Fell and its lower sibling, Swarth Fell Pike, escorted by a fenceline. Near the top of Swarth Fell Pike, where there is a fine view of the infant River Rawthey, there are two large cairns, reached by stiles. From the lower of these we can now head back to the start, northeast across tussocky ground to either Near or Far Cote Gill, both of which lead unerringly to the disused quarry with only the waterfall to negotiate, by a narrow path on the left as you go down.

Walk 29: The Vale of Eden: along the High Way

Maps: OS Landranger 1:50,000 series: Sheets 91 – Appleby-in-Westmorland and 98 – Wensleydale and Upper Wharfedale

Start: Hawes: Car park adjoining National Park Information Centre in the old station yard. GR 876899. Toilets.

Finish: Kirkby Stephen

Distance: 25 kilometres (15 miles)

Ascent: 310 metres (1000 feet): many undulations

Type of walk: A long, linear and energetic walk through arguably the most attractive of the dales. The route, in the main known as the High Way and now used as part of the *Alternative Pennine Way* (Denis Brook and Phil Hinchliffe), from Hawes, follows a fairly clear and well-established trail frequently used by Lady Anne Clifford. On its journey it enters the Vale of Eden, where it runs down to The Thrang and Pendragon Castle before resorting to farm fields and pathways for the final stretch to Kirkby Stephen. With appropriate transport the walk may be terminated at Pendragon Castle or Nateby.

On the trail of Lady Anne Clifford

Born at Skipton Castle on 30 January 1590, Lady Anne Clifford was the third, and only surviving child born to George Clifford, 3rd Earl of Cumberland and his wife Margaret Russell. When the family moved to London, Lady Anne went too, and was brought up around the Royal Court and in the family's country houses. Here, evidently, she learned a remarkable self-assurance and determination that was to be her characteristic hallmark, and to cause to be left in the memories of the people of the Yorkshire Dales and Eden in particular a surprising force of personality that is still felt today.

Fortunately, and it is well attended with fortune, the trail of Lady Anne Clifford across Yorkshire, Westmorland and Cumberland is one of fascination and considerable interest, and well suited to study on foot.

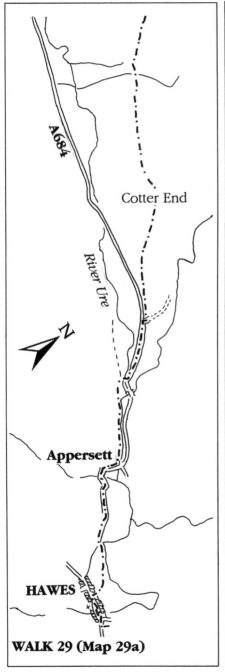

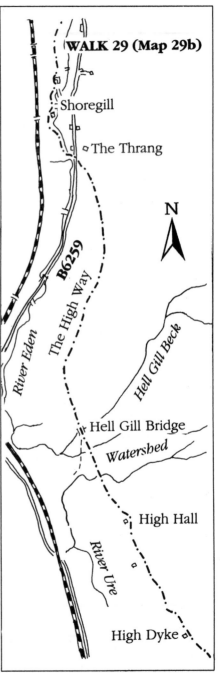

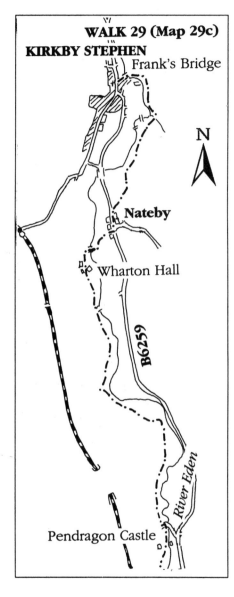

WALK 29 (Map 29c)
KIRKBY STEPHEN
Frank's Bridge
N
Nateby
Wharton Hall
B6259
Pendragon Castle
River Eden

When Lady Anne was fifteen her father died. Naturally, as was her right, she expected to inherit her father's estate, but to her dismay she discovered he had not entrusted it to her, the estate, of vast lands in Cumberland, Westmorland and Yorkshire, passing instead to his brother and his brother's son. From that moment, Anne's purpose in life came to be one of regaining her inheritance. She did stake a claim to the estate, but her conviction was not one shared by the king, James I, by the church, or by either of her husbands.

It was during her second marriage that Lady Anne not only acquired the surname with which she came to be associated, Pembroke, from the Earl of Pembroke and Montgomery, but also the inspiration to start on works of restoration, for which she became famous.

Although her claim was never recognised, Lady Anne did in the end inherit the estate. Her cousin Henry died without heirs in 1643, and she was the only legitimate successor, a circumstance which she must have regarded as Divine intervention. In 1649 she finally came back north to begin the work she had longed to carry out for well over forty years. She was then 60 years old, but her energy, for so long fettered by her life and husbands, made short work of the shackles, and she spent the next 26 years rebuilding churches and castles, often at a time of continuing disquiet in the country. This was Cromwell's time, and such displays of aristocratic wealth were unpopular; Cromwell by all accounts threw his hand in, leaving the fearsome determination of Lady Anne to its own way.

It was that same determination that caused her to disregard her family's appeals to take life easy, but, she said, she might as well die on her horse litter as in her bed! Not inappropriately, she died, at the age of 86, in the room in which her father had been born.

The walk along part of Lady Anne's way, begins in the town of Hawes, by a small back street a short distance west of the one way system. This leads north (briefly) to a group of shops, and a car park belonging to the Fountain Hotel. Keep on beyond the car park, between buildings to emerge into open fields. Soon the route reaches the line of a dismantled railway. Cross this and turn left eventually to join the A684, which is followed as far as Appersett. Stay on the road, which crosses Widdale Beck, to a stile, over which the path follows the line of a wall, parallel to the road. When you reach the River Ure, follow it, roughly northwestwards until it deviates sharply, and here enter woodland by a stile..

When you leave the woodland follow the continuing path to an access track, and here turn right to return to the A684. Head left along the main road as far as the Cotterdale road. Turn right here, and then left to climb above the A684 on an indistinct trod.

Ahead the route lies up Cotter End, with a wall on your left. You are now on the High Way. At a gate, press on steeply to gain Cotter End, beyond which the onward route is obvious, passing High Dyke, Shaws and High Hall to cross the descending River Ure not far from Hell Gill Bridge, which marks the boundary between North Yorkshire and Cumbria.

Continue along the High Way, with superb views all around, keeping with it as it gradually descends to meet the valley road at The Thrang. The Thrang, an imposing building, was built in 1838, for the minister at Mallerstang Church.

Your acquaintance with the valley road is brief, leaving it almost immediately through a gate on the left to drop down to the River Eden, a fine moment.

Cross the river by a bridge just below Deep Gill, and turn right, to follow its true left (west) bank to a farm. Pass through the farmyard and turn right for a short distance, then leaving the access track to cross a field on the left. Beyond, the path continues beside the river to Shoregill. To the north of Shoregill, take the middle of three gates and continue with a wall on the right, and keep on, over stiles, to rejoin the river, still following a wall. Cross the wall by a gate, and continue along it, cross an in-flowing beck and climb gently. From this slightly raised position, there is a good view of the ruins of Pendragon Castle below, one of Lady Anne's finest achievements.

Eventually, the path reaches a narrow lane. Go left along the lane, round a hairpin bend, to reach open land, and here leave the road on a track across pastureland. Follow the track left as it heads for a gate not far from Lammerside Castle. Climb easily to the castle. Pass through a gate and go ahead for a few strides before turning right to descend to a field corner.

A series of stiles and gates and farm tracks eventually bring you to Wharton Hall, a fine building dating from the fourteenth century, and still in active use. Walk down the access track to a gate on the right, and cross a field to a rickety bridge, then bear half left, rising gradually to meet the B6259 at Nateby. The final approach to Nateby is not clear across the fields, but a convenient stone stile, more easily noticed, gives access to the rear of a public house!

Head down the road, as if going to Kirkby Stephen (which indeed you could), but turn right along a walled path that is quite often flooded, and invariably muddy. At a fork, take the right branch, and continue muddily down a narrow path that reaches a tributary of the River Eden, crossed by a footbridge, beyond which you follow the banks of the Eden, and a field margin, to Frank's Bridge on the edge of Kirkby Stephen. Cross the bridge and ascend into the town.

Walk 30: Great Whernside from Nidderdale

Maps: (1) Most of the walk is accommodated on OS Landranger 1:50,000 series: Sheet 98 – Wensleydale and Upper Wharfedale; (2) OS 1:25,000 Outdoor Leisure Map: Sheet 30 – Yorkshire Dales – Northern and Central areas

Start: Car park, near Scar House Reservoir. GR 069767. Toilets. There is a toll for gaining motorised access to Upper Nidderdale, payable as the water authority's lands are entered at Lofthouse.

Distance: 18.5 kilometres (11.5 miles)

Ascent: 375 metres (1230 feet)

Type of walk: A tough and uncompromising walk across rough and in places untracked terrain. Not to be undertaken lightly, and demanding good navigational skills if visibility is poor, especially on the summit plateau and the descent. Dedicated moorland wanderers and bog-trotters will find this walk of vintage quality, a challenge, and one that offers immense rewards. Not all of the walk follows rights of way, though there are paths throughout, suggesting that considerate walkers will be tolerated.

The Nidderdale Round

It was always a mystery that Nidderdale never found its way into the Yorkshire Dales National Park. Upper Nidderdale in particular, upstream from Pateley, in terms of landscape heritage is every bit as fine countryside as any afforded the special protection of national park status, with immense variety of landscape, and much that is unique and worthy of protection. In the end the corridors of power endeavoured, forty years after the national park was confirmed, to redress the situation by designating Nidderdale as an Area of Outstanding National Beauty.

The River Nidd, which spends its infancy high on the northeast shoulder of Great Whernside, is neither among the longest nor the most spectacular of Dales rivers. Indeed in places, as if afraid of all the attention it might otherwise receive, it disappears underground, as at Goyden Pot, to creep shyly along underground passages to next

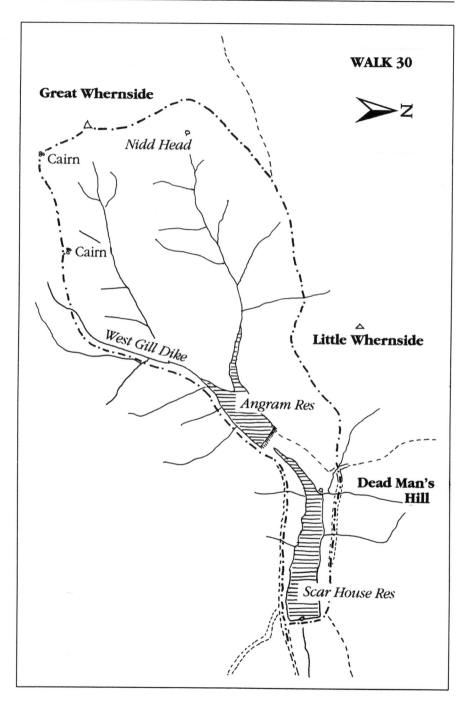

WALK 30

N

Great Whernside

Cairn

Nidd Head

Cairn

West Gill Dike

Little Whernside

Angram Res

Dead Man's Hill

Scar House Res

see the light of day at Nidd Head springs just south of Lofthouse village. In Lofthouse itself the road crosses a dry river bed by a bridge, a certain indication that caves lurk beneath. From here a private road, at the start of which we must pay a modest toll, pursues a narrow and evenly graded course to the large car park near Scar House Reservoir, following the line of a railway built to service the construction of the dams.

Walkers wanting to examine Goyden Pot, in reality a cave, not a pot-hole, will find a convenient picnic area just beyond Limley Farm. From the road the cave entrance yawns black against the white cliff of limestone, but should not be entered when any stream is flowing into it, for that heralds a potential rapid expansion into a river, an awesome sight when it does flow, and one best observed from a safe distance. If it is completely dry, the Pot is well worth a visit, and may be explored with care by torchlight.

In dry weather the sight of a dried-up river bed of washed boulders is curious and puzzling; matters are worse downstream of Goyden Pot, where the river bed, so long deprived of its ancient river, is floored with grass, a sure sign that an overflow due to complete flooding of the cave system is a rare event.

In long forgotten days of jaggermen, pack-ponies and pedlars, Nidderdale was a veritable crossroads of the Dales, a network of ancient packhorse routes crossing in all directions – north by South Haw and Great Haw to Colsterdale and Coverdale, by Little Whernside to Kettlewell, and by How Stean Gorge, Riggs Moor and Meugher to Yarnbury and Grassington in Wharfedale. By these ancient ways we can fashion tours to our own liking, taking in the rolling vastness and soaring fellsides, with an eye for the dancing of sunlight on peaty becks, and an ear for the sound of silence.

Upper Nidderdale and the source of the Nidd

We begin from the car park and soon cross the dam of Scar House Reservoir, constructed in 1936 to serve the needs of Bradford. Beyond the dam we turn left on a rough track, Carle Fell Road, an ancient market road by which cattle drovers and traders would travel to markets and fairs at Masham. Towards the end of Scar House Reservoir this trail climbs steeply northwards to cross into Coverdale by Dead Man's Hill, and from here we pursue a less conspicuous path westwards to the boggy col between Little Whernside and Great Whernside.

Once described as "the modest maiden of the Pennine dales, and an altogether delightful region for those who love Nature in her softer moods", Nidderdale possesses a gentleness that contradicts its own harshness. Nowhere is this better seen than during the gradual transition from the wooded ravine north of Lofthouse to this remote spot high among the feeder streams that flow helter-skelter from the moors.

For all that, Dead Man's Hill gets its name from a triple murder in 1728 when three decapitated bodies, presumed to be the remains of Scots pedlars murdered by robbers, were discovered. An alternative account suggests they were lured to a farmhouse, and their heads severed to prevent identification. Even in those far off days bureaucracy had its slice of the action, and the Middlesmoor registers record the payment of fees to the coroner, the sexton, and other people concerned with the reinterment of "three murder'd bodies found burrd on Ledge Edge without heads."

Beyond this gruesome spot, at the col beyond Little Whernside, a wall is encountered, and we follow this uphill until close by the tiny spring that is the birthplace of the Nidd it deflects sharply westwards to drop to the head of the Coverdale Pass. From this divergence we must now head east of south, rising slightly, to the trig pillar among the deposit of boulders forming the summit, where we may well meet walkers who have ascended by the 'tourist' route from Kettlewell. To the north rises the mound of Buckden Pike, with the boggy expanse of Yockenthwaite Moor beyond. A few paces west and we gaze down on the beauty of Upper Wharfedale, unlike Nidderdale an animated and touristy thoroughfare, hemmed in by the great upland divide of the Birks Fell-Horse Head ridge.

'Whernside', derives from the Old English, *cweorn-side*, meaning the hill from which millstones come, and while a few abandoned millstones still scatter the Wharfedale slopes of Great Whernside, I have yet to discover any on the Nidderdale side, and find it hard to believe that rock underlies the boggy summit of Little Whernside at all. We are left to assume that the millstones of *Great* Whernside were in some way superior to those quarried from Whernside at the head of Ribblesdale, which is a higher mountain.

Continue east of south now, holding to the highest ground to avoid the clutches of some less than obvious muddy stretches, we reach a cairn (GR 006733) near a fenceline. Now begins what is frankly the most demanding part of the walk, albeit downhill, and possibly some of the roughest, toughest, tumbling terrain in the whole of the Pennines.

Follow the fenceline east to a small pile of stones (GR 019736), near the point where the fenceline (and national park boundary) dog-legs right. Leave the fenceline now, and make for the southern spur of Angram Reservoir (pre-dating Scar House Reservoir by 22 years) by way of West Gill Dike. There is a wet path descending eastwards that will assist progress, but this is difficult to locate and should not be especially sought out. Rough peat hags topped by heather and tussock grass tumble all around, dipping unpredictably into groughs and water channels that can deflect us from our course. As the reservoir is approached a wall guides us safely down to its edge, or we may aim to follow the stream down to the weir at the southern inflow to the reservoir. Once beside the reservoir a broad track leads to Angram dam and the metalled roadway linking the two reservoirs, from where it is a pleasant stroll back to the car park.

Walk 31: Grassington to Hawes

Maps: (1) OS Landranger 1:50,000 series: Sheet 98 – Wensleydale and Upper Wharfedale; (2) OS Outdoor Leisure Map 1:25,000 series: Sheets 10 and 30 – Yorkshire Dales, Northern and Central, and Southern areas.

Start: Grassington, Wharfedale.

Finish: Hawes, Wensleydale.

Distance: 43 kilometres (27 miles)

Ascent: 1065 metres (3495 feet)

Type of walk: A long and at times arduous walk, and, in its entirety, only appropriate to strong and experienced walkers. Although the stretch between Grassington and Cray tends to be fairly popular, once the moors of Yockenthwaite are entered into the likelihood of early salvation in the event of an emergency is a distant prospect.

A Capital Walk

Long undisputed as the 'capital' of upper Wharfedale, Grassington is a fascinating village, and an important settlement, notably during Iron Age times. Further north lies Hawes, the 'capital' of upper Wensleydale, and an important market town of considerable antiquity. Between the two communities lies some of the most tempestuously beautiful landscape in the Yorkshire Dales, from the serene limestone escarpments of Wharfedale, to the wild moorlands that form an intransigent barrier between the two dales. To traverse that landscape is to experience quintessential Dales country: at either end relaxing, comforting and intoxicating extravagance, in between demanding, lonely moorland isolation that calls for considerable navigational skill. Escapes there are in plenty, but to pursue the course faithfully calls for commitment and endurance. Strong walkers might tackle the whole crossing in one day, but there is far more to be said for a two-day expedition, breaking the journey at a remote inn (Cray), or a wild camp on the edges of Yockenthwaite Moor, or by descending to the head of Wharfedale in search of other accommodation.

Enormously popular with motorised visitors, Grassington is essentially a place of the hills, and the base for the Yorkshire Dales National Park Authority. It is, as Ella Pontefract in her authoritative, but long out of print, book on *Wharfedale* opines "a stalwart, hardy place with the enduring spirit and windswept air of the upper dale."

Within but a few minutes its touristy bustle may be left behind for an elevated scamper along limestone edges that can prove alarmingly deceptive in misty conditions.

The Town Hall in Grassington, such as it is, lies at the top end of the main street, beside a fine chestnut tree planted in 1887 to commemorate Queen Victoria's Golden Jubilee, and here, at a crossroads, Chapel Street leads left, out of the village. When, in a short while, the lane turns sharply left, leave it for a signposted path entering a farmyard on the right. This leads to a track through a farm gate after the last building. Beyond the gate, follow a wall to arrive at three gates in close proximity, the middle one of which gives on to a field, across which a gap stile allows passage to the next pasture.

The on-going route is fairly clear, crossing pastures, and leading eventually to Lea Green (GR 997657). Lea Green is the vast field system of an ancient British settlement, thought to be Iron Age, but sometimes claimed to be Romano-Celtic, suggesting that the Romans found it already in working order, and left the inhabitants to continue peacefully with their farming.

Once on the edge of Lea Green a broad track is crossed, continuing ahead on a green track up a slight rise. A near parallel wall appears on the right and is followed at a distance, until path and wall meet near a dew pond. A nearby stile takes the route onwards, skirting well-defined limestone outcrops, and crossing a ruined wall to a gate. More stiles and fields follow, past an old lime kiln, and by an easy path to the head of Conistone Dib, a natural dry gorge descending steeply on the left. Ahead a bridge leads on to a brief enclosed way to reach an old packhorse road, Scot Gate Lane.

Across Scot Gate Lane a signpost indicates a green track running beneath Hill Castles Scar to the eminence of Conistone Pie, a small rocky knoll crowned by a large cairn. Visible from many parts of the dale, Conistone Pie resembles, from a distance, a man-made tower, yet closer acquaintance reveals it to be a perfectly natural limestone sculpting. It is a commanding viewpoint, permitting a forward view, up the length of Wharfedale to the distant skyline of Yockenthwaite Moor, while nearer to hand the vertical and overhanging cliffs of Kilnsey Crag seem plausible enough at this safe distance.

A level grass-covered ledge leads on above Swineber Scar, and ahead to a stile by a gate on Highgate Leys Lane near a small plantation of pine trees. Beyond the gate a track leads down to a back lane linking Conistone and Kettlewell.

Nearby Scargill House is now a Christian retreat and conference centre, and a short way further on a signposted path on the right, leads by a series of stiles and enclosures to the edge of Kettlewell at a narrow green lane, pressing on, past the King's Head to reach the main road through the village. Kettlewell may be reached rather more speedily without leaving the road, if the call of the bar introduces a note of urgency.

Kettlewell is a tough, abiding place, a delightful jumbled village that has survived the ravages of time and tourism, and remains much today as it has been for three or four centuries.

Near the Bluebell Inn turn right to follow a back road out of the village, at a crossroads keeping ahead until the road swings steeply, very steeply left, to gain the end of Top Mere Road (shown but not named on the 1:50,000 map) at a bend.

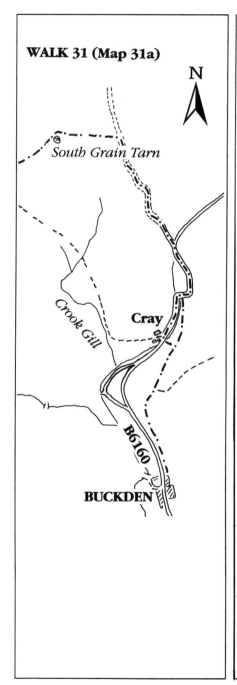

WALK 31 (Map 31a)

N

South Grain Tarn

Crook Gill

Cray

B6160

BUCKDEN

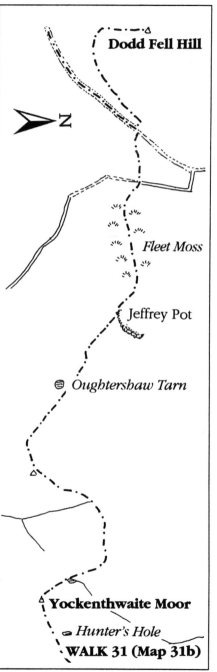

Dodd Fell Hill

N

Fleet Moss

Jeffrey Pot

Oughtershaw Tarn

Yockenthwaite Moor

Hunter's Hole

WALK 31 (Map 31b)

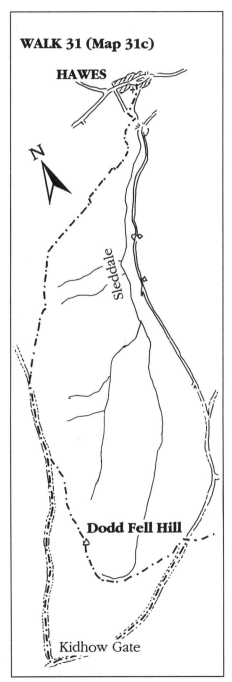

WALK 31 (Map 31c)

HAWES

Sleddale

Dodd Fell Hill

Kidhow Gate

Gradually the gradient along this rough track eases as it surmounts a tongue of ground sandwiched between the Wharfe and a tributary, Cam Gill. Eventually constraining walls are left behind for a steady plod across open moorland to an ancient path, Starbotton Road, crossing it near a small hummock. The road, a speedy way back to the safety of Wharfedale, if needed, is otherwise ignored and a stile located behind the hummock. Once across the stile, the ensuing wall is followed across Tor Mere Top, to Buckden Pike, a seemingly endless dual with boggy and untamed terrain. Between Starbotton Road and Buckden Pike the route does not follow a right of way, but it is a route that has been in use for many years. Considerate walkers will ensure that it continues to be so. If you wish to avoid this section, then leave Kettlewell for Buckden using the Dales Way, which takes a low level route along the true right (west) bank of the River Wharfe.

The top of Buckden Pike is a flattish, grassy affair, with wide ranging views. From here a descent, initially northwest, then southwest, sets off bound for Buckden. Part way down, where it joins the level upper section of Buckden Rake (GR 941784), it is possible to divert northwards, heading for the tiny cluster of buildings at Cray, a remote spot perched on the steeply descending highway from Aysgarth in Wensleydale. Overnight accommodation may be had at the White Lion Inn (Tel: 0756 760262), for those who do not wish to descend to Buckden.

The crossing of Yockenthwaite Moor that follows is demanding, both in terms of energy and navigational skill; walkers venturing this way in less than good visibility may never be seen again! Even on a clear day, Yockenthwaite Moor raises its moments of self-doubt.

Thinking about the final pull to Tor Mere Top

Two possibilities await: one is to pass behind the pub at Cray, the White Lion, going as far as Crook Gill and there ascending along the gill (so far as it is safe to do so) until easier ground is found on the approach to the summit plateau. The other, and marginally easier (but longer) choice is to ascend the road, as if heading for Wensley-dale, until a minor, enclosed track leaves it (GR 943804), left. Follow this out on to Cray Moor until the restraining wall ends. In an emergency, or a simple change of mind, this old track can be followed across into Raydale, making for Stalling Busk, Semer Water and Countersett, from where Hawes is easily reached by a back road, via Burtersett.

More valiant souls, on reaching the open track, should head west for South Grain Tarn and then southwest, rising gently through peat hags and groughs, many of which are eroded to bedrock. The impoverished trig pillar on the summit will no doubt come as welcome relief.

A circuit now follows, around the head of Deepdale Gill, not to be shortcut. The boundary shown on the 1:50,000 maps roughly delineates the route to follow, but need not be adhered to religiously. Once safely beyond the top of Yockenthwaite Moor, its confusing peaty channels and featureless terrain, things improve, navigationally, at least. Other than after prolonged wet weather, the subsequent wall-following, past

Oughtershaw Tarn and on to Fleet Moss, is nothing like as dire as Yockenthwaite Moor's reputation might lead you to believe.

A prominent, and surprising, escarpment, Jeffrey Pot Scar, marks the start of Fleet Moss, across which progress is invariably wet, along an almost non-existent line of fence posts, finally to gain the sanctuary of the Hawes-Buckden (Beggarman's) Road at its highest point, Long Slack Gate (GR 860838).

From this point a wall may be followed westwards to meet the Roman Road at North Gate (GR 853841, but not named on 1:50,000 maps) from where a direct and trackless ascent may be made, northwest, to the summit of Dodd Fell Hill. From the top of Dodd Fell Hill head west of north to follow its broad ridge down to intersect the Pennine Way.

Rather more straightforward, especially after the crossing of Yockenthwaite Moor, but again longer, is to follow the Roman Road left to Kidhow Gate (GR 830834), where the Pennine Way is encountered, and can be followed, right, all the way across the northern flank of Dodd Fell Hill, to Gayle, a suburb of Hawes, before reaching the village itself. Signposting ('Pennine Way') indicates the onward route at points of uncertainty.

An alternative, and no less pleasant, finish may be accomplished from Long Slack Gate, by following the road, right, for about 1 kilometres to the start of the steep descent, by road, to Hawes. Here, you can join Walk 26 on its final stage, over Drumaldrace, a fine, if tiring finish to a very long walk.

Walk 32: Wharfedale and Littondale: the Birks Fell ridge traverse

Maps: (1) OS Landranger 1:50,000 series: Sheet 98 – Wensleydale and Upper Wharfedale; (2) OS Outdoor Leisure map 1:25,000 series: Sheet 30 – Yorkshire Dales – Northern and Central

Start: Buckden village car park. GR 942774. Car park charge. Toilets.

Distance: 18 kilometres (11.25 miles)

Ascent: 740 metres (2430 feet)

Type of walk: A demanding walk of great beauty, splendid Dales' walking offering views of old favourites from a different angle. The crossing of the ridge has to be repeated later in the day, a real leg wobbler. There are two significant ascents – 320 metres (1050 feet) from Raisgill to Horse Head Gate, and 355 metres (1165 feet) from Litton to Firth Fell.

Up and over and back again

Sandwiched between Langstrothdale and Wharfedale on the north and east, and Littondale to the south the Birks Fell ridge has long been a popular traverse. Monks and corpses first crossed between the valleys long ago for their respective reasons, now the journey represents one of the finest Dales' outings for walkers of all shapes and sizes.

The walk begins at Buckden, for the convenience of its shops and car park, but Yockenthwaite, Halton Gill and Litton may be used just as well, and the walk undertaken in either direction. From Buckden it is of no consequence which way round you go, this description travels anti-clockwise, and such is also recommended if starting at Litton or Yockenthwaite; from Halton Gill, clockwise has the edge.

Traditionally the ridge is known as the Birks Fell ridge, even though the highest point of it is a little visited spot, Sugar Loaf – a consequence of old mapping techniques versus modern. But since we visit neither summit the distinction is unimportant.

From the car park we head towards the village and then turn immediately right on the minor road to Hubberholme. Shortly after the bridge over the Wharfe a signposted path, the Dales Way, takes us around a loop of the river rejoining the road a short distance further on. This is a pleasant introduction, ambling alongside the river, often patrolled by dippers and grey wagtails, and little more time-consuming than a walk along the road. We are eventually forced on to the road for the stretch into Hubberholme. Here the church, a rather low, squat building, is of some interest, and stands on the alleged site of an Anglo-Norse burial ground. In 1743 the Reverend Miles Wilson announced that his services at Hubberholme would be "once every Lord's Day in the afternoon, except in the winter quarter, when it is in the forenoon every other Sunday, because it is with great danger and difficulty I pass over very high mountains and large drifts of snow to the chapel."

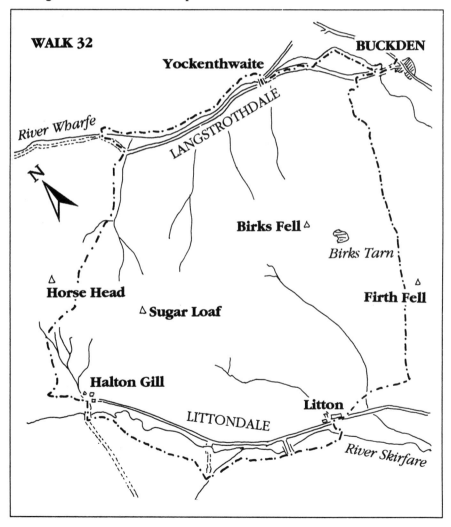

At Hubberholme we cross the river and continue on the north, true left, bank as far as Yockenthwaite, where a bridge permits a return along the minor road for a short distance to Raisgill, a neat collection of cottages and farm buildings.

A signposted track, an ancient monastic way and packhorse route, leaves the road and winds upwards on to Horse Head Moor, generally following the line of Hagg Beck. There are tremendous retrospective views here, improving with ascent, of Yockenthwaite Moor and Buckden Pike. A short boulder hop takes us across a tributary of Hagg Beck, before the long but now relaxed climb to Horse Head Gate. It is for the suddenness of the view that awaits you at Horse Head Gate that I prefer this anti-clockwise circuit. Before you rise Darnbrook Fell, Fountains Fell, Pen y Ghent and Plover Hill, with the conspicuous summits of Ingleborough and Whernside further distant – quite breathtaking. The trig point on the summit of Horse Head is a few minutes, 400 metres, north, while the highest point of the ridge, Sugar Loaf, lies a little further (900 metres) in a southerly direction.

Looking across Hagg Beck to Sugar Loaf, the highest summit along the Firth Fell – Horse Head ridge

Now, after a rest and a cup of coffee, comes a decision. How do your legs feel? The point is that with a long descent to Halton Gill awaiting, and the climb back up from Litton to come, Horse Head Gate marks the point of no return. Anyone with the least concern about their ability to plod back up the ridge from Litton should head for Sugar Loaf, and continue instead along the ridge until the path from Litton is encountered near the top of Firth Fell, there resuming the walk. No rights of way exist along the ridge, but sensible walkers have been crossing it for years without problems, and it forms a very satisfying walk in itself, whether from Wharfedale or Littondale. Have no fear then that you will be letting yourself down if you don't complete the full circuit; the ridge route is quite delightful, and you can always return another day to complete it from the other valley.

From the gap in the wall that constitutes Horse Head Gate it is all downhill to Halton Gill with our first glimpse of Littondale's patternwork of fields improving as we go. Ahead of us the minor road to Stainforth snakes off to pass between Pen y Ghent and Fountains Fell near Dalehead Farm.

Halton Gill lies at an ancient packhorse crossroads, tracks radiating in almost all directions serving settlements at Hawes, Bainbridge, Middleham, Horton-in-Ribblesdale and Settle. Now it seems anything but the Piccadilly Circus it once was. Many of its buildings date from the seventeenth century, converted to meet the demand of present day travellers for self-catering accommodation and country retreats. I often wonder if country life is as bad as the empty, decaying buildings imply; if the simple ways of a rural existence are any less satisfying than those of a sophisticated urban environment. Something has happened to take the countryfolk away from their heritage, and something else to draw the townspeople from their crowded conglomerations in search of peace and refreshment. Or is it that we all want what we haven't got?

For a short distance we follow the minor road towards Stainforth until it crosses Halton Gill Bridge. Then a good path takes us across numerous fields to Nether Heselden and Pen y Ghent Gill, crossing the River Skirfare by a footbridge at Litton. The whole of this walk through Littondale is stunning, and, hopefully, a fitting preparation for the ascent that follows. By no means the largest community in the dale, Litton has given its name to a valley once known as Amerdale, and Vendale in Kingsley's *The Water Babies*.

On a hot summer's day the Queen's Arms at Litton is altogether too tempting, whether it is beer, tea or coffee you want; it does a fair old trade in winter, too.

Just beside the pub, whose origins date to 1842, a signposted bridleway leads to a green rake slanting across the hillside, first crossing Crystal Beck and then continuing to tackle the steep hillside in an oblique manner. Finally it changes direction and heads straight as a die for the top of the ridge. The distance is a little more than one kilometre from the change of direction, but it will seem much more, and the ascent can weaken a flagging spirit.

Once across the summit of the ridge, achieved near the trig on Firth Fell, it is all downhill, for a short distance following the line of a wall, then passing through a gap in it to chase a line of poles all the way to the woodlands that surround Redmires Farm. It is a long descent, with Buckden village in sight all the way, and seeming to get no nearer. But eventually it does, and a farm track drops us quickly to Redmires and back on to the minor road to Hubberholme just west of Buckden Bridge.

Walk 33: Wharfedale – Ilkley to Grassington

Maps: (1) OS Landranger 1:50,000 series: Sheets 98 – Wensleydale and Upper Wharfedale, and Sheet 104 – Leeds, Bradford and Harrogate; (2) OS Outdoor Leisure Map 1:25,000 series: Sheet 10 – Yorkshire Dales – Southern area (from Bolton Bridge northwards only)

Start: Ilkley, at the Old Bridge over the Wharfe, not far from the Parish Church. Toilets nearby.

Finish: Grassington

Distance: 28.5 kilometres (18 miles)

Ascent: 275 metres (900 feet): numerous minor ups and downs en route make a more precise calculation difficult

Type of walk: Essentially a linear riverside walk of great delight, following the first stages of the Dales Way, an 130 kilometres (81 miles) trail from Ilkley to Bowness on Windermere in the Lake District.

Unashamedly beautiful

Wharfedale is an animated thoroughfare, one of Nature's most endearing creations; green pastures framed by limestone walls, a long, narrow valley surrounded by high fells, and unashamedly beautiful. Through its midst flows the River Wharfe, one of few English rivers to possess its own Roman goddess, Verbeia. If the river is any testament, Verbeia was a most beautiful woman, yet she must have had her dark side, for the Wharfe is in places treacherous and fierce.

The walk begins in the ancient town of Ilkley, world-renowned for its moor. Known by the Romans as Olicana, it has also variously been known as Olecanon, Illicleia, Hilleclaia, Illelaya, Illeclat, Illeclay, Yelleilaia, Yelkeley and Hekeley. Before the Romans came the land around Ilkley was under the control of the Brigantes, numerically the largest tribe in Britain though rather loosely knit and unreliable. Under the Anglo-Saxons, Ilkley became a manor, held by the Archbishop of York, and later passed through various ownerships, serving time as a seat of justice for the Forests of Yorkshire. The manor rolls covering the twelfth to the seventeenth century still survive, and make interesting reading. One entry records: "No tenant shall receive or harbour vaccabund or arrogant lyers but which are known to be borne within this wapentake, nor keep any Drabes or evell condicioned women . . ." Fear of domestic reprisals precludes speculation as to what condition of a woman could possibly be described as evil!

By 1709 Ilkley had become "a very mean place . . . dirty and insignificant . . . chiefly famous for a cold well, which has done very remarkable cures in scrofulous cases by bathing, and in drinking of it." Today it is a mecca for historian and rambler alike, and a springboard for a host of fine walks.

From the Old Bridge we set off upstream along a surfaced path on the south side of the river. Soon we reach Ilkley Tennis and Squash Club where the path (signposted) goes left through a gate for an encounter with a succession of pastures before briefly meeting the Wharfe again.

Our first objective is the busy village of Addingham, but shortly after reaching the road, which we are forced to follow for a while, the route is signposted (right) along the access road to Low Mill Village, a truly impressive and sensitive example of what a little imagination can do to restore and preserve the character of old mill cottages and buildings. Our route passes through the village, exiting via a narrow passageway on to a broad track that leads us to the Old Rectory, sitting on a raised mound, its gardens filled with a splendid and unexpected collection of wildfowl from many parts of the world – silver pheasants, Chinese and Canada Geese, guinea fowl, white-fronted geese, Muscovy ducks, peafowl, and, if you are lucky, the magnificent display of white peacocks.

Once beyond this unique collection a flight of stone steps on the right takes us down to a small humped bridge, where we follow a path, left, past Addingham church, with its rather-too-large blue-faced clocks.

By following the path, half left, we locate a narrow passageway over another humped bridge between cottages that brings us to a road, where we turn right. A short stretch alongside the road leads back to the Wharfe, where a flight of steps (signposted) heads downwards. Ignoring the iron suspension bridge, continue, always in company with the river, through another small estate of improved cottages in to a caravan site, from the middle of which a path takes us back to the river's edge and once more through riverside pastureland.

There is a surfeit of barbed wire along this stretch, serving no apparent purpose, and the route could be improved by its removal or replacement with less damaging material. At one point, as if to emphasise the point that much of the Dales Way is a negotiated thoroughfare, we are forced back on to the road for five strides before being allowed to follow the edge of the adjoining pasture, when a simple stile would have served to keep walkers and traffic apart.

Eventually, we rejoin the B6160, and many walkers here turn right and follow the road to Bolton Bridge, at least until a gap in the roadside wall on the right permits an escape and a more direct line to the bridge. But for a B-road, this is extremely busy at most times of the year, and possesses numerous blind bends that render it hazardous for pedestrians. Thankfully, there is an alternative way, which I much commend; it involves a little ascent, but at least when we are compelled to rejoin the road it is for

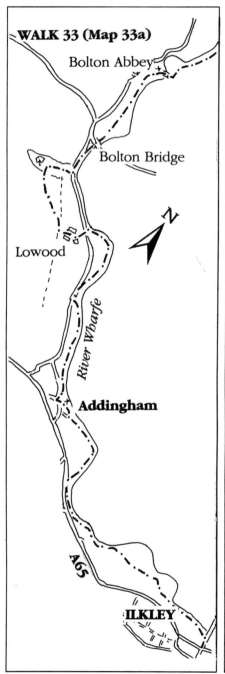

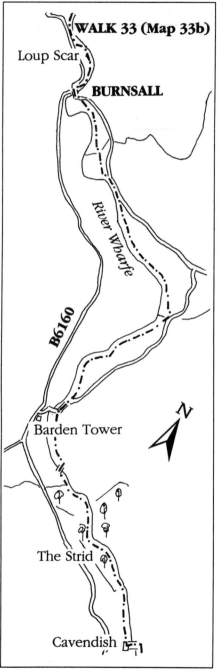

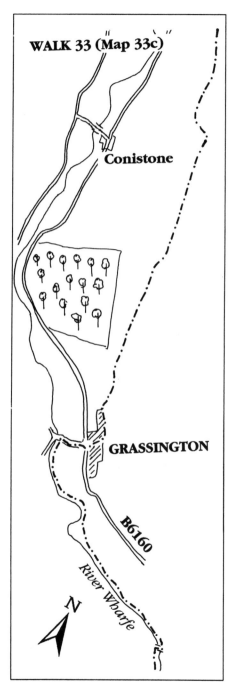

WALK 33 (Map 33c)

Conistone

GRASSINGTON

B6160

River Wharfe

N

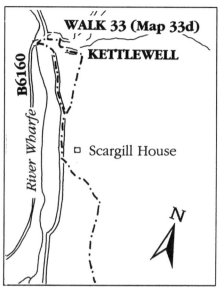

WALK 33 (Map 33d)

KETTLEWELL

B6160

River Wharfe

□ Scargill House

N

the shortest possible distance. So, on reaching the road, instead of heading right, go left for thirty metres to pursue a footpath to Lobwood House farm. Press on past stables and through the farmyard, invariably muddy, to reach the abutments of a former railway line, beyond which a path goes right, across a pasture, to a high point above Eller Carr Wood (not named on the 1:50,000 map) from where there is a splendid view of this stretch of the Wharfe. The way now descends to enter Lob Wood where we pass beneath a railway viaduct. Logically, it might be supposed that a walk along the disused railway line would serve equally well, as indeed it does, but there is no right of way here, and the line is often waterlogged and muddy. Once beneath the viaduct we can swing round on a pleasant path through woodland to rejoin the B6160. Now we have no choice but to tackle the road, but we are doing so along a much safer stretch, and can leave it after little more than two hundred metres by a gap in the wall to a footbridge and a short amble to Bolton Bridge.

From Bolton Bridge (reconstructed in 1993) where we reach the edge of the Yorkshire Dales National Park, we continue with the Wharfe's west (true right) bank as far as the village of Bolton Abbey, with the imposing ruin of its priory (not in fact an abbey) well worth the minimal detour.

The priory was built in the 1150s by Augustinian canons, led by Prior Reynald, who found conditions at nearby Embsay unfavourable. The land on which the priory was built was endowed by Lady Alicia de Romille (or Rumilly) for, as she put it "the well-being of my soul and those of my forebears and descendants." Lady Alicia was daughter of Robert de Romille, a Norman who overran the Skipton area after 1066.

Even with a home in such a delightful spot, the canons did not confine themselves to a cloistered life, which in any event meant an unremitting round of worship, seven times a day, seven days a week, and included Matins, which for them meant leaving their beds at 2am, but taught, ran hospitals, sheltered travellers and themselves travelled far afield to conduct services in parish churches and carry out other parochial work.

After a history of worship and fellowship, often halted by poverty, illness, and marauding Scots, the priory was threatened with obliteration under Henry VIII's dissolution of the monasteries. Thankfully, in spite of the devastation of much of the building, the nave remained intact, and became the focal point of worship for local people, which is how you will find it today.

Near the priory we cross the Wharfe for the first time, by a wooden bridge, and continue upstream through woodlands. A minor road is encountered for a brief spell as we reach Pickles Beck, before leading us to Cavendish Pavilion bridge at the entrance to Strid Wood. These are private woodlands and contain a network of paths laid out in the early nineteenth century by the Reverend William Carr, who spent over 50 years at the priory church. Strid Wood now contains a Nature Trail and a small charge is usually made for the rights of passage.

Shortly after leaving Strid Wood, the route recrosses the river and continues to Barden Bridge. Once more a short stretch of roadway enables us to return to the riverbank, with which we stay for some distance, observing only minor deviations, as at Howgill, to deal with inflowing streams. With time on our hands a diversion to inspect Barden Tower is worthwhile. Now an imposing ruin it was formerly used as a hunting lodge by the Cliffords of Skipton; it was restored in 1659 under the orders of Lady Anne Clifford, the only surviving child of the third Earl of Cumberland and later Countess of Pembroke, who had quite a thing about restoring derelict castles often in direct opposition to Cromwell himself. She spent many of her remaining years at Barden, until her death in 1676.

As the river wanders attractively on beyond Howgill we remain close by its banks, short-cutting a loop at Woodhouse Farm, before pressing on to Burnsall Bridge, which we cross to reach the village. A little off-route lies the village of Appletreewick, from whence came Yorkshire's answer to Dick Whittington, William Craven, born in 1548. Around 1562 William was sent to London as apprentice to a merchant tailor, and in due course entered into business at a great mansion house in Watling Street. In 1594 he gave the enormous sum of £50 towards the building of St John's College, Oxford, and in 1600 was elected Alderman for Bishopgate. A year later he was chosen Sheriff of London, and in 1603 knighted by James I. In 1610-11 he became Lord Mayor of London; whether he had a cat as a companion is not recorded.

At Burnsall we rejoin the riverbank, now on its western side, and continue to Loup Scar where the river flows through a limestone fault, a place of great summer appeal. Onwards the path drops pleasantly to a suspension footbridge below Hebden village. We cross the bridge and continue once more on the Wharfe's true left bank, with which we remain as far as Grassington, the "capital" of Upper Wharfedale, a thriving community with all the services a walker could require. Grassington's main focal point is its cobbled town square, but there is much more of great historical interest awaiting the traveller with time to explore. In spite of its hustle and bustle, this is a place to sit quietly for a while to watch the world go by, and think of how you are going to get back to Ilkley.

Note of natural history interest: The botanist in search of plants that enjoy damp riverside or pastureland conditions will be well pleased with this walk, and likely to encounter much that will delay progress. The same holds true for bird-watchers; on one occasion the author noted almost 40 species of bird, including goosander, tree creeper, grey, yellow and pied wagtails, dippers, kestrel, peregrines, buzzard, curlew, golden plover, warblers – wood, willow, garden and chiffchaff – and most members of the tit family – great, blue, coal, willow, marsh and long-tailed.

Walk 34: Rogan's Seat and Upper Swaledale

Maps: (1) OS Landranger 1:50,000 series: Sheet 91 – Appleby-in-Westmorland, and Sheet 98 – Wensleydale and Upper Wharfedale; (2) OS Outdoor Leisure Map 1:25,000 series: Sheet 30 – Yorkshire Dales Northern area

Start: Muker. GR 910979. Car park. Toilets.

Distance: 19 kilometres (12 miles)

Ascent: 500 metres (1640 feet)

Type of walk: Of varied interest, particularly to industrial archaeologists. Wonderful scenery, fine panoramas, and a contrast between the relics of an industrial age and riverside loveliness that makes this walk especially worthwhile.

Of perfect harmony between man and nature

Once a busy industrial valley, Swaledale is a favourite of many walkers, its extravagant beauty, especially in the higher reaches of the dale, having acquired for it the epithet "Herriot Country", a distinction it shares with Wensleydale through the books and television films of James Herriot. Upper Swaledale, where this walk is set, is remote and arouses a feeling that here at least there exists perfect harmony between man and nature.

Everywhere empty moorlands and derelict mine workings are a stark and constant reminder of the demise of the great industry that once found its centre here and of the community life it sustained. Throughout the valley allotments, smallholdings and small farmsteads proliferate, kept long ago by men who worked in the mines and managed the farms to supplement their income.

Upper Swaledale in particular is very much a place for the walker rather than the motorist, its many side valleys, all of them beautiful, may only be reached on foot, their secrets accessible only to the pedestrian.

The walk begins from Muker, one of the most photogenic villages in the Dales, a huddle of cottages around their church, everything just where it should be. Even on a rainy day, an alternative walk up the Pennine Way to Keld and back by Kisdon Force and a riverside path, is pure delight: on a fine springtime day it is breathtaking, small wonder the originator of the Pennine Way, the late Top Stephenson, thought this to be perhaps the loveliest stretch of his long green trail.

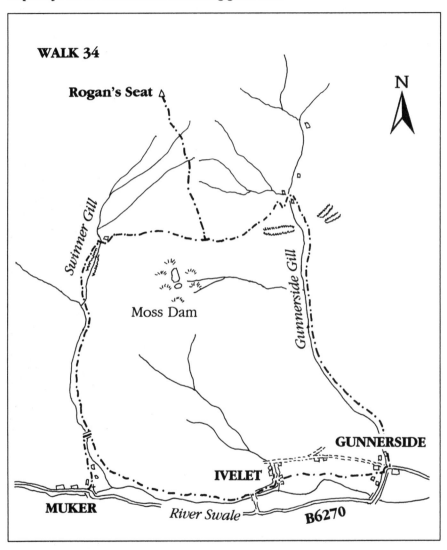

From the car park in Muker follow a track north to cross the Swale by the Ramps Holme footbridge, and then follow the river eastwards across meadows, through Ivelet, to Gunnerside. The bridge at Ivelet is an attractive single arch construction on the old corpse road used from communities higher up the dale to Grinton near Reeth, at one time the only place with hallowed grounds.

From Gunnerside we head north into Gunnerside Gill, a place where even the non-industrial archaeologist cannot fail to be impressed by the artefacts of an industry that died about the turn of the century. This is an evocative place, the ruinous smelt mills, the adits, the chimneys, water-wheel pits, spoil heaps, and, grooving the hillsides, the artificially-created "hushes", great channels formed by the scouring action of water as it coursed the steep slopes to expose the lead ores. It is an awesome, moving sight, inhabited now only by ghosts and distant memories. There are numerous guides to lead-mining in Swaledale and elsewhere in the Pennines, but the rigours and hardships of the miners is powerfully related by the late Thomas Armstrong in his novel *Adam Brunskill*.

Gunnerside nestles comfortably among the hills

A waymarked path goes up the east side of Gunnerside Gill from the bridge in the village over Gunnerside Beck. Soon we are in pleasant woodland, barely glimpsing the industrial remains, and with only the sound of fast-flowing water for company. Eventually we are free from the woodlands and out in the open, the first real evidence of the mining before us. A steep-sided gill appears across the valley, Botcher Gill Nook, and beyond the valley narrows and the ground starts to rise to the most conspicuous of the great hushes; two, three, maybe more appear on our side – Gorton Hush, Friarfold, Bunton – while opposite the unmistakable gash of North Hush is plain for all to see. Due west of North Hush a broad path crosses the moor to the head of Swinner Gill, and this is our objective, but to reach it we must first continue north to cross the gill near Blind Gill. If the force of water prevents this, an alternative way, albeit a tiring one, is to continue as far as the Blakethwaite Mine and its dams and to ascend over very rough ground, due west, to the summit of Rogan Seat.

Otherwise we ascend from Blind Gill on to the slopes of Lownathwaite, where we encounter a path which has ascended the western slopes of Gunnerside Gill, by way of Jingle Pot Edge and Botcher Gill. Almost on the highest point of the crossing between Gunnerside and Swinner Gills a branch track, maintained to the benefit of the shooting parties that make use of these active grouse moors, heads north to Rogan's Seat, and a more desolate spot you are unlikely to find. The summit is broad, flat and featureless, and the highest point, if you can locate it, marked by a small cairn on a broad peaty uplift. A larger cairn nearby is marginally lower.

The outward trek to Rogan's Seat is simple enough if lacking in interest, and needs now to be retraced to the junction of the tracks. Here we head west once more to the top of Swinner Gill where a sign directs us to a pleasant path plunging into a superb gorge to find more evidence of lead mining. A cave, known as Swinner Gill Kirk, was once used as a church in the days when religious gatherings were not so readily tolerated.

The next section, down Swinner Gill, is steep and precarious, following a narrow path along the edge of crags and introducing a tinge of excitement.

Little time is then needed to reach the valley bottom by the River Swale just where it leaves Kisdon Gorge, and from there a good path allows us to amble peacefully back to Ramps Holme Bridge and Muker.

Walk 35: Ward's Stone

Map: OS Landranger 1:50,000 series: Sheet 102 – Preston and Blackpool

Start: Lee Bridge, GR 567552. There is limited parking near Lee Bridge. Alternative starts may be made from the Jubilee tower (Clougha Moss Car Park), GR 542573, which necessitates 5.5 kilometres (3.5 miles) of pleasant downhill or level road walking to begin, or from Tarnbrook, GR 587557, putting the road walking at the end.

Distance: 18.6 kilometres (11.6 miles)

Ascent: 470 metres (1540 feet)

Type of walk: A gentle introduction along the Tarnbrook Wyre leads to a splendid dash of waterfalls, beyond which a path ambles upwards across the slopes of Tarnbrook Fell to the summit. A boggy section ensues to Grit Fell and on the descent to the Jubilee Tower, followed by a relaxing stroll downhill. Impressive panorama. Most of the walk is along agreed access routes from which walkers may not deviate.

The indigo hills

Lying well to the side of the main line of the Pennines, the secret, folded hills of the Forest of Bowland (pronounced "Bolland") have paradoxically long been popular with the Lancashire countrygoer, who tends to know of them rather better than most. Gazing down on the county's coastal plain, and always regarded as properly belonging to Lancashire, this ancient hunting forest was for nigh on eight hundred years within the jurisdiction of Yorkshire, with but the royal park and chase of Little Bowland lying within Red Rose country. And while the bureaucratic dictates of the 1974 reorganisation of local government boundaries shamefully transferred much of Lancashire to other counties, notably Cumbria, Merseyside, Greater Manchester and Cheshire, at least the Forest of Bowland was put properly in its place.

Often, after a journey north, it is these indigo hills, resting beside the M6 motorway, that mark the last stretch of my homeward flight, raising spirits, and chastising my wilful neglect. For long the Pennines' only Area of Outstanding Natural Beauty, these rounded hills are walking country of the highest order. Steady breezes from the Irish Sea caress their slopes, folded gently into crystal-streamed valleys, where the life of the farming communities goes its placid way, much as it has done for countless years.

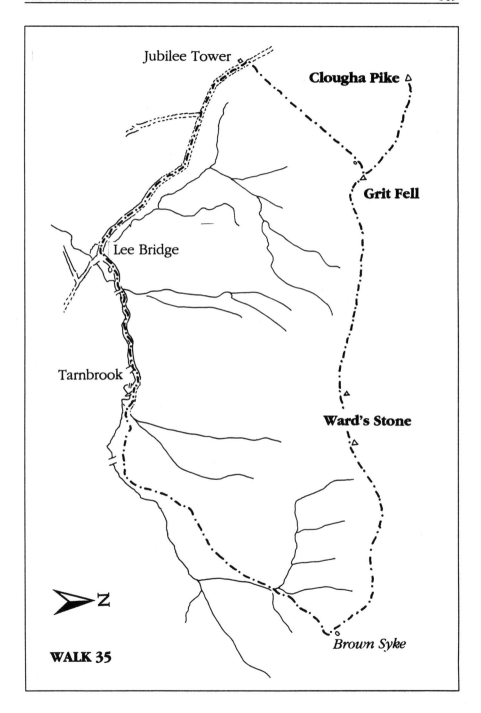

Jubilee Tower

Clougha Pike △

Grit Fell

Lee Bridge

Tarnbrook

Ward's Stone

N

Brown Syke

WALK 35

Possessing much of Pennine character, with tussock grass, peat, heather and gritstone abounding, this is a region of strange appeal, a part of that great range that wants to be loved, to be "part of the scene", and yet it offers no large centres of tourist or visitor interest to draw people to it, and lies within a mesmerising network of minor roads of seemingly haphazard design.

Sadly, too, its destiny is marred by the severest access restrictions found anywhere in the Pennines, most of its highest ground being denied to walkers, with more "Private" and "Keep Out" notices per square mile than anywhere in Britain. It is remarkable that with the attentions given may parts of the Peak during the '20s and '30s, and indeed the West Pennine Moors (not that far away) just before the turn of the century, so little concern seems to have been expressed, even now, about what the late Tom Stephenson called "Forbidden Land". Sixteen years of hard negotiation were needed to secure the limited access areas around Clougha Pike and Fair Snape Fell (see Walk 37), in a vast wilderness dominated by grouse that are hard-faced enough to chuckle at you quietly and tell you repeatedly to "go-bak, go-bak".

Ward's Stone

The circuit of Ward's Stone, the highest of the Bowland summits, is thankfully available to walkers, a fact however that only serves to illustrate what we are missing.

From Lee Bridge a metalled roadway follows the Tarnbrook Wyre and leads to the hamlet of Tarnbrook, once the centre of a small industry manufacturing gloves and felt hats, and here the roadway gives way to a broad farm access track. Follow the track as it ascends the broad flank of Tarnbrook Fell, the slopes of Wolfhole Crag strongly profiled to the northeast across the dip of Gables Clough and Gavells Clough.

For a while the path escapes the infant Wyre, but rejoins it as the two force a way through a narrow ravine, the latter forming a spectacular series of cascades. Above the falls, we cross the stream and follow a line of posts (usually topped with yellow paint) to ascend northeast to the col between Wolfhole Crag and Ward's Stone in the vicinity of a small puddle, Brown Syke, which comes and goes as the water retention properties of this vast sponge dictate. Near the col a fenceline and dry-stone wall meet, and we here turn left, generally west, following the wall to a stile across a fence. Cross the stile and follow the fence, now southwest, and uphill, until we find ourselves channelled neatly to a point (where fences meet), crossing the fence again by a stile. The trig marking the summit of Ward's Stone is only a short distance away.

Two trigs adorn the summit plateau of Ward's Stone, the most easterly being one metre higher, but it certainly doesn't look it. The plateau is largely bare, though dotted with outcrops of gritstone boulders, and on a clear day the crossing to the second trig is uneventful, allowing time to contemplate the fine panorama north and east to the Three Peaks of Yorkshire and northwest to the whole of the Lakeland fells.

Thus far we have been following an agreed access strip, and this now continues west to a minor summit, Grit Fell, just beyond which our route abruptly changes direction, heading southwest and dropping in a straight line to the Jubilee Tower on the Quernmore road. Walkers with time to spare will find the short extension from Grit Fell to take in Clougha Pike a worthwhile deviation.

As we descend from Grit Fell we soon encounter a massive cairn, labelled "Shooters Pile" on the map, a useful spot for a breather and from which to contemplate the startling expanse of Morecambe Bay and the far rolling fells of Lakeland. A vista of remarkable contrast.

On, down to the Clougha Moss car park and the Jubilee Tower, erected in 1887 by James Harrison of nearby Hare Appletree Farm in commemoration of Queen Victoria's Jubilee. A simple downhill stroll, following the road, soon brings us back to Lee Bridge.

Walk 36: Whitendale and Brennand

Map: OS Landranger 1:50,000 series: Sheet 103 – Blackburn and Burnley

Start: Slaidburn. Car park by the river. GR 714523.

Distance: 19 kilometres (12 miles)

Ascent: 485 metres (1590 feet)

Type of walk: An excursion into the heart of Bowland, and involving two ascents, though neither is arduous, such effort as is required being far outweighed by the sheer beauty of this isolated corner of England.

Journey to a lost world

Though it is now rather better known than of old, walkers who want to get away from it all should make a visit to the lonely valley of Whitendale, not by the easy access road, north from Dunsop Bridge, but over the hill of Dunsop Fell when the emerald and fertile pastures hidden among this tightly enclosed sanctum spring upon you with a suddenness that takes your breath away. Here is an enchanting lost world, a place of peace and quiet, its green fields a stark contrast to the brooding hills all around.

The walk begins in the village of Slaidburn, once the administrative capital of the Forest of Bowland, its court-room now embodied in the Hark to Bounty Inn, which before 1875 was known simply as the Dog Inn. The renaming of the inn lies at the door of a visiting squire who from a pack of hounds giving voice in the roadway outside the inn is said to have detected the voice of his own dog and exclaimed in delight: "Hark to Bounty".

Leave the car park and turn right to climb past the war memorial and the Hark to Bounty. Continue ahead for 1½ kilometres (1 mile) to a road, Wood House Lane, which goes to the right. Ignore this lane and continue for another 300 metres to a rough farm track on the right, leaving the road after a bend, at GR 693531. Ahead is the solitary building of Burn Side, to the right of which we pass as the track heads for wild country. Now the steepness of Dunsop Fell greets us, tackled by the narrow ridge separating the lower ground just crossed and a narrow, steep-sided valley, Dunsop Brook, beyond. As more level ground is reached the path, such as it is, swings northwest across the top of Dunsop Brook. A short distance further, near the highest point of Dunsop Fell, we cross a narrow mossy-banked stream, with a wall coming in

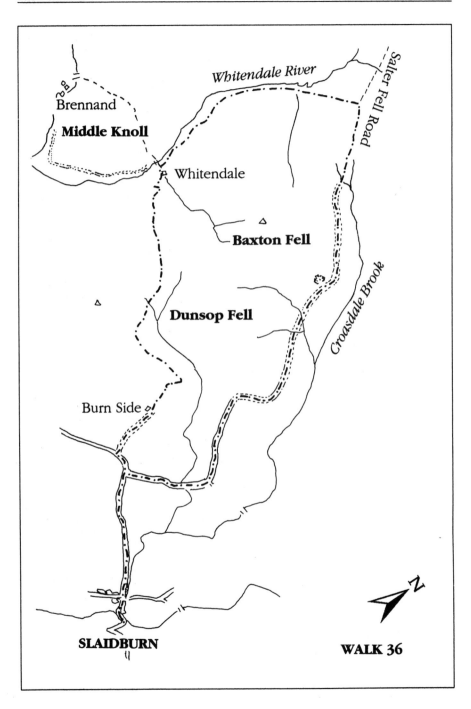

Brennand

Middle Knoll

Whitendale River

Salter Fell Road

Whitendale

△
Baxton Fell

△
Dunsop Fell

Croasdale Brook

Burn Side ⌀

SLAIDBURN

N

WALK 36

from the left. Gradually move towards the wall to a concealed gate at Dunsop Head, a fine vantage point, and if the weather allows, a good spot for a moment's rest. The apparent close proximity of other Bowland hills is surprising: Totridge rises to the south with Fair Snape Fell's sweeping ridge behind it (Walk 37). Further north lie Ward's Stone (Walk 35) and Wolfhole Crag.

From Dunsop Head to Whitendale Farm the route has been waymarked by the water authority, and with their assistance we continue for a while on more or less level ground before descending, with the mound of Middle Knoll ahead and left, separating the valleys of Whitendale and Brennand. To the left of Middle Knoll the rivers of the two valleys unite to flow as one, Dunsop River, south to join the River Hodder at Dunsop Bridge.

Approaching Whitendale Farm the path passes through a carpet of heather, the route plotted by stone cairns and waymarking posts, and it is finally by a grouse-shooters' track that we reach the farm. Here we pass through the yard with buildings to our right, and then turn right at a junction to cross a bridged tributary which puts Whitendale River on our left. Now we head north along the line of the river, past a bridge (do not cross it) to a forked pathway beyond a gate, where we keep left. The path begins to climb as we head for Hornby road, better known as the Salter Fell track, a salt packhorse route of uncertain date. Still we continue to climb, and after passing through newish plantations the ground becomes uneven.

Higher up the path fades, as it had done earlier, but keeping the river nearby watch for a cairn that in summer may be concealed among the ferns, shortly after which we ford a stream. Now is the time to leave the stream, though still maintaining much the same direction, and to tackle a fairly rough section (still waymarked by posts) until we encounter Hornby Road rather suddenly.

To the left the track heads for Hornby in the Lune valley, but our way goes right, roughly following the course of Croasdale Brook, but remaining high above it. Continue past quarry workings on the shoulder of Baxton Fell and lower down cross Black Brook at New Bridge (not named on the 1:50,000 map). This old road has been metalled, but is now in a state of disrepair. Even so, it speeds us down, around Low Fell, to a five-barred gate, and beyond we join the upper section of Wood House Lane, by which an easy return is made to Slaidburn.

Variant: Once in the valley of Whitendale, a short diversion may be made around (by a good track) or over (by a bridge and a good path) Middle Knoll into the adjacent and equally delightful valley of Brennand. The top of Middle Knoll is very boggy, and should only be tackled when the ground is firm or frozen. Then, having satisfied our curiosity we may return to Whitendale Farm and resume our journey. This addition will add about 4 kilometres (2.5 miles) to the distance, and 105 metres (345 feet) to the ascent.

Walk 37: Fair Snape Fell: South Bowland Round

Map: OS Landranger 1:50,000 series: Sheet 102 – Preston and Blackpool

Start: Langden Brook, near Sykes and the Trough of Bowland. GR 632512. Off-road parking near access road to waterworks.

Distance: 20 kilometres (12 miles)

Ascent: 455 metres (1490 feet)

Type of walk: An invigorating walk over wild upland, concluding in a splendid low-level return through meadows and woodland. The walk may be reduced by 6 kilometres (3¾ miles) by retreating along the outward route from Fair Snape Fell.

The heady heights of Bowland

Bowland has nothing to do with bows and arrows; its name comes from 'bu' land, being cattle country. Nor is it a 'forest' in the commonly accepted sense, deriving the title from 'foris', meaning land set aside for the royal sport of hunting. Anglo-Saxon kings hunted here before the Normans came and laid siege to the surrounding area of the Fylde, so devastated in 1065 by rebellion that it was rendered useless for anything but forestry. In time, Bowland came to Royal hands during the reign of Edward II, and thence to Henry of Lancaster, so becoming a Yorkshire domain in a Lancashire dukedom, and seemingly set fair for the squabbles between the two counties that were to follow. During the Wars of the Roses, the king himself was hunted, while for the ordinary people the Wars, in essence a squabble between two rival families, were a protracted and tedious affair. Even now, at the highest point of the Trough of Bowland, a forlorn and redundant boundary stone marks the former dividing line between the counties of the Red and White Roses.

The 'Trough' itself is a quite dramatic crossing, the route by which ill-fated Lancashire witches were transported to the gallows at Lancaster Castle in 1612. Take this route on a bleak winter's day and the hillsides seem to press in on you, possessing more than a hint of darkness. Yet on a fine summer's day the transformation is remarkable, and the heather-decked slopes and bubbling becks play host to hordes of visitors, picnicking, paddling, strolling, sleeping or simply staring in wonder beside the roadways.

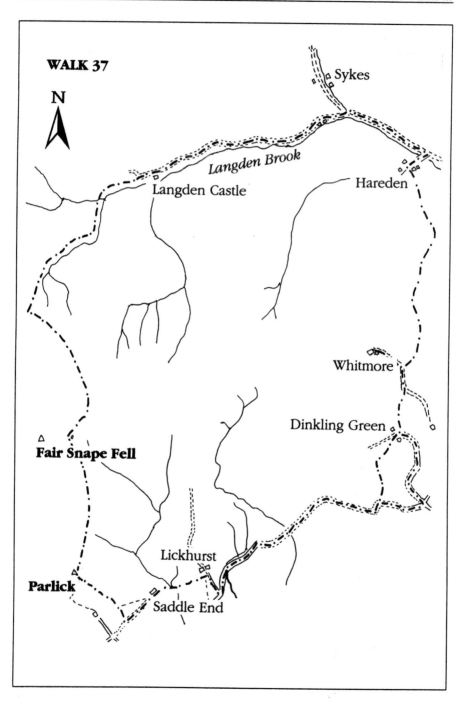

WALK 37

N

Sykes

Langden Brook

Langden Castle

Hareden

Whitmore

Dinkling Green

△

Fair Snape Fell

Lickhurst

Parlick

Saddle End

For all its surrounding bleakness, the Trough has always been a busy route. Not only men working the Forest came this way, but traders crossing between Clitheroe and Lancaster, and less affluent wayfarers struggling from abbey to abbey in search of food and lodging. It was, too, a convenient access route for reiving Scots, as they swept southwards on hit-and-run raids, and predictably for both sides in the Civil War between men of Lancashire and Yorkshire.

Parked near Langden Brook, close by Sykes, on a fine day (even in winter) surrounded by day-trippers swigging hot coffee and tea from a mobile hamburger stall, it is hard to imagine that only a short distance away lies one of the remotest and wildest corners of high Bowland.

Along the die-straight access road to the former Preston Water Works (now in the hands of North West Water), flanked by a splendid display of bushes and trees, we soon reach the open dale. Across the brook the slopes of Hareden Fell rise steeply, and ahead, the stream twisting about in its stony bed like an irascible serpent, every bend reveals a new prospect, drawing us further and further into the distant purple recesses of Bleadale and Fiendsdale. A broad upland access track leads deep into the valley, further than we need to go, and so affords a speedy start to our walk.

Langden Castle, a pretentious name for a barn, gazes out across Langden Brook into Bleadale, separated from our onward route by the huge mound of Bleadale Nab. Beyond Langden Castle, as the access track starts to rise, a signposted path starts across the fells to the distant hamlet of Bleasdale.

Langden Castle

Langden Brook, encountered a short while later, when in spate can be awkward to cross, for there is no bridge, but normally there is no problem fording or boulder-hopping to the opposite bank to gain the conspicuous ascending path as it climbs to the moorland plateau above. Here, for a while, some effort is called for, but the steepness, such as it is, is short-lived and leads to an exhilarating traverse on a more-or-less horizontal path, tracking shelf-like high above a quite unsuspected steep-sided ravine, finally to emerge in a no-man's land of shallow peat groughs and bedrock, fragrant heather all around and the call of grouse, curlew and buzzard overhead, punctuated by the shrill interruptions of meadow pipit and twite.

Suddenly, as Lancashire writer Jessica Lofthouse puts it: "We are above the world, ringed round by a vast Homeric sea of high fells, wave beyond wave of blue, purple, indigo." And so it is, for the heady heights of Bowland, seeming to roll away forever, are as far away as can be from the distant towns and cities whose smoke screens layer the sky.

Finally, out of the groughs we come to a fence, once the boundary between Lancashire and Yorkshire, reeling about drunkenly as if uncertain of its direction. A stile continues the onward path as it descends Holmes House Fell to Bleasdale, but our route lies along the fence, a safe and certain guide in mist to the massive cairn, topped by a large post, which marks the highest point of Fair Snape Fell. There is no clear indication which side of the fence is the permitted access route, for we have now left the public right of way followed from Sykes. The summit cairn lies on the easterly side of the fence, and an approach on that side brings you into conflict with fewer messy peat groughs than the more evident path on the opposite side.

There is a trig on Fair Snape Fell, but it lies some ten metres lower than the true summit, and our route lies over the nearby stile on to the access land of Wolf Fell, where a broad track leads down by Saddle Fell to Saddle End. This same point may be reached, however, by a diversion from the summit of Fair Snape Fell to the trig pillar and then by a splendid, descending ridge to Parlick, a shapely outlier, lonely mountain cwms on either hand and a splendid view across the farms and meadows of the Ribble valley. From Parlick a number of routes connect with Saddle End.

A selection of footpaths and tracks ensue. On a hot summer's day a visit to Chipping would be in order, where refreshments are available. Otherwise, our task is to link the farms of Lickhurst, Dinkling Green, Higher Fence Wood and Hareden. Most of the footpaths marked on the map are still evident on the ground, and only desperation or the onset of the foulest of weather would force us on to the road to Dunsop Bridge.

It is a great pity that access cannot be won to the fine summit of Totridge Fell, for this would make a superb round. As it is the higher slopes of Mellor Knoll, with the end in sight, offer a tranquil spot from which to gaze upon the confines of the Trough.

An easy stroll along the road soon returns us to the starting point at Sykes.

Walk 38: Pendle Hill

Map: OS Landranger 1:50,000 series: Sheet 103 – Blackburn and Burnley

Start: Nick of Pendle, north west of Sabden village. GR 771385. Room to park a few cars.

Distance: 10.5 kilometres (6.5 miles)

Ascent: 260 metres (855 feet)

Type of walk: Normally little more than a pleasant stroll over elevated moorland, leading into a sheltered ravine that brings you to the very brink of the eastern escarpment. Not at all demanding, but with tremendous views; ideal for a short, clear winter's day.

Affectionately yours

Once described as a living creature stretched in sleep, Pendle Hill dominates the surrounding countryside and has long aroused great affection among the people of Lancashire. One 17th century parson, Richard James, observed that Pendle stands "rownd cop, survaiying all ye wilde moore lands", and though from the valley seeming to have a fine ridge it is actually flat-topped. Nevertheless, it is a fine, shapely hill, of which it was claimed that its "broad, round, smooth mass is better than the roughest, craggiest, shaggiest, most sharply-splintered mountain of them all." A well-padded hill covered in grass and ling with barely a tree in sight, Pendle Hill is alas nothing like as high as it was once thought to be, and though steep-sided, it is easy of access and gentle on the legs.

Gazing down on the ancient town of Clitheroe, Pendle Hill is surrounded by lovely villages, one in particular, Downham, being the setting for the film *Whistle down the Wind*, and the ancestral home of Lord Clitheroe, whose family have been lords of the manor since the 16th century.

South of the hill is the village of Sabden, famous as the scene of the Lancashire or Pendle Witches, about whom Harrison Ainsworth wrote in his novel *The Lancashire Witches*, and Robert Neill in *Mist over Pendle*. Sabden was industrialised by the Cobdens, who began in business as cotton manufacturers in the 1820s. Later, the village had a touch of light fantasy threaded into its fabric, as if to set off the grimness of its industry, by claiming to be the only villages to possess its own treacle mine. Old handloom-weavers, it is said, used to weave a biscuit known as parkin, using oatmeal as the warp and treacle as the weft!

Nearby, a short distance east of Barley is the village of Roughlee where the Nutters lived. They were locally an important family, and a sensation was caused when Alice Nutter, a wealthy and refined woman, was denounced as a witch. She was put on trial in the company of the disreputable Demdike and Chattox families, and was so unlike them in manner and means that it is thought she may have died to protect her Catholic friends. The famous trial of the Pendle witches occurred in 1612, and while the families may indeed have been in league with the Devil, the greater likelihood is that they were simply two quarrelsome families who contrived their own downfall, at an especially sensitive time in England's history, by hurling accusations of evil practice at each other.

Set slightly to one side from the main thrust of the Pennines, it is the sheer bulk of Pendle Hill which commands attention and respect, "lying like a leviathan basking in the sunshine" *(The Lancashire Witches)* it does indeed often give the impression that one day it will rouse itself and lumber off to pastures anew. Reaching north east for more than 14 kilometres (almost 9 miles) from the outskirts of Whalley, and rising 500 metres (1640 feet) from the Ribble valley, Pendle Hill is a summit with a skirt of lonely moors – Downham, Worston, Mearley and Barley – one which cannot be ignored; nor should it be.

Pendle Hill

There is a popular ascent from Barley (GR 823403), passing the Ogden Reservoirs and ascending Ogden Clough, but the open aspects of the approach from the Nick of Pendle, high on the road from Clitheroe to Sabden, are fine, easy and invigorating, and give a more elevated start.

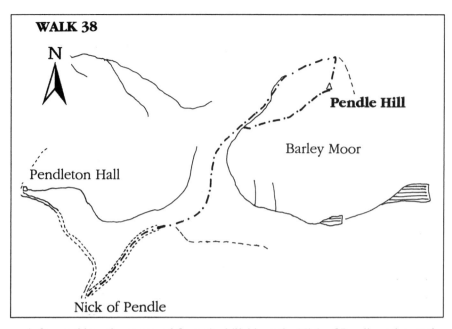

WALK 38

N

Pendle Hill

Barley Moor

Pendleton Hall

Nick of Pendle

A few parking places carved from the hillside at the Nick of Pendle gather at the base of a broad track setting off northeast across Pendleton Moor and Apronfull Hill (not named on the 1:50,000 map), and this leads on to Spence Moor before degenerating from firm going to something rather more boggy. Apronfull Hill is a Bronze Age burial site, but is renowned in legend as the spot where the Devil gathered a brimful of stones with which to bombard Clitheroe Castle, breaching the wall of its keep and creating the opening known as the Devil's Window.

As we cross to Spence Moor a valley, Ashdean Clough, opens up on the left, and ahead rises the broad summit of the hill. On reaching Ogden Clough the path encounters a dilapidated wall, and a short distance down into the clough may be seen a path curving with the line of the stream away towards the summit. Either the continuation of our original path (rather boggy) or the Ogden Clough path (drier) will lead onwards to a point due west of the summit, from where a direct and boggy ascent may be made. There is however a better alternative to hand, and this simply stays with the stream, soon being forced almost into its bed as a dry-stone wall appears on the left, and following the stream on one side or other until it reaches its source. At this point we can continue uneventfully along the line of the wall, safely in mist, to the very edge of the eastern escarpment, and here turn south on a broad green path to the summit trig.

Historically, this was one of many beacon hills throughout the length and breadth of Britain, and not surprisingly commands a 360° panorama taking in the industrial townships and agricultural plains of Lancashire, the coastline of the Irish Sea and the distant hills of the Lake District and Yorkshire.

A simple return by the outward route, or initially due west using the direct stretch from the bed of Ogden Clough, will have us back at the Nick in less than an hour.

Walk 39: Blackstone Edge from Hollingworth Lake

Map: (1) OS Landranger 1:50,000 series: Sheet 109 – Manchester; (2) OS Outdoor Leisure Map 1:25,000 series: Sheet 21 – South Pennines

Start: Ealees Car Park, Hollingworth Lake. GR 939153. Free parking. Toilets. Refreshments.

Distance: 10 kilometres (6 miles)

Ascent: 330 metres (1080 feet)

Type of walk: A moorland walk of no great difficulty, shaking off the shackles of urbanity. Historically interesting and a firm favourite since Victorian times. In spite of a covering of blanket peat the going, even along the summit ridge where the Pennine Way is encountered, is nowhere arduous, and only one short stretch is not on a footpath of one kind or another.

Down there is Yorkshire. Down there is Lancashire

Up here is the top of the world – "the Andes of England" as Daniel Defoe, writing of his second journey through England and Wales, called it. Sandwiched between the Peak National Park and the Aire Gap, this vast moorland rises defiantly from the industry-scarred valleys below. In *Britannia*, William Camden, an eminent Elizabethan antiquary, called all this area "Blackstone Edge", though properly the Edge will be found to be a short, gritstone-crowned ridge overlooking Littleborough. In the good old days, the ridge formed the boundary between Yorkshire and Lancashire; now what was Yorkshire is West Yorkshire, and what was Lancashire is – well, anyone's guess since the bureaucratic contrivance that in 1974 became Greater Manchester ceased to exist. For me this is still and always will be Lancashire.

The ascent of Blackstone Edge has been popular since Victorian times, as Davenport's Guide (see Bibliography) published in 1860 testifies. Yet with only the accounts of Celia Fiennes (who came in 1698 and found Blackstone Edge to be "a dismal high precipice") and Daniel Defoe (who in 1724 found the character of the country so awe-inspiring – "the most desolate, wild and abandoned country in all England" – that it made the horses uneasy and frightened the dog) to go on it is a wonder anyone ever ventured this way again. Admittedly, contemporary records suggest that both Fiennes and Defoe had something to complain about, although Defoe, who encountered snow in August, discovered that the natives had the answer to the "acute and piercing" cold: " . . . the store of ale which flows plentifully . . . seems abundantly to make up for all the inclemencies of the season, or difficulties of travelling." But theirs is only one side of the story, for mild Spring days and the Summer sun, aired by gentle breezes portray a different scene, one of uninterrupted views, of long, leg-swinging days tramping the moors, of peaceful, sheltered corners, the song of the skylark and the call of buzzards and curlew overhead.

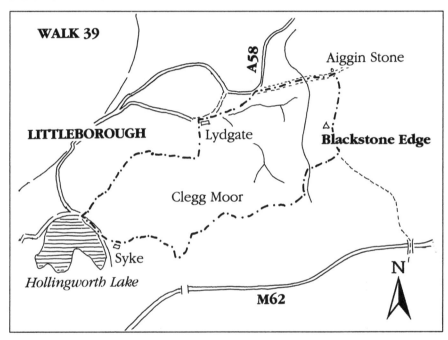

The walk begins at Hollingworth Lake, constructed in 1801 as a compensation reservoir to keep the levels of the Rochdale Canal topped up. To the Victorians, it was better known as a source of pleasure and entertainment, of steamboat rides, dancing, merrymaking and drinking. In terms of popularity not a lot has changed since then, and most weekends will find the lake and its environs thronged by escapees from the surrounding urban jungle.

From the car park a broad track leads northeast beneath Cleggswood Hill; when this veers right, leave it to follow a paved way (waymarked) across a field where picnic tables border a rippling stream. Cross a narrow footbridge and continue with the stream, passing through gates, until a minor road is reached near Lane Foot Farm (not named on the 1:50,000 map). A neat, wooded valley runs left here to the Littleborough suburb of Ealees, and another, less immediately obvious, to the right of the great prow of hill directly ahead of us. To reach it, proceed left, alongside the stream, for a short distance until a yellow waymark directs you up a flight of steps, towards the farm, before veering across the lower spine of the ridge into the adjacent valley. Another wooden bridge takes us across the valley stream. This narrow valley and its nearby counterpart are quiet now, sylvan glades, but at one time busy with coal mining, mining made easy by the presence of the coal seams at very shallow depth, often reaching the surface, and accessible simply by digging into the hillside, techniques known as "Light Holes" or "Breast Eas".

Soon we reach the edge of a golf course, with the main track going left around it. But here we pass through a gate to follow a path across the course, soon becoming a broad track along the edge of one of the fairways, the access road to nearby Owlet Hall. Visible throughout virtually the whole of the walk, our objective, Blackstone Edge and the adjoining Clegg Moor are now an impressive battlement fretting along the distant skyline.

Once beyond the golf course, we go left on a metalled roadway to the tiny community of Lydgate on Blackstone Edge Old Road. The houses here were built by Sir Alfred Law of Durn and Lydgate Mills, who was MP for the High Peak Division of Derbyshire. Nearby Lydgate Mill is a typical early example, built where it could make most effective use of water from Red Brook for power. The mill's "Tenterground" was on the south-facing hillock on the other side of the stream. Here woollen cloth was stretched on hooks to dry and bleach in the sun – hence the expression "on Tenterhooks".

At Lydgate we turn right, passing by the houses, to gain an undulating path alongside a wall, and finally to come within a few metres of the A58. Here we begin the steepest part of the walk, pursuing a line of great controversy. On the map the line is marked as a Roman road; but is it? – one of the problems left by our ancestors to trouble the minds of latter-day experts. That it was a medieval packhorse route is not in question: in 1286 there is reference to a complaint from one Richard Wood to the Sowerby Constables which mentions his mare being used to carry salt over Blackstone Edge. Similarly, in 1291, Richard de Radeclive and Hugh Elland were granted permission to levy custom for two years on goods for sale carried over "Blacksteynegge".

The earliest suggestion that this route might be of Roman origin was made by William Stukely in 1725, with many subsequent opinions supporting or rejecting this claim. The point of controversy lies in the way the road is paved. Sometimes referred to as *Dhoul's Pavement*, a corruption of *Devil's Pavement*, it is some 5.5 metres wide (18 feet) with kerbs, and a fine example of ashlar paving. Down the centre of the road is a shallow trough either cut or worn in the stones, as to the purpose of which many theories have been advanced, the most commonly accepted that it acted as a guide for vehicles descending the incline, which in places is quite steep, achieving a gradient of 25% (or 1 in 4). The road is in many respects Roman in construction, and could have formed part of a route from Manchester (Mancunium) to York (Eboracum) or Ilkley (Olicana). Not far away was found the silver arm of a statue of Victory, to which was attached a silver plate inscribed with a dedication to Valerius Rufus of the Sixth Legion, which accompanied Hadrian into Britain in AD 120, and was stationed in

Northumbria, at York and at Ribchester. So, the balance of probability suggests Roman antecedents, but no one really knows.

At the high point of the road, the Pennine Way, that symbol of man's freedom to roam, crosses on its way north over Chelburn Moor to the White Horse Inn on the Halifax road. At this juncture stands a prominent stone, the Aiggin Stone (pronounced "Aijin"), inscribed with a Latin cross and the initials "IT" – a Roman navvy's autograph, perhaps, or, more likely, the handiwork of one of the nineteenth and twentieth century vandals whose names are etched into numerous road blocks and especially on the summit rocks all along Blackstone Edge – Timothy Iveson, 1826; Abraham Rhodes, 1838, and Loft Lads, 1864, to name but a few.

Between the Aiggin Stone and the top of Blackstone Edge we traverse an area of peat and gritstone, pursuing a line of cairns, and nowhere encountering trying conditions that cannot be evaded. The summit trig is perched atop a massive gritstone boulder, and awkward to attain. All the summit rocks here are excellent vantage points from which to survey the bracken-clad hillside rolling gently towards the intake fields and distant Hollingworth Lake. Several of the boulders display fine examples of splash erosion and chemical weathering in the form of bowl-shaped hollows or pot-holes. The largest outcrop has, inevitably, attracted a name, and is known as "Robin Hood's Bed". The name of Robin Hood occurs quite frequently throughout the southern Pennines and the Peak, formerly a vast tract of land stretching form here to the East Midlands, the medieval hunting forest of Sherwood.

Robin Hood is not a name invented to adorn a legend, for he was almost certainly a Yorkshireman who died and is buried at Kirklees Priory, near Brighouse; Maid Marion came from Wakefield, Little John is buried at Hathersage. After 600 years fact and legend have become inseparable, and who would want to destroy the myth? Nevertheless, Robin Hood was an outlaw of a kind common in years past, a moss trooper perhaps who would have found these Pennine fastnesses ideal, easily defended bases for foraging and marauding expeditions – taking only from the rich and giving to the poor, of course.

From the summit of Blackstone Edge the Pennine Way slips muddily towards the Trans-Pennine motorway (M62) and the distant transmitter on Windy Hill. But we must now ignore this and remain instead with the rocky escarpment of the Edge until the opportunity presents itself to descend across untracked ground towards the mound of Clegg Moor. To be sure of finding the right line, we can take a more or less westerly direction, and will then in due course encounter the man-made leat, Broad Head Drain, which we can follow until it loses itself on a shallow marshy col. At this point an initially indistinct path traces a line across the edge of Clegg Moor. A short-lived line of cairns points us in the right direction, and once around the bulk of Clegg Moor the immense view over Hollingworth Lake to Littleborough, Rochdale and Oldham opens up. A small pool, Dry Mere, hides in a grassy basin, and the nearby heathery slopes are an ideal spot to relax and while away some time before committing ourselves to the final stage of the walk, which will take us back to the mêlée of querulous day-trippers sauntering along the lakeside 'promenade'.

Continue, then, down the rough track passing Dry Mere to reach a broad, graded track extending, right, back to Lydgate. Cross this, and bear left on a grassy trod until it descends in a broad sweep to a stony track leading us to the cottages at Syke. It is but a short stroll along a pleasant country lane to regain the lakeshore a short distance south of the Ealees Car Park.

"Robin Hood's Bed": Blackstone Edge

Walk 40: Stoodley Pike

Maps: OS Outdoor Leisure 1:25,000 series: Sheet 21 – The South Pennines

Start: Hebden Bridge. GR 992272.

Distance: 11 kilometres (7 miles)

Ascent: 310 metres (1015 feet)

Type of walk: Most of the walk uses walled tracks and pathways. There is a little moorland walking, but even this uses the Pennine Way, and is well-trodden.

Gritstone needle

The Battle of Waterloo (18 June 1815) was the culminating conflict of over 20 years of warfare against Revolutionary and (from 1799) Napoleonic France. Napoleon, however had been defeated in 1814, and exiled to Elba, and this event prompted the construction of a monument to peace on the site now occupied by Stoodley Pike. Unfortunately, Napoleon escaped and returned to France in March 1815, overthrew the restored monarchy, and began his reign of a 'Hundred Days'. Work on the monument to peace was halted, but completed shortly after Napoleon's defeat at Waterloo. In 1854 the monument collapsed, and the present tower, solid, soot-blackened and with few outstanding features, save its internal staircase to a balcony, was built two years later. It stands about 38 metres (125 feet) tall, and is one of the most well-known landmarks in the Pennines. For Pennine Wayfarers, it is a taunting, tantalising, towering edifice that never seems to come any closer. Those not engaged in such demanding leisure pursuits will find the following walk to Stoodley Pike much more easily accomplished: it concludes with a pleasant walk down a length of the Rochdale Canal.

Hebden Bridge is a traditional mill town snugly accommodated in the confines of the Calder Valley, a busy community, proud of its heritage, and of the friendly welcome it extends to visitors: any preconception that here is where you will find the stark, grimness of an industrial past, is soon dispelled. Modern-day Hebden is full of bright shops, cafés, restaurants and pubs.

Until the beginning of the 19th century, nearby Heptonstall was the centre of activity, a hilltop village housing weavers and farmhands alike. As elsewhere, the Industrial Revolution, that great transition from an agricultural nation to an industrial one, concentrated developments on the availability of water, and so a string of cotton mills sprang up along the valley. Hebden prospered, and became an international

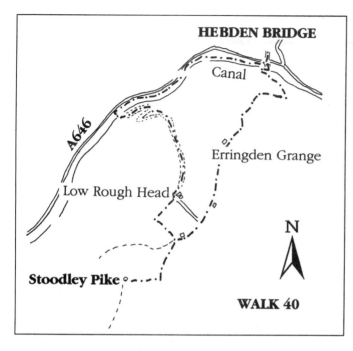

centre for the manufacture of a thick-twilled, short-napped, cotton cloth known as fustian, until foreign competition brought about its demise.

The Pennine Way choses not to descend to Hebden Bridge, passing by the town to the west, but the presence of Stoodley Pike and a wealth of moorland pastures sees to it that Hebden receives its share of visiting walkers.

The walk begins from the town centre, where there are a number of small car parks. Leave from the main crossroads, down Holme Street, as if heading for the Little Theatre. At the end of Holme Street, just after the former Hebden Bridge United District Secondary School, turn left (signpost) to pop up on to the towpath of the Rochdale Canal at Black Pit Lock No. 9. Rochdale Canal is one of the earliest trans-Pennine canals, opened in 1804.

Cross the canal and turn right to cross Black Pit aqueduct, and then left over a canal overflow. A short flight of steps, turn right at the top, leads up to a back road. Go left along the road to cross the railway. A short way further on, at the end of Palace House Road, turn right, up a walled track, with sparse woodland above and a fine retrospective view of the Calder Valley beginning to open up. Continue ahead, climbing easily, and ignoring footpaths right and left to reach a surfaced section of the track, that deteriorates to a footpath on reaching the first of the trees.

Keep following the footpath to a junction and go right, along the line of a fence. At the next bend, go left with the path, keeping to the higher of two paths to reach a walled track, from where there is a good view of Heptonstall Church on the hill across the valley.

Follow the walled track, which passes beneath a tunnel carrying a farm access track, and at a crossroads take the track ahead, beneath electricity pylons, on to a broad, walled track that is cobbled in places. A couple of hundred yards further on Stoodley Pike comes into view on the distant skyline.

When the track reaches a T-junction, turn right, and continue to a gate. A few yards further on you reach a metalled road at another crossroads. Keep ahead (signposted: 'Stoodley Pike') on to Kilnshaw Lane, with the Pike now directly ahead across a pattern of walled fields. Now simply stay on Kilnshaw Lane, past Erringden Grange and Kilnshaw Farm, ignoring tracks on the left, to reach Swillington Farm. Just beyond Swillington Farm you reach the Pennine Way, which goes left, up to Stoodley Pike, and right, down to the Calder Valley.

Stoodley Pike

Turn left, following the Way on to the moors beneath a prominent outcropping of gritstone known as the Doe Stones. The path is in part gravelled, and leads to a stile over a wall. Turn right across the stile, to a gap stile, beyond which a broad, gritty trail leads directly to Stoodley Pike, and the opportunity to take a break and admire the austere Pennine landscape that rolls away as far as you can see.

Retrace your steps to the junction near Swillington Farm, cross the main track, and descend with the Pennine Way (which is now followed all the way to the valley) to a gate. Keep ahead, alongside a wall, to a step stile on the right. Cross the stile, and the next field to another stile, and here keep on beside a wall to reach a farm access track near Low Rough Head Farm (shown but not named on the map). Go left around the farm to follow a delightful track down into Callis Wood, a pleasant spread of alder, beech and holly trees. Just as you leave Low Rough Head Farm, look for some low grassy ridges in the adjoining fields. These are ancient cultivation terraces, dating probably from medieval times, and possibly earlier.

There are fine glimpses through the trees of Callis Wood across the patterned fields to Heptonstall. Keeping always to the main track, you reach a lower track running left to a farm. Leave the track here, and descend through thin woodland (still on the Pennine Way) to rejoin the farm access. Ignoring tempting footpath signs on the right, continue down the main track to a bridge over the Rochdale Canal, not far from Rawden Mill Lock No. 12.

A simple canal-side stroll is all that is now required to take you back to Black Pit Lock, and a return along Holme Street into Hebden.

Walk 41: Withins Height

Map: OS Outdoor Leisure Map 1:25,000 series: Sheet 21 – The South Pennines

Start: Ponden Reservoir. GR 995373.

Distance: 7 kilometres (4 miles)

Ascent: 190 metres (623 feet)

Type of walk: Delightful wandering across the Haworth Moors, visiting places of interest to followers of the Brontë sisters. Nowhere is the walking difficult, but boots are recommended.

In Brontë Country

Haworth, and the moors beyond, will always be associated with the Brontës, a uniquely-gifted family growing up in the emotionally repressed conditions of Victorian times. Most people remember the names of Anne, Charlotte and Emily for their literary endeavours, though there were three more children in the family – Maria and Elizabeth, both of whom died in childhood, and the only boy, Branwell, who squandered his many talents.

The girls were born in Thornton, Yorkshire, daughters of Patrick Brontë, an Irish clergyman, and his Cornish wife, Maria. Their mother died of cancer in 1821, not long after Anne was born, the year (1820) in which they moved to Haworth. After their mother's death, the children were looked after by an austere aunt, and their only escape lay in writing and the exploration of the countryside around their home. It is across this same countryside that the following walk roams, visiting the so-called Brontë Falls, and Top Withins, thought to have inspired Emily's *Wuthering Heights*.

Taking care not to cause obstruction, there is room to park a few cars near the dam of the Ponden Reservoir. Begin by crossing the dam wall to reach the Pennine Way. Across the reservoir stands Ponden Hall, built in 1680, largely restored in 1801, and later said to have been the inspiration for Emily's Thrushcross Grange.

On reaching the end of the dam wall, turn left, and immediately right (signposted: Pennine Way, Brontë Way, Haworth, 3m. The signposts on the Haworth Moors also cater for Asian visitors, and bear two Oriental ideograms, which simply mean 'Path': they mean 'walk' and 'way').

The onward route leads past Rush Isles Farm, following a walled track, and climbing by a long flight of steps (often running with water) to a row of cottages, seen ahead on the skyline. Near the cottages, cross a step stile and turn left along a broad

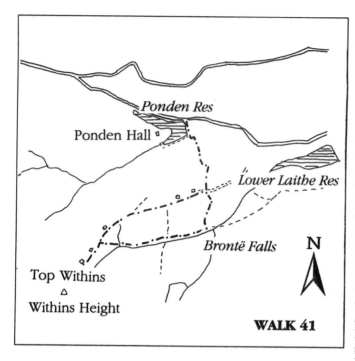

Ponden Res

Ponden Hall

Lower Laithe Res

Brontë Falls

N

Top Withins

Withins Height

WALK 41

track leading to a minor back road at Buckley Green. Here turn sharp right, pass Buckley Green, and in a few strides turn left, alongside a wall, to begin ascending open moorland. Eventually, after a dilapidated cross wall, the path enters an enclosed stretch, ending at a stile. Over the wall to the left, the view towards Haworth is notably of the small village of Stanbury and Lower Leith Reservoir.

After the step stile, the path meets a broad track going left and right. To the right lies the line of the Pennine Way, but for the moment, continue ahead, across the track, and on to a grassy trod through heather (signposted: Brontë Falls). Another broad track is soon encountered. Keep ahead here also, following the path as it runs down to a wall (stile), beyond which lies a small pasture. Cross this, keeping to the left of a nearby mound and to the right of the ruins of Hill End Farm, to reach another wall. Ahead, and to the left, the Brontë Falls come into view, a fine splash of white water where a number of streams descend from the moorland defile of Harbour Hole. The Brontë sisters knew the falls as 'The Meeting of the Waters', and they may be reached by continuing past the derelict building of Virginia Farm, and down the ensuing field to a gate. Beyond the gate drop again, across a collapsed lateral wall to a rash of embedded boulders before reaching the clapper bridge across South Dean Beck, that has acquired the name 'Brontë Bridge'.

To inspect the falls, cross the bridge and turn left to reach the foot of the shallow ravine of the falls. Near the path stands a chair-shaped rock on which has been carved 'C. Brontë DWW', and a plaque affixed to a boulder bears the words of Psalm 104. From this position you can see another plaque set in rock beneath the Brontë Bridge, commemorating the destruction of the bridge by a flash flood on 19 May 1989, and its rebuilding in March 1990.

Retrace your steps up to the gate below Viriginia Farm, and there go left on a slanting path (signposted: Top Withens 1 mile). Maps and most books spell Withins with a second 'i'; the signposts replace this with an 'e'. Either way, it probably means 'a place where willows grew'.

As the path levels, keep ahead through a gap in a wall, and then pursue it alongside on-going walls to a brief descent to reach a ladder stile across the intake wall.

In the far distance, just below the skyline, the dark shape of Top Withins looms, easily reached by a gently rising footpath that meets the Pennine Way — here a paved walkway — near the razed farm, Withins. Turn left and walk up to Top Withins.

A plaque on this bleak building reads: 'This farmhouse has been associated with Wuthering Heights, the Earnshaws home in Emily Brontë's novel. The buildings even when complete bore no resemblance to the house she described, but the situation may have been in her mind when she wrote of the moorland setting of the heights.' Anyone hoping to visit a shrine, will be disappointed with Top Withins, but the setting is quite splendid, and it is not difficult to understand how these moors came to feature so vividly in the works of the Brontë sisters, for whom they were a constant backdrop.

The way down follows the Pennine Way, past the top of the path by which you ascended from the Brontë Falls, and continuing easily first across tussocky moorland and then through banks of heather to reach Upper Heights Cottage. Above the door is the datemark '1761', and a mysterious face.

Immediately after Upper Heights, turn left to reach Lower Heights Farm, and continuing gently downwards to meet the outward route. Turn left, cross the stile, and retrace your steps to Ponden Reservoir.

Walk 42: The Saddleworth Edges

Map: OS Landranger 1:50,000 series: Sheet 100 — Sheffield and Huddersfield

Start: Binn Green picnic area. GR 018044 (shown but not named on the map). Small car park that fills up early. Toilets. Additional parking at Dove Stone Reservoir, with access at GR 008040.

Distance: 13 kilometres (8 miles)

Ascent: 255 metres (835 feet)

Type of walk: Easy approach alongside reservoir, leading to rocky clough and a short, grassy pull to the edge walk proper. A good path leads round the rim of the sprawling peaty plateaux, passing some interesting gritstone formations, notably The Trinnacle, with splendid airy views. Long descent from Chew Reservoir on service road.

On the northern edges of the Peak District

Mention the Peak District and most walkers will think first of the dark, peaty plateaux of Kinder and Bleaklow, as well they might, for these two massive, sprawling areas form a considerable heartland of the National Park.

Further north however the Pennine Way, still very much in the infancy of its northwards flight, traverses another less well known plateau that leads to the Wessenden and Saddleworth Moors, on along Blackstone Edge, Stoodley Pike, the 'Brontë' Moors, and ultimately to the more pleasant, more pastoral scenery of Malham and the Dales. This unshapely mass, drained by countless streams and brooks, culminates in Black Hill, a summit very aptly named, and one not to be grappled with after prolonged wet weather. It is a strange black morass seldom visited other than by walkers tackling the Way, and only then with a keen sense of determination to pass on quickly.

Yet only a short distance west, where the plateau drops abruptly to the heavily-populated valleys around Mossley, Greenfield and Uppermill, is to be found one of the most endearing walks in the whole of the Peak District, known locally as the Saddleworth Edges. It is, in contrast to the starkness above, a place of unexpected beauty in a rough hewn sort of way, and represents for the people of eastern Lancashire an entire Lake District on their own doorsteps.

On reflection it is hardly surprising that the difficulties met with in the higher reaches of some Peakland summits have led walkers to evolve a necklace of walks around their edges, where the ubiquitous peat has drawn back like a receding hair line

The author on The Trinnacle, Ravenstone (Photo: Tom Perry)

to expose the bare millstone grit beneath. These are most conspicuous along the eastern side of the Derwent valley – Margery Hill, Back Tor and Stanage – and on Kinder and Bleaklow. But the Saddleworth Edges too, attended by man-made reservoirs and fretting at the suburbs of Oldham, have long been popular with local walkers, and rightly so.

Walkers whose mission in life is conditioned by the need always to reach a summit may argue that these concocted "edge" walks simply snap at the heels of Peakland mountaineering rather than getting to grips with it. But there is a strange and fascinating aura about the bleak moorland fringes, one which often outweighs the dubious merit of battling with the unremitting terrain higher up.

The reservoirs – Greenfield, Yeoman Hey and Dove Stone in particular – are immensely popular at weekends almost throughout the year, but few visitors undertake more than a stroll beside them, leaving the grand balcony above free for more energetic souls. Motorists travelling along the A635 between Greenfield and Holmfirth may scarcely give a second glance to this apparently uninviting landscape, where the dark brown caps of peat have a sorry look about them. Walkers prepared to venture this way however will find the recesses of Greenfield Brook and Birchin Clough, and the walk which ensues, full of interest, with a wide range of birds – buzzard, kestrel, sparrowhawk, skylark, golden plover, wheatear and meadow pipit – for company.

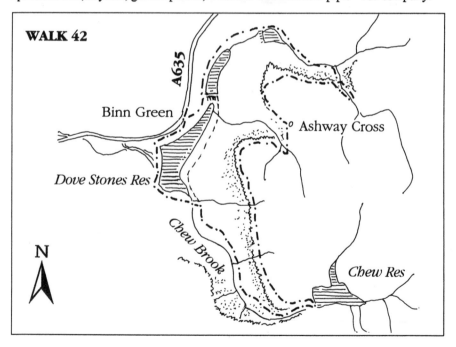

The walk begins at the Binn Green picnic area on the A635, just out of Greenfield. A flight of steps leads down into a small copse of conifers, and to a squeeze stile giving access to the reservoir road. The route turns left here and descends to Yeoman Hey Reservoir, constructed in 1880, and visited 101 years later by the King of Tonga, Taufa'ahau Tupou IV. Yeoman Hey may seem a bit out of his way, but he had been in London for the wedding of Prince Charles and Lady Diana Spencer, and was invited to tour the reservoirs by a contractor who had built a wharf in Tonga some years earlier.

Follow the service track around the left (western) side of the reservoir. Above us rises a conifer plantation, known as Bill o'Jack's, after the former innkeeper William Bradbury of the Moor Cock Inn, until 1935 to be found along the Holmfirth road. He and his father Jack met an untimely death in 1832 at the hands of unknown assailants, and were buried at Saddleworth church.

Continue, in company with the relief channel, until in due course you reach Greenfield Reservoir (1903). As we leave the reservoir behind we enter Greenfield Brook, a place of delightful cascades frowned down upon by the dark cliffs of Ravenstones, prominent among which is the curious tower of The Trinnacle, perhaps the most impressive feature along the Edges.

A short distance further on Greenfield Brook divides into Holme Clough (left) and Birchin Clough (right). Close by, a dark tunnel captures the waters of Birchin Clough and sends them tumbling underground to the Dove Stone Reservoir. Do not be tempted to explore!

Cross the top of the tunnel, to follow the course of Birchin Clough, a short scrambly route, crossing and recrossing the stream with varying degrees of difficulty according to the levels of rainfall, but eventually entering a narrow section above a small cascade. The path, much less obvious now, presses on along the line of the brook, but it can be abandoned almost anywhere to strike up the hillside on the right to a conspicuous path doubling back along the line of Birchin Clough. From this elevated vantage point a spectacularly expansive panorama unfolds across the bleak and barren tops of the Saddleworth Moors, quite unsuspected from below, with wild and rocky valleys reminiscent of remote Scottish glens.

As we pursue the edge path so the rock architecture improves until quite soon we reach The Trinnacle, a fine free-standing pillar of rock, split, as its name suggests into three. Walkers with a good head for heights will experience no difficulty clambering on to the highest point, but as is often the case with rock climbs, getting down is more problematic than going up.

The Trinnacle marks the true start of the edge walk, and from here a good path wanders onwards in splendid airy fashion to our next objective, the Ashway Cross, a memorial to a Member of Parliament killed in a shooting accident. But not long after leaving The Trinnacle, by way of diversion, seek out a narrow path ascending left to a large cairn, Major's Cairn (not mentioned on the map). Major was a dog, and with his owner spent a good deal of time wandering these moors. If the path is missed (easy to do) the cairn can be found in a matter of minutes by ascending left from the edge path through the heather at almost any point. From the cairn a good path leads down to the Ashway Cross.

From Ashway Cross the path bends to cross Dovestone Clough, before resuming its progress along the edge above another fine escarpment of gritstone faces. Further on yet another memorial is encountered, this time to two climbers killed in 1972 in the Dolomites, and beyond that is to be found a quite unique dwelling, Bramley's Cot, constructed against a face of rock in a most ingenious way. In its present incomplete state it is tempting to think "Cot" means that it was half a cottage! But there was a time when it was sufficiently complete to see service as a shooting lodge.

Continue along the marginal path with a few unavoidable patches of peat to contend with, noting the obvious gully across the valley, Wilderness Gully, scene in 1963 of one of England's largest avalanches in which two climbers were killed. The path continues along the edge until finally we reach Chew Reservoir, constructed in 1912, the highest reservoir in England.

By following the reservoir service road a speedy descent to the valley bottom may be made, to be greeted in summer by shoals of would-be adventurers gathered around the dam of Dove Stone Reservoir and along its shores. From the dam it is only a short walk back to the Binn Green picnic area using either the broad path beside the reservoir, or ascending to a stile above the unusual circular overflow to gain a path back to the start.

Walk 43: Kinder –
The Southern Edges

Maps: (1) OS Landranger 1:50,000 series: Sheet 100 – Sheffield and Huddersfield; (2) OS Outdoor Leisure Map 1:25,000 series: Sheet 1 – The Peak District: Dark Peak area; (3) Harveys Walker's Map: Dark Peak North

Start: Edale car park. GR 125853. Ample parking (charged). Toilets. Refreshments available nearby. National Park Information Centre at Fieldhead.

Distance: 13 kilometres (8 miles)

Ascent: 480 metres (1575 feet)

Type of walk: A pleasant meadowland introduction leads to an energetic ascent of Jacob's Ladder and on to the southern rim of the Kinder plateau. A clear path (infinitely more substantial when the ground is frozen) then takes you easily into a gritstone wonderland and across the top of Crowden Brook and Grindsbrook Clough.

On the edge of time

There must have been a time when the hamlets of Edale and Grindsbrook Booth passed their days in quiet pursuit of their pastoral obligations. Cloistered in a backwater among the high surrounding mountains, they doubtless echoed to the sound of sheep and the occasional "jaggernaut" of packhorses carrying salt to Yorkshire from the mines of Cheshire, and wool on the return trip. Now the echo is of booted feet and the excited chatter of less commercial trekkers setting off on journeys both long and short. For Edale it was decreed would be the southernmost point (and for most, the start) of the Pennine Way, when perhaps a more purist start would have had its origins further south, where the true overtures of the Pennines are composed. But walkers were ascending the moorland plateau of Kinder from Edale long before the Pennine Way became a reality, and we must retreat at least to the sanctuary of the nineteenth century before we find a setting free from the inquisitive and those in search of upland enjoyment.

Today, the popularity of this fascinating region is such that it could, with some justification, demand "Keep Off: Your feet are killing me!". Yet even if walkers were

excluded entirely from the worst sections it is unlikely that the ground would recover
for many years, and this is one of the major problems facing the Peak National Park.
Thankfully, their collective wisdom has set about to devise a programme of solutions
which yield a sustainable benefit to walkers, while attempting to preserve the wildness
of the terrain in a manner which satisfies the aspirations of all who visit it. What I find
remarkable is that people come to the Peak, ascend Kinder and Bleaklow further north
only to complain later about how awful the landscape was. This, admittedly much-
tramped landscape is a legacy, part of our geological and geographical heritage, and
those who are unable to accept it as such should refrain from coming here in the first
place. Kinder will never be a place of towering Alpine *aiguilles* or soaring *arêtes*, but
it holds no less reward, and no less merit for being simply, Kinder.

One of the ways improvement may be made is to reroute (permanently or tempo-
rarily) the worst stretches, and present day walkers will find themselves persuaded to
pursue what was the bad weather start to the Pennine Way rather than plough
unceremoniously through the worst clutches of Crowden Head en route to Kinder
Downfall. This bad weather start has long been a more picturesque alternative, and
provides a fitting introduction to a fine circular walk around the southern edge of the
plateau, where the going underfoot has some stability at least.

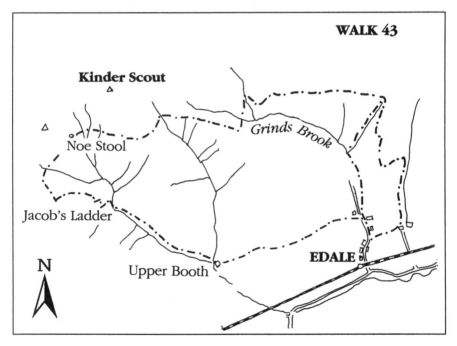

From the car park we head up the minor road to Grindsbrook Booth where the
Pennine Way officially begins (or ends) at the Old Nags Head Inn. Here we turn left
to reach a gate giving on to a narrow ascending track flanked by stands of hawthorn,

holly, rowan, birch and ash. Shortly, the path diverts left across a stile (signposted "PW Upper Booth"), and follows an uneventful, but very relaxing, route to Upper Booth, interrupted only by a succession of stiles of varying degrees of complexity and constriction. The view across the green lushness of Edale (the Noe valley) to the great Lord's Seat – Mam Tor ridge (see Walk 44) is excellent.

At Upper Booth we reach the minor road from Barber Booth and here turn right across a bridge to continue to Lee Farm. Beyond Lee Farm the valley begins to narrow, until suddenly we are at the foot of a stepped incline, at Youngate Bridge. The bridge spans the waters descending from the Kinder plateau, and is a fine resting spot before the ascent of Jacob's Ladder.

We are here on an ancient packhorse route, and the original line may still be seen setting off left along a walled track before turning again in a sweep that takes the sting out of the gradient. The herders who used to control these packhorse trains were called "jaggers", and one, Jacob Marshall, is reputed to have elected to take a direct line to the top of the hillside so that he could have a few moments to smoke a pipe before his packhorses arrived, hence the name, Jacob's Ladder. The condition of the Ladder has been much improved in recent years, but it is still a bit of a pull before we feel that the rocky profile of the Swine's Back ahead is getting any nearer.

As the gradient finally eases the packhorse trail continues ahead to Edale Cross, an ancient boundary marker. Just before Edale Cross the Pennine Way swings north, and passes to the right of Swine's Back. We follow this line, but very soon leave it to bear right on a good path around Edale Head.

The terrain here is quite remarkable, everywhere the landscape is slashed into peaty groughs that make navigation even in good visibility a nightmare for anyone incautious enough to venture away from the obvious pedestrian ways. As we continue, we start to encounter the weird forms of gritstone blocks sticking up from the peat, reminders that here we are on the edge of an ancient time, that these very gritstone gargoyles have their origins in the sandy water margins of a prehistoric ocean.

The first notable outcrop along the path is Noe Stool, which viewed from its northeast side has the likeness of a Toby Jug. A little way on, another form carries the name Pym Chair, another of symmetrical composition is known as The Pagoda, while yet more, a veritable landscape garden of them, bear the name Wool Packs. Much time can be spent pottering about these intriguing outcrops, and whichever way the wind blows certain shelter may be found for a short halt.

To one side of our route Crowden Tower commands a fine panorama, but ahead we descend sharply to negotiate Crowden Brook, a task demanding some ingenuity (or wet feet) after wet weather. On exiting Crowden Brook, bear slightly right to regain the edge path, but with Grindslow Knoll still half a kilometre (quarter of a mile) ahead take a path, left, to the head of Grindsbrook Clough. A large cairn marks the top of the clough, and here we cross the original line of the Pennine Way. If bad weather should suddenly set in, an escape down Grindsbrook Clough is perfectly feasible, only becoming problematical when the stream freezes solid, and even then may be safely negotiated with care.

Our onward route lies across the top of the clough, skirting the northerly tip of yet another clough before ascending slightly to the minor top, Hartshorn. A line of exciting crags line the fringe of the drop to Grinds Brook, before we pass around Golden Clough to a cairn marking the start of the descent of the rocky spine of Ringing Roger, in turn bringing us to The Nab, an excellent vantage point, more than justifying a postponement of the final descent. Below The Nab a zigzag path finally brings us down to the pastureland above Grindsbrook Booth, where the National Park Authority has an Information Centre.

Noe Stool, Kinder

Walk 44: The Great Ridge – Lord's Seat – Mam Tor

Maps: (1) OS Landranger 1:50,000 series: Sheet 110 – Sheffield and Huddersfield; (2) OS Outdoor Leisure Map 1:25,000 series: Sheet 1 – The Peak District: Dark Peak area; (3) Harveys Walker's Map: Dark Peak South

Start: Edale car park. GR 125853. Ample parking (charged). Toilets. Refreshments available nearby. National Park Information Centre at Fieldhead.

Distance: 27 kilometres (17 miles)

Ascent: 790 metres (2590 feet)

Type of walk: A long and energetic walk, but with ample opportunity for abbreviation and the concoction of shorter circuits. Some suggestions are detailed at the end of the walk. The centre-piece of the walk is the long ridge of Rushup Edge which links with the Mam Tor-Lose Hill Pike continuation, a fine and airy traverse of a major geological divide between the Dark and White Peak areas. In full, this represents a demanding walk for strong walkers, of varying interest throughout.

Noe way round

To the miners who long ago moved northwards, seeking hidden lead in the limestone bedrock of the Peak, the great ridge of Rushup Edge must have seemed a formidable barrier, the end of everything. What a surprise it would have been to have climbed ever higher over wiry, unfamiliar tussock grass to crest that long divide and seen, not a higher continuation of the white rock plains they were leaving behind, but "a wide deep valley, sombre and swampy, over-shadowed by huge buttresses . . . which look like the bastions of eternity." For here the lands of the Peak divide, Dark and High to the north, White and Low to the south, a demarcation nowhere more graphically illustrated, as if indeed the Almighty had said that's enough of that, now we'll have some of this! – and drawn a line across the landscape as might an accountant across a column of figures. In the peak this great crest is quite special, one of few real ridge walks in the region, an enfolding arm sweeping protectively around the Noe valley. Within its embrace the ridge created a hidden retreat, long ago carved by glaciers, that

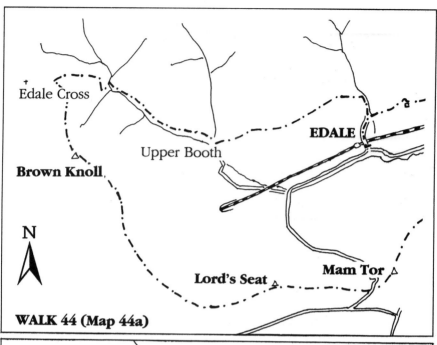

Edale Cross

Upper Booth

EDALE

Brown Knoll

N

Lord's Seat   **Mam Tor**

WALK 44 (Map 44a)

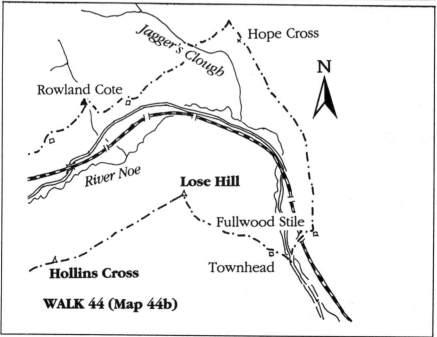

Jagger's Clough   Hope Cross

Rowland Cote

N

River Noe   **Lose Hill**

Fullwood Stile

Townhead

Hollins Cross

WALK 44 (Map 44b)

only gradually opened up as packhorse routes fed the flickering flame of commerce between east and west, presaging the road and railway links that finally announced to the outside world the cluster of sheltered communities that even now make up the valley.

The walk here described begins in that sheltered valley and forms a happy association of relaxing valley pathways and airy ridge walking, with numerous opportunities to shorten the walk if the greater round is too demanding or a less time-consuming excursion required. Even as it stands, little ingenuity is required to figure out how to enlarge the walk further by scampering up The Nab and Ringing Roger to the Kinder plateau above Grindsbrook and then pursuing the Southern Edges (Walk 43 in reverse) to Edale Cross.

The walk begins in Edale and starts northwards to the community of Grindsbrook Booth where, opposite the Old Nag's Head Inn we head left along the alternative, and now to be preferred, start to the Pennine Way (Northbound). Pleasant pasturelands ease our way to the cluster of buildings at Upper Booth, from where we continue westwards into the enclosing folds of the upper Noe valley. Prominent gritstone outcrops, for which the Peak is renowned (among other things) dot the skyline, measuring our progress as we tackle the rungs of Jacob's Ladder, finally, at GR 081861, to follow a wall which zigzags roughly southwards to the domed summit of Brown Knoll.

Brown Knoll is the highest point of the journey, though the panorama is dominated by the higher swell of the Kinder plateau to the north which from here appears at its highest and most mountainous, especially in winter when the whole expanse lies buried beneath crisp and gleaming snow. The western slopes of Brown Knoll nurture the infant River Sett, and roll downwards to South Head where in days of landowners intolerant of (then) trespassing ramblers a gamekeeper would pass his Sundays waiting quietly with dog and gun to deter walkers bound for Edale Cross or the confines of Roych Clough, and to Mount Famine — named from some imaginative association with the Antarctic volcano of the same name.

From Brown Knoll a path descends gently southeastwards to meet an ancient route, Chapel Gate, not far from the A625. At this point, too, for possible future reference, we encounter the arrival of a direct ascent from Upper Booth, a variant shortcut referred to later. Chapel Gate is the oldest way from Edale to Chapel (i.e.-en-le-Frith), taking its leave of the Noe valley at Barber Booth.

A wall now leads us gently across Rushup Edge, across the Bronze Age round barrow that marks the summit of Lord's Seat. The barrow is associated with the hill fort we are about to encounter on Mam Tor, though there is little to tell us who the "Lord" was, a tag first attached as long ago as 1620. From Rushup Edge you can just see the defile of Winnats Pass, thought to have been formed under the sea rather than as the product of a collapsed cave system. As with the route through the Noe valley, Winnats, too, for centuries saw service as an important trade route between east and west, and became the route adopted by a new turnpike road in 1750 linking Manchester and Sheffield. Barely half a century later this was superseded by a new and less severe road looping beneath the unstable cliffs of Mam Tor, which 165 years later, in 1978, landslipped parts of the road into oblivion, causing traffic to revert to the time-honoured passage through Winnats.

Such landslips, for which parts of the Great Ridge are notorious, have also carved into Rushup Edge, and as Mam Nick is approached the ridge narrows appreciably, honing an awareness of steep descents on both sides. A slanting path descends to Mam Nick, through which a minor road squeezes into the confines of the Vale of Edale. A few paces along the road and we cross by a broad stile to a flight of steps leading us unerringly to the summit trig pillar on Mam Tor.

The majestic summit of Mam Tor rests on a base of Edale shales, soft, crumbly rocks formed from the mudbanks of an estuary over 300 million years ago. As a result, when these slates become wet, they tend to lose cohesion and much of their bearing strength. Above the Edale slates lie layers of the sandstones and gritstones that make up the Millstone Grit series, each layer discernible by its coloration and their respective resistance to the effects of eroding winds, rain and frosts. It is the capacity of the Mam Tor shales to crumble and slide, and the suddenness of winds which make an approach to the edge overlooking Castleton an unwise venture that could conclude with an unwelcome and potentially fatal fall.

Commanding such a prominent position it is hardly surprising that Mam Tor became the location of a late Bronze Age hill fort, the largest in Derbyshire, of which there is evidence to date it as circa 1200 BC, though the visible ramparts that remain today were probably dug up by Iron Age people who inhabited the region until the Romans made their presence felt in the first century AD.

The ridge path continues in splendid fashion, dips to Hollins Cross, where there is a memorial to "Tom Hyett of Long Eaton", and then rises across a much narrower section to the base of Back Tor. A steep pull, now eroded, takes us to the top of this shattered section of the ridge before a relatively easy crossing to Lose Hill Pike (pronounced "loose"), on which there is a topograph. Below the summit stands Losehill Hall, built in 1882 as a private residence, later to become the first residential centre established by a National Park Authority in Britain when it opened in 1972.

Lose Hill also bears the name "Ward's Piece", and commemorates a famous campaigner for walkers' rights, G.H.B. Ward, who was born in Sheffield in 1876, and in 1900 established the Sheffield Clarion Ramblers. In 1912 he formed the Hallamshire Footpaths Preservation Society; in 1926, the Sheffield and District Federation of Ramblers Associations, and was the first Chairman of the National Standing Council of Ramblers Federation (later the Ramblers Association) when it was formed in 1931. Ward was a formidable walker well into old age, a fine orator and prolific writer. The part he played in many of the early struggles for access contributed to his being elected a Fellow of the Royal Geographical Society in 1922 and to the award of an Honorary Degree of Master of Arts of Sheffield University in 1957. "Ward's Piece", near the summit of Lose Hill, was presented to him in the presence of 2000 ramblers on 8 April 1945, to be passed to the National Trust. He died in 1957, though his slogan, "A rambler made is a man improved" lived on for many years on the cover of the Sheffield Clarion Ramblers' Handbook.

The shattered front of Back Tor

From Lose Hill we descend by a conspicuous track southeastwards to enter an old lane and pass Townhead to reach the Edale road. Here we go left across Townhead Bridge, and take a right branch to Fullwood Stile Farm.

An ancient track, dating at least to Roman times, heads north from Fullwood Stile to a gate beyond which we continue to climb to Hope Cross (marked as "Guide Post" on the Outdoor Leisure Map), a restored medieval signpost. A short way further we reach a junction of ways, at which we should make for Jaggers Clough, a name reminding us of the packhorse traffic that passed this way years ago. A good path continues to Rowland Cote Youth Hostel, passing in front of the buildings and pressing on across pastureland to enter a lane into Ollerbrook Booth. Many of the tiny communities in the Peak carry the suffix "booth", a name originally meaning a safe enclosure for domestic livestock. More pastureland and a footbridge over Grinds Brook allow us to climb a slope leading to the Old Nag's Head Inn, where a left turn will take us back to the Edale car park.

Variants: The full circuit, which is a demanding undertaking, may be shortened and varied by one or more means:

1. From Upper Booth descend to a footbridge across the River Noe. Climb the opposite bank to a stile and cross a field, keeping to the right of Highfield Farm, and continuing to Tagsnaze Barn. Press on, using stiles, to reach Dalehead and go in front of the house (this is National Trust property) to a gate. More stiles follow until an indistinct footpath can be gained and followed upwards until finally it disappears altogether until Chapel Gate is reached at a sign on a cairn. A short distance south we join the path from Brown Knoll.

2. From Lose Hill Pike retreat along the ridge to Back Tor, and descend to the col, from where a good path drops obliquely to Back Tor Farm and Back Tor Bridge, shortly to join the road for the final stretch to the Edale car park.

3. Tackle the Mam Tor – Lose Hill section only using the track through Harden Clough, keeping right on an ascending path when the track bends left. This ascent brings you to the road just below Mam Nick, and may obviously be used to opt for Rushup Edge instead, descending either to Upper Booth or over Brown Knoll to Jacob's Ladder.

Many more permutations are possible for this popular ridge walk, allowing the day to be abbreviated or lengthened to suit one's needs or abilities. One thing remains certain, however; even in the poorest of weather, the Great Ridge provides a great outing and a great experience.

Walk 45: Back Tor and Derwent Edge

Maps: (1) OS Landranger 1:50,000 series: Sheet 110 – Sheffield and Huddersfield; (2) OS Outdoor Leisure Map 1:25,000 series: Sheet 1 – The Peak District: Dark Peak area; (3) Harveys Walker's Map: Dark Peak North

Start: Fairholmes car park. GR 173893. Ample free parking. Toilets. Refreshments, Information centre.

Distance: 16.5 kilometres (10 miles)

Ascent: 330 metres (1080 feet)

Type of walk: An entertaining walk, beginning along the shores of the Derwent Reservoir, and then by the sinuous Abbey Brook to a boggy moorland crossing, finishing with an easy amble beside the Ladybower Reservoir. Interest is maintained throughout, the twists and turns of the Abbey Brook divide drawing you onward into its depths, and the summit plateau is dotted with the weird shapes of weathered gritstone.

On the edge

On a fine weekend in summer the Fairholmes car park is thronged not only by walkers but also by visitors who come to hire bicycles on which to jaunt around the reservoirs. Fairholmes is a large car park, but even so it sometimes fills to overflowing, and with so many bodies about you might well consider there to be little prospect of any peace and tranquillity you may have sought; judging by the hubbub and the general cacophony of anticipation you could be right – the children are excitable, too. Mercifully, experience has shown that very few of these fair weather wanderers ever venture into the depths of Abbey Brook, an excellent reason to my mind for putting boots on and getting smartly under way, a little distance can be very soothing on the ears.

These eastern moors of the Peak, Howden and Derwent, while not quite reaching their highest point during this walk, fall steeply to the Derwent valley though never quite aspiring to the precipitous gritstone escarpment we find further east along Stanage Edge. They remain nevertheless firm favourites with walkers seeking peace or the company of like minds. Though by no means certain, the highest stretches of the moors, unlike the valleys below, may never have been entirely covered by glaciers, leaving the gritstone monoliths we find today projecting above an ocean of ice, exposed to the winds and rains of a bitterly cold environment.

Derwent Reservoir

These lands of the Derwent were once among the most prized possessions of the monks of Welbeck Abbey, who derived their title towards the end of the twelfth century, during the reign of Richard I. Sheep farming, a profitable enterprise for the monasteries, largely determined the pattern of settlements in the valleys, principally during the thirteenth and fourteenth centuries, and these remained very much intact until the Derwent Water Board (as it then was) drowned the valley between 1912, when the Howden Dam was built (followed by the Derwent Dam in 1916), and the end of the Second World War when the Ladybower Reservoir was constructed.

Our first objective is the divide of Abbey Brook, a long and deep sided valley separating the wild Howden Moors from the more popular expanses of Derwent.

Leave the car park and head towards the dam on a minor road. When the dam is full the overspill is a fascinating sight, contrasting sharply with the serene beauty of the reservoir and the conifer-clad hillsides beyond. As we complete a long bend in the road, which continues to where once stood the hamlet of Derwent, we take a slanting

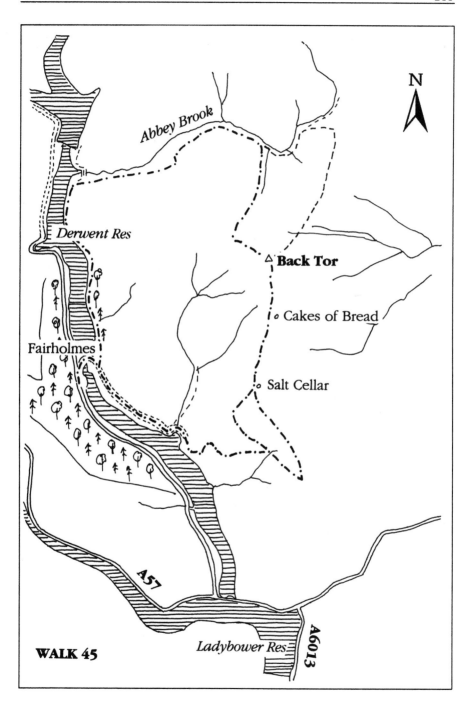

N

Abbey Brook

Derwent Res

△ **Back Tor**

○ Cakes of Bread

○ Salt Cellar

Fairholmes

A57

WALK 45

Ladybower Res.

A6013

path ascending, left, through plantations and finally bringing us to a broad track beside the dam wall.

The next section, a little over two kilometres (about 1¼ miles) calls for little expenditure of energy, ambling pleasantly beside the reservoir. There is a strong temptation to dawdle and delight here as hawks, that could be kestrel or buzzard, or the rarer goshawk, quarter distant slopes, a constant symphony of birdsong filters from the trees, and a family of stoats, if we're lucky, invoke panic among nesting blackbirds and thrushes. Alas, the sound of bicycle bells is likely to interrupt our meditation, and on some days the ascending branch into Abbey Brook (signposted: Bradfield and Strines) cannot come soon enough.

A short, sharp pull is the opener to Abbey Brook, but once gained we immediately sense the promise this enchanting valley holds. Beginning as a broad-based valley, wooded in its lower reaches, Abbey Brook, unlike many of its contemporaries and lesser cloughs does not immediately pan out into bleak, boggy moorland. Instead it describes a pattern of its own, fairly direct in the early stages, until Cogman Clough is reached, and on across a stretch of springy turf where some old, scarcely discernible enclosures may be found. Later, the valley narrows, enticing the walker into its embrace, sustaining its mystery beyond Wild Moor Clough and the outcrop on the other side of the brook known as Barristers Tor. Nearby, a geological weakness has allowed the waters of Sheepman Clough to fashion their own ravine, and here we take our leave of Abbey Brook, heading now along and above the clough on a track less evident than the maps suggest (but clear enough) until a large cairn marks a change of direction on Lost Lad Hillend (not named on the 1:50,000 map).

Suddenly the view opens up, a virtue endorsed by the erection of a topograph on nearby Lost Lad by the Sheffield Clarion Ramblers in memory of W. H. Baxby. The summit is named after a shepherd lad lost in the snow, and from it a broad path dips a little and reascends to struggle on through deteriorating underfoot conditions to Back Tor, a now conspicuous outcrop topped by a trig pillar.

Walkers who enjoyed the confines of Abbey Brook will find that from the confluence with Sheepman Clough they can continue ahead towards the watershed rather than make for Lost Lad. The on-going path is narrow, but quite clear, and continues across Hobson Moss to Agden Bridge among the far-off side valleys of Bradfield Moor. Once you reach the upper limit of Abbey Brook and approach the watershed, watch for a broad, wet path (not shown on the 1:50,000 map, but coinciding with the boundary of the National Trust land) that provides you with an alternative approach to Back Tor. This variant adds about one kilometre to the overall distance.

The final conquest of defiant Back Tor demands a little mild scrambling, its trig pillar being splendidly placed on the very top of a fine array of weathered gritstone. This is one of the Peak's finest vantage points, a splendid accumulation of the ancient bones of our landscape. In a narrow niche a touch of romance arouses finer feelings as you discover that Mary and Jack became engaged here, on 5 March 1933. Nearby, some remarkably perceptive vandal of yester-year reminds us that "When Nature created Man, it created a Monster" — with any luck, he slipped climbing down and sprained his ankle!

A steady descent leads on from Back Tor and intersects a path that has ascended through Shireowlers Wood from the reservoir track we used earlier in the day. What remains of Bradfield Gate, a solitary pillar, supports a signpost confirming that walkers travelling that way are still en route for the distant village of Strines, and its thirteenth-century inn.

Ahead and to the left of our path more gritstone outcrops appear, rudely fashioned by the ancient hand of time into forms that have become known as the Cakes of Bread. A little further and we reach the rocks of Dovestone Tor, sibling of Back Tor, but smaller and less impressive. Nearby, yet another weather-worn sculpture, the Salt Cellar, requires less imagination than many named outcrops on these vast moors, and gazes down on what remains of the lost community of Derwent, submerged forever by the rising waters of Ladybower.

From the Salt Cellar return to the main path and continue east of south to White Tor and on to yet more gritstone gargoyles, the Wheel Stones, fancifully thought to simulate the wild flight of a coach and horses across the moor. Soon we encounter another trans-moor track, this time linking Derwent and Moscar, and we can follow this, initially northwest, until we meet a dilapidated wall at Grainsfoot Clough, with the path continuing beyond, falling gently, to the edge of the wooded plantations which flank the eastern side of the Derwent valley. By way of a minor diversion, but worth knowing about in extremely warm weather, the path alongside the wall which descends southwest from the Salt Cellar brings you to a lateral farm track where you will find a most delightful spring of refreshingly clear water issuing from the hillside. I can't vouch for its purity, but it tastes delicious and makes superb ice cubes if transported home in redundant vacuum flasks. It you elect to sample the water you should then continue southeast along the farm track until, at Grainsfoot Clough, you meet the Moscar path.

Descend easily to the plantations, the dry-stone wall along the northern edge of the footpath having been completely rebuilt by conservation workers in 1989. Eventually, we cross Grindle Clough, and a short way further pass between some ancient barns (one bears the date "1647") to traverse a steep slope (slippery when wet), following the line of a fence until we can cross the pasture diagonally downwards to a stile on the reservoir road. Now all that remains is a simple and delightful stroll around Mill Brook inflow back to Fairholmes at the end of a walk arguably as fine as any in the Peak.

Walk 46: Stanage Edge from Hathersage

Maps: (1) OS Landranger 1:50,000 series: Sheet 110 – Sheffield and Huddersfield; (2) Harveys Walker's Map: Dark Peak South

Start: Hathersage. GR 232815. There is a substantial car park near the fire station in the village centre, reached by a side road at the southern end of the village. Toilets are located in the main street.

Distance: 17 kilometres (10 miles)

Ascent: 300 metres (985 feet)

Type of walk: A splendid and airy walk high above the valley, approached easily through farmland. There are a few uphill rises, but these are neither long nor steep. At all other times the going is easy.

On the crest of a wave

Fretting over the Hope and Derwent valleys like a wave about to break, Stanage Edge, defines the western edge of Hallam Moors as they clamber indolently from the suburbs of Sheffield, and marks a strong contrast with the lands of the Low Peak. To the south, as far as the eye can see, lies a pastoral landscape of walls and rolling greenness, culminating at the natural gateway to the High Peak, Hathersage, a peaceful settlement clustered around its church in whose churchyard, it is claimed, lie the remains of Little John, Robin Hood's trusty lieutenant. While here, spreading northwards as far as the eye can see, wild moorland rises in brooding darkness to the heights of Derwent Edge, Kinder, Bleaklow and beyond.

Sadly, many walkers intent on visiting Stanage Edge ignore Hathersage altogether, making with indecent haste for the car parks that fester alongside the minor road linking Burbage Rocks and Bamford Edge. Such impatience forces a premature introduction to Stanage which wants for the fascination of seeing one's objective from afar and working steadfastly through the valleys below to reach it.

Stanage Edge, the longest and most impressive of all gritstone escarpments, has its place, rightfully, in the annals of rock-climbing history, having been explored since the late nineteenth century, and still capable of entertaining modern rock gymnasts. But it is remarkable, too, in affording lesser mortals, those who like their feet firmly on more or less level ground, a splendid and airy walk, full of interest, easy of access, and with a fine panorama.

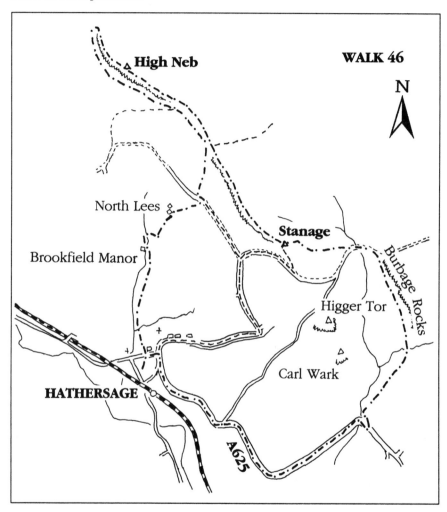

There is a car park in the village centre (GR 232815), near the fire station, and on leaving it turn left and in a short while pass through an alleyway leading on to the main road through the village (toilets down the road to the left). Cross the road (or, if you visited the toilets, follow the cobbled passageway just past the Post Office) and enter Baulk Lane. This metalled road soon degenerates into a broad farm track, passing the village cricket green, where, if you undertake this walk on a summer Sunday, you could well spend a pleasant half hour or so before the homeward journey, relaxing to the sound of leather on willow and cries of 'Run, you idiot' floating over the conveniently low hedgerow. Onwards the track climbs very gently, until, at a signpost in mid-pasture, it branches half left and descends to a stile giving on to a path passing behind Brookfield Manor. Continue ahead to a minor road, Birley Lane.

A small stream flows nearby, Hood Brook, this is a favoured haunt of dippers and grey wagtails, and the surrounding trees play host to almost all members of the tit family. Continue, right, along Birley Lane until you can go left, uphill, on a track leading to North Lees Hall.

The Hall, an austere edifice, was built by the Eyre family in the sixteenth century, the family and their strong Roman Catholic beliefs having been banished from the district by the proud and narrowly Protestant people of Derbyshire. The Hall is now owned by the National Park authority and leased as a farm and guest house, and the farm buildings house the remains of a Roman Catholic chapel built in 1685, only to be sacked in 1688. The tall, three-storeyed, castellated tower is said to have provided the setting for Thornfield Hall in Charlotte Brontë's *Jane Eyre*, Charlotte having spent three weeks in Hathersage in 1845.

Pass behind the Hall and ascend a rough flight of stone steps to gain a track across a field and leading to a small plantation, bordering a cascading stream. There is a relaxed air about this short stretch through the plantation; Stanage Edge is now more prominent high above, a spectacular frieze of rock decorating the skyline, and the shelter of the trees provides refuge for woodpeckers, tree creepers and the occasional nuthatch.

As you emerge from the plantations on to the old turnpike road that ran from Ashopton (long since submerged under Ladybower Reservoir) to Sheffield, the true magnitude of Stanage Edge, hitherto only glimpsed above the trees, at last becomes obvious, stretching away to the right to Burbage Rocks and left to the identifiable beak of Crow Chin and High Neb. It is one enormous wall of rock invariably festooned with the ropes and jingling paraphernalia of rock climbers and echoing to their calls.

From here the choice of direction is yours, left or right, but a start at the High Neb end affords a convenient and alternative return to Hathersage later in the day to simply retracing one's outward steps. So, set off along the road, left, for only a short distance until after about 100 metres, and just before the Hollin Bank car park (shown but not named on the 1:50,000 map), a path climbs right across open pasture. Follow this and ascend easily to a small copse directly beneath the rocks of the Edge, and as you emerge from the sparse shelter of the trees you find yourself on a path composed of gritstone blocks, now worn smooth by countless generations of feet, that ascends to the rim of the escarpment. This is known as Jacob's Ladder (not to be confused with the track of the same name west of Edale) and is probably no more than an ancient trod or causeway that has been paved. There is about it however a similarity with the so-called 'Roman' Steps in Cwm Bychan in the Rhinogs of Wales.

Once on the escarpment edge continue northwest (left) with the path, but almost immediately throwing away all the height you have just gained by descending a broad track of loose stones to pass beneath the escarpment of High Neb. Shortly after a wall and stream descending on your right leave the main track and cross a stile on to a narrower but clear path through bracken. This leads quickly into the midst of a profusion of millstones, lying about the hillside as their makers left them, some lying flat, some half buried, others leaning, yet more stacked as if in some ancient wheel repair depot, one even with a smiling face (the graffiti-mongers get everywhere!). Many possess centre holes, others are blank, the odd one or two only half finished, and here and there lie square blocks yet to be tackled; fifty, a hundred, perhaps, lie scattered about, a sad testimony to the end of an era.

Millstones, Stanage

Continue on the path through this millstone graveyard, the prominent 'beak' of Crow Chin above you, allegedly named by a millstone cutter who is said to have mistaken the protruding rock for the beak of a giant crow bearing down on him: you can see the similarity, but I can't help wondering what millstone cutters drank in those days! Away from this abandoned factory the path passes on pleasantly, in due course to meet the A57 at Moscar, but you should keep your eyes open for a grassy path ascending, right, through a break in the rock wall, and this by a gentle uphill plod brings you once more to the rim of the escarpment a short distance northwest of the trig point on High Neb, the highest point along the Edge.

Along this section of the Edge you may notice a series of basins scooped out of the rock, some with curved lines rather like upturned cat's whiskers. All of them are numbered, the first one you will find is 17, though there are in total one hundred, and this numbering is the clue that tells you they are man-made. They are in fact drinking bowls for grouse, sculpted at the beginning of this century by two gamekeepers who were paid one old penny a time for their construction, to ensure the precious birds had a plentiful supply of water. It was a nice idea, but it doesn't quite work, for when the birds need the water most, in summer, they are quite often bone dry.

From High Neb follow the edge path on a long and splendid traverse to the highest, and at this remove quite distant, point on Stanage. The scenery, especially that formed and framed by the weathered rocks of the escarpment, is consistently splendid, and the marvellous view a generous reward for so little effort; small wonder then that Stanage Edge is a popular promenade. Near the top of Jacob's Ladder a road, the Long Causeway, a Roman road, leads northwest across Hallam Moors to Redmires reservoirs, and affords an easy ascent to walkers based in Sheffield.

Along the way there are many points where you can sit and watch the antics of rock climbers, with varying degrees of amusement according to their talents. Robin Hood's Cave, a conspicuous balcony with a large flat roof, is worthy of exploration, and it seems quite plausible that this legendary hero might have resorted to the cave as a hideaway, though there is no evidence to support this.

Like High Neb, the highest point at the opposite end of the Edge, is also marked by a trig point, and forms the culmination of the long and easy crossing. Here the turnpike road climbs to meet the escarpment near Burbage Rocks, and you can follow the path from the trig until you meet this road. Continue along it to the second bridge, where a gate gives access to the Duke of Rutland's Drive, a green and gentle track running beneath Burbage Rocks which may now be followed to its junction with the A625 at GR 263806. A couple of miles of easy strolling will now take you back to Hathersage.

Repeated faulting has, however, added an interesting dimension to the landscape above Hathersage, providing a series of table-like hills – Higger Tor, Carl Wark and Winyards Nick. These flat-topped hills, with gently sloping concave sides, rise impressively from the moorland, and a network of paths makes them easily accessible. Walkers with energy to spare should not miss them. Less energetic souls will find a shorter finish in the descent from the top of the Ringinglow road, beneath Higger Tor, direct to Hathersage Booths.

Walkers who want to shorten the walk a little can find a way down from the trig on Stanage Edge (retrace your steps a short distance to locate the line of descent), down to the road, and by descending, right, and following the signposts for Ladybower you will arrive at the track through the woodland above North Lees Hall, and by doing so retrace your outward journey.

Walk 47: Kinder Downfall from the Sett Valley

Maps: (1) OS Landranger 1:50,000 series: Sheet 110 – Sheffield and Huddersfield; (2) OS Outdoor Leisure Map 1:25,000 series: Sheet 1 – The Peak District: Dark Peak area; (3) Harveys Walker's Map: Dark Peak North

Start: Bowden Bridge car park, Sett Valley. GR 048869. Parking is limited, so an early arrival is recommended. If the car park is full, retreat to Hayfield and park there. Refreshments available at Bowden Bridge.

Distance: 12 kilometres (7 miles)

Ascent: 450 metres (1475 feet)

Type of walk: A deceptively energetic walk, at least until the Kinder plateau is reached. Progress then very much depends on the condition of the peat bogs, although most of the worst can be avoided by courting the frayed edges where the bare bones of weathered gritstone make for an easier passage. From Kinder Low the going is virtually all downhill and delightful.

That old black magic

Very little time will pass, I suspect, before even the rawest of recruits to hill-walking in the Peak will learn of and seek out Kinder Downfall, for there can be few places more dramatic, more inspiring, more renowned than this, the highest of waterfalls in the Peak. Given the preponderance of wearying bleak black bog which northbound Pennine Wayfarers unavoidably encounter in the early stages of their flight, this rocky gash, where the River Kinder plunges over the lip of a massive amphitheatre of weathered gritstone, must come as a brief and welcome interlude. Whether their minds can detach themselves sufficiently from their mission to appreciate the grandeur of the setting is another matter, and I have witnessed many such heavily-laden souls stoically press on, grim-faced with barely a moment's pause.

No, to gain the most from the Downfall it must become the object of your mission, not a mere incidence en route, for then it can be experienced rather than given a passing glance. And of the many approaches, that from the Sett Valley above Hayfield is to be preferred, certainly for a first visit. That many agree with this assertion will become self-evident if you arrive late at Bowden Bridge in the hope of finding somewhere to

park. If perforce you are obligated to park in Hayfield, an alternative start to the walk
is detailed at the end.

The car park at Bowden Bridge, once a small quarry, featured in the Mass Trespass
on Kinder in 1932, an act documented in the late Tom Stephenson's *Forbidden Land*
and Howard Hill's *Freedom to Roam*, and over which, even now, there are mixed
views as to its efficacy. Resentment had been growing for some years at the denial of
access to large areas of the Peak, jealously guarded by owners and their gamekeepers,
and it seemed inevitable that major and deliberate conflict would arise sooner or later.
The very path along which we start this walk, from Hayfield to the Snake Inn, was
itself hard-gained from local landowners by our forefathers as long ago as 1897, and
came only a year after the great right of way battle on Winter Hill in the West Pennine
Moors, one of the biggest 'mass trespasses' in British history, but in hill-walking
folklore much overshadowed by the Kinder Trespass thirty six years later. But it all
serves to highlight the rights to walk freely won by our forefathers, for they too loved
the hills, often their only escape from a difficult and demanding daily round, and
walked right stoutly themselves.

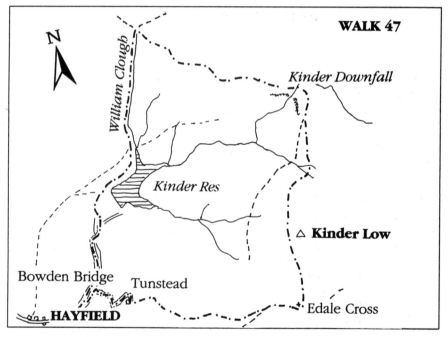

From the Bowden Bridge car park (see commemorative plaque to the trespass on
quarry wall, the original mould of this plaque is now in the Edale Information Centre)
turn left along Kinder Road, and follow this as far as the entrance to the grounds of
Kinder Reservoir. Here go right across a small arched bridge over the River Kinder,
and only a short way further on leave the road through a small gate on the left to follow

the banks of the Kinder. A few minutes of burbling brook brings us to a second bridge by which we recross the river to regain the minor road we left earlier. That we could have walked up the road will here be obvious, but it is not a right of way, and the path by the side of the river is by far a more soothing option, and easier on the feet.

On our right are the main gates to Kinder Reservoir, and just to their left we pass through a small wooden gate giving on to a rising path beside a wall. Initially uphill, this path soon reaches a small crest from where there is a fine view over the reservoir to the distant Kinder Scout plateau, with Kinder Downfall, our objective, tucked away to the left.

A short distance further on a rising track on the left is met, and while this may be followed, turning right along the shelf of White Brow as it reaches higher ground, there is no real advantage in doing so, and the height you will have gained will all be surrendered later in the walk only to be regained again.

Continue ahead instead, following the path around the reservoir until we reach the foot of William Clough, the folds of which can now be seen ahead. Two other paths, reached by a bridge across the stream flowing down William Clough, take you by different routes to Kinder Downfall, and are equally popular. For historic reasons, if nothing else, we follow the line of the 1897 path, into William Clough, crossing and recrossing the stream until, as we near its summit (Ashop Head), the clough divides. Take the right fork and ascend to Ashop Head where the eroded Pennine Way descends the steep brow on our right and meanders off to the left, heading for Featherbed Moss and the top of the Snake Pass. Ahead the Snake Pass continues north and then east into Ashop Clough and the upper reaches of Woodlands Valley.

Our route, however, lies up the boggy steepness southeast of this mini-crossroads, an ordeal in wet weather, but mercifully short-lived, and after crossing a fence leading to the rim of the Kinder plateau. What follows is a fairly dry path undulating through and around outcrops of gritstone boulders, bringing the conspicuous ravine of the Downfall ever nearer.

There are many exciting vantage points both before and after we cross the River Kinder from which to view the Downfall, but extreme caution is demanded of photographers and anyone seeking descents into the amphitheatre, which for the most part don't exist or are only accessible to experienced scramblers. If in doubt, stay on firm ground. Whether the Downfall puts on a show will largely depend on the extent of rainfall over preceding days, and it is not uncommon to find the River Kinder reduced to a mere trickle.

At the risk of spoiling spectators' pleasure, walkers visiting Kinder Downfall when the river flows strong and the prevailing southwesterly wind whips across the valley should be wary of the fact that the wind has a knack of spuming the downfalling waters high into the air, back above the falls, to besiege any luckless soul attempting to cross the river above the falls. On this notoriety rests many a man's mirth, and many an incautious traveller's drenching. Be warned!

Cross the shallow river and shelter for a while among the rocks to take in the jewelled eye of Kinder Reservoir and the distant industrial badlands and urban conglomerations of South Lancashire, Cheshire and Greater Manchester.

We resume our journey, heading south on the Alternative Route to the Pennine

Way to reach the ravine of Red Brook, from where a path descends obliquely to the valley. But we continue instead, around Red Brook, shortly to reach the trig station on Kinder Low. On a clear day, when the ground underfoot is exceptionally dry, you can divert from Kinder Low to seek out the three cairn-topped mounds of peat from all the hundreds of mounds of peat that mark the triple summit of Kinder Scout itself, but only an expert navigator or a madman would attempt such an undertaking in poor visibility.

From Kinder Low we continue south, passing to the right of Edale Rocks, to descend by a wall to reach Monk's Road, an old packhorse route to the Yorkshire markets from Hayfield and the Sett Valley, near Edale Cross, a boundary marker of the medieval Royal Forest of the Peak.

We return to the valley by heading west from Edale Cross, following the ancient track until we reach Oaken Clough where we can go right, over a stile, to cross the ensuing hillside on a clear path, making for Tunstead Clough Farm, our progress through walls eased by a succession of gates or stiles. The way around the farm follows its access road and brings us down easily to the valley bottom, alongside the River Sett. The Bowden Bridge Car Park is only a short distance away.

Alternative start from Hayfield: If the car park at Bowden Bridge is full many walkers simply park untidily and often obstructively along the road, which is narrow enough without the further impediment of cars. It is better, and certainly less obstructive, to return to Hayfield and park there.

By then walking along Kinder Road you will come to the start of the Snake Path, the 1897 path, which leaves the roadway at GR 041868 and sets off up and across the hillside ultimately to join the horizontal path across White Brow, mentioned above. This alternative start adds negligible ascent and little distance, and affords a return from Bowden Bridge along the southerly bank of the River Sett to Hayfield.

Walk 48: The Roaches Crest

Maps: (1) OS Landranger 1:50,000 series: Sheet 118 – Stoke-on-Trent and Macclesfield, and Sheet 119 – Buxton, Matlock and Dove Dale; (2) OS Outdoor Leisure Map Sheet 24 – The Peak District: White Peak area

Start: Roach End. GR 996645. Limited parking.

Distance: 16 kilometres (10 miles)

Ascent: 405 metres (1325 feet)

Type of walk: A lofty, but not too energetic, parade across one of the first ramparts of the southern Pennines. Good paths throughout, superlative views, and always full of interest.

Where opposites meet

These proud ramparts may well have been the first glimpse Stone Age Man had of upland Britain as he set out northwards from the great continent of Europe, into this new and bleak landscape, an awesome sight tens of thousands of years ago, and one that must have filled his mind with foreboding, for nowhere else is the contrast between lowland and upland quite so pronounced. Even now the scene is no less dramatic; south and west lie the cultivated landscapes of a softer, man-managed Britain, while northwards the land displays a sterner countenance, as beneath our feet and all around the dark gritstone that heralds the Peak draws an unmistakable line on the geographical map of the countryside, a frontier where opposites meet.

The Roaches (a name deriving simply from the French: 'rochers' meaning 'rocks') is a craggy whaleback, dominating the borders of Staffordshire north of Leek. With its siblings, Ramshaw Rocks and the shapely and dignified Hen Cloud, the Roaches resemble a range of mountains in miniature, and have long found favour with the rock climbing fraternity. Even at this lowly altitude, among the foothills of the Pennines, the strong characteristics that hallmark the range are very much in evidence, none less so than the tremendous feeling of space and openness which so typifies Pennine country. This is most noticeable gazing west, a panorama in which the radio telescope of Jodrell Bank is prominent, directing its gaze to rather greater distances than we might see. On a good day you may be able to pick out the Clwydian Hills and the domed summits of the Berwyns up to 100 kilometres (60 miles) distant.

The walk that follows is essentially a figure-of-eight, and embraces not only the Roaches Crest and Hen Cloud, but the fine continuation northwestwards of the ridge

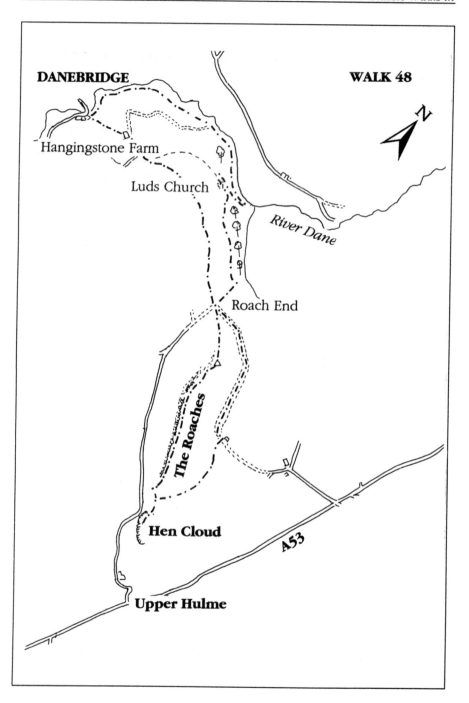

to the Dane valley, which marks the boundary between Staffordshire and Cheshire. Because there is limited parking both in Danebridge and at the southern end of the ridge, the latter tending to be bagged early in the day by rock climbers, a start is recommended from Roach End, in the middle. There is still limited parking even here, but more of it, while a start from this mid-point enables the walk to be curtailed should the need arise; it also means you can tackle the walk any way round you prefer, each of the four possibilities seeming to illustrate totally different aspects of this delightful region.

From Roach End a stony path ascends easily enough by a wall, picking a way through a collection of weathered gritstone monoliths for which the Peak is famous, and in no time at all delivering us to the trig pillar marking the highest point. Here, for the first time, we may begin to appreciate the wide panorama, our eyes unavoidably drawn to the elegant form of Tittesworth Reservoir and the town of Leek beyond it, the shapely cone of Shutlingsloe to the northwest, and, northeast, the mound of Axe Edge overlooking the old market and spa town of Buxton.

A gentle descent now leads us south along the Crest, with ample opportunity to inspect the cliffs rising from the ancient larch plantation below. The path is never in doubt, crossing and recrossing a collapsed wall until we reach quite unexpectedly a small tarn called Doxey Pool, lying in a shallow basin where a layer of peat overlies the sandstone beneath, effectively preventing natural drainage. It has been suggested that the pool was named after the daughter of Bess Bowyer (of whom more anon), but since it is recorded in the Domesday Book as 'Dochesig' this seems most unlikely.

The Crest path now descends to a sharp natural break in the otherwise continuous cliff face, and we can descend a gully (near the end of a fence) to pass beneath the cliffs of the Upper Tier. We are now very much in the domain of the rock gymnast, massive cliffs, vertical and overhanging rise above us, intimidating. Inevitably our attention will be drawn to a most daunting overhang, a massive ceiling of rock projecting from the cliff face; if you are lucky you might see climbers in varying states of panic tackling a route put up in 1952 by the late Don Whillans, and called The Sloth, which somehow negotiates the overhang. Unless possessed of a death wish, The Sloth is not for us anything more than a pleasant coffee break, after all a little armchair rock climbing never did anyone any harm!

Now we follow the Rockhall Steps which take us down to the Lower Tier where we will find Rockhall Cottage, a weird abode built into the cliff, and not surprisingly the home of a succession of eccentrics. Originally this would have been a game-keeper's cottage, but it was occupied for nearly a century by Bess Bowyer, daughter of a noted moss trooper, Bowyer of the Rocks, once a real terror in the locality. Nor was Bess any more law-abiding for she reputedly sheltered smugglers, deserters and thieves. It is said she had a beautiful daughter, after whom the Doxey Pool is supposedly named, who could often be heard singing among the rocks in an unknown tongue. Eventually, the daughter was abducted, and old Bess, distressed and discon-solate, languished and died.

We continue along the track beneath the cottage, later turning left at a wall. From a stile there is an obvious ridge path ascending to the top of Hen Cloud, demanding only a little extra effort, but offering an immense panoramic reward. Hen Cloud, its name deriving from the Celtic *clud*, meaning a rock, hence 'High Rock', is unusual in the Peak, being one of only a few peaks of any distinction, standing alone and aloof at the end of the Roaches ridge.

The crags of the Five Clouds along the Roaches edge

On returning to the stile we can pursue a path through a succession of fields, aiming ultimately to intersect the minor road near Shaw House. From there follow the road, no less pleasant for being shared with the occasional car, back to Roach End.

We embark on the second half of this delightful walk by squeezing through a narrow gap in the wall to cross a small enclosure to a stile. Beyond the stile a good path takes us with leg-swinging freedom along the crest of a gentler ridge, later following the edge of a neat escarpment punctuated by gritstone outcrops, until we arrive at a gate and stile. A clear track goes right here, along the line of a wall, and will bring you directly to Lud's Church; if time is short, this is the way to go. Otherwise, go left and descend, alternating stiles and gates, to Paddock and Hanging-stone Farm until we reach the road about 100 metres south of Danebridge village.

Pass through Danebridge and follow a muddy lane to a stretch of woodland along the south bank of the River Dane. The path continues east towards Back Dane (fine view of Shutlingsloe beyond the wooded slopes of Wildboarclough), and from there on towards the Gradbach footbridge. Here we change direction abruptly and head west once more, ascending through the depths of Back Forest, to reach Castle Cliff Rocks, a fine viewpoint over the Dane valley. From this pleasant spot seek out the higher of two nearby paths and follow this until a dark and mossy cleft appears unexpectedly on the right. At first there appears nothing to it, but on venturing within we find ourselves in a different world, a narrow, mysterious, dank and green chasm, twisting this way and that, its walls as near vertical as makes no difference and dressed in moss, lichen and wild garlic. This is Lud's Church, supposedly the Green Chapel of the classic poem *Sir Gawain and the Green Knight*. It was formed by a major landslip, and hemmed in by its confining walls one can almost feel the spirits of years gone by reaching out to us. During the reign of Henry V, the Lollards, precursors of the Reformation, held their forbidden conventicles here, and gave name to the place, where later Squire Trafford of nearby Swythamley Hall leapt his horse fifteen feet over the gap.

A short flight of stone steps leads upwards out of this amazing grotto into pretty woodland above, through which a broad path, contouring southeastwards, always near the upper limit of the woodland, brings us to a signpost indicating the direction of Roach End. Lower Roach End farm, a lonely isolated dwelling, is prominent now as we ascend a stony track beside a wall until, with Roach End in sight, a narrow squeeze stile allows access to the farm road for the final few paces.

Walk 49: Lathkill Dale

Maps: (1) OS Landranger 1:50,000 series: Sheet 119 – Buxton and Matlock; (2) OS Outdoor Leisure Map 1:25,000 series: Sheet 24 – The Peak District – White Peak area.

Start: Monyash; there is a small parking place a short distance up the side road to the left of The Hobbit Inn, with additional limited roadside parking. GR 150667.

Distance: 19 kilometres (12 miles)

Ascent: 240 metres (800 feet)

Type of walk: Quite simply a walk of outstanding beauty. There are few dales that can compare with Lathkill, part of which was declared a National Nature Reserve by the Nature Conservancy Council; a place of pilgrimage for botanists, ornithologists and lepidopterists. Though capable of complete reversal, the walk begins across limestone pastureland and investigating two tributary dales before finally admitting itself to the confines of the River Lathkill at Alport.

Derbyshire Dales Delight

Lathkill Dale is a place where the writer must labour long hours inventing superlatives to supplement the supply he or she will have exhausted well before describing as much as half the journey along the dales' length – but then you can go too far with superlatives, especially when 'a tapestry of Nature's richest invention' says it all!

That any place can arouse the fevered eloquence of one skilled with words is largely a subjective matter, after all, one man's meat is another man's poison. But Lathkill Dale owns more than enough qualities to spur even the grumpiest among us to concede it is outstandingly beautiful. Here wooded slopes, weirs and clear sparkling waters are but the framework on which Mother Nature has indeed hung out her finest work.

Our walk begins in the village of Monyash, about 7 kilometres (4 miles) by crow from Bakewell. Like many villages in the Peak, Monyash was granted a market charter during the Middle Ages, 1340 in fact, which gave it the right to hold a weekly market and a fair twice a year; the old market cross still stands at the centre of the village green, near The Hobbit Inn. Of course, this applied to the days when a market was a

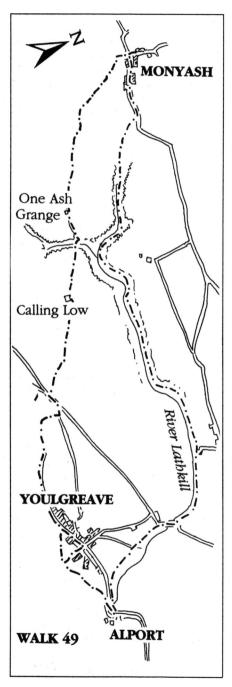

MONYASH

One Ash
Grange

Calling Low

YOULGREAVE

River Lathkill

WALK 49   ALPORT

real market, and not some modern-day counterpart eschewing unwanted bric-a-brac from the gaping maws of car boots.

During the fourteenth and fifteenth centuries Monyash lay on an ancient way from Derby to Manchester, which linked it with neighbouring villages. Later still, packhorse trains carried salt along a trail just south of the village en route from Leek to Bakewell, while drove herds were a familiar sight (and sound) in the village, which in 1765 also found itself on the turnpike from Newcastle under Lyme to Hassop, a route used to convey pottery ingredients to North Staffordshire and pottery products back the other way. Quite a busy little place in years gone by, the centre of much quieter attention now, unless your arrival coincides with the occasional ghetto blaster ghoul that chances this way in search of someone's peace to invade.

From the car park head down the road to the market cross, and continue ahead at the crossroads (Rakes Road) to pass a large pond on the left around which the road sweeps. As the road bends right, leave it along a minor road (signposted, as is much of this early stage of the walk: 'Limestone Way' – the Limestone Way being a splendid walk linking Matlock and Castleton). As the minor road, too, curves away, continue ahead along a broad track between dry stone walls, that later narrows. At the end of this lane, near the head of Fern Dale, cross a stile by a gate, and keep to the right edge of the pasture for a short stretch to another stile across a wall. A green path leads us half left across the ensuing field to yet another stile, beyond which two fields are crossed, keeping to their left edge, until we are again required to cross into the adjacent field, following its right hand edge to a gate giving access to One Ash Grange Farm.

There is a remarkable peace about this gentle introduction, suave, green and seductive, an overture to something exciting, suspected but as yet unseen.

One Ash Grange was established in the twelfth or thirteenth century to supply Roche Abbey in Yorkshire with wool. It was a deliberate policy of abbeys founded after the Norman Conquest to organise a network of isolated farms to supply produce for their own consumption, and this was often done quite ruthlessly, evicting local peasants under the provisions of thirteenth century enclosure legislation as need dictated. Later peasant descendants were also to have a hard time under the strictures of the Enclosure Acts of the fourteenth, eighteenth and nineteenth centuries. That many of the surrounding pastures were used for sheep is evidenced by the noticeably larger fields which predominate south of the Lathkill compared with those to the north.

On entering the farmyard, go left at a camping barn, and follow a track until a waymark sign locates a stile above a steep flight of steps to a small field, beyond which we enter a narrow ravine to emerge on a rocky ledge beneath a cliff. We are entering Cales Dale, and by following the path to the left a direct entrance may be made into Lathkill Dale. But our route lies across the dale, up a flight of steps (slippery when wet), and across ensuing fields to pass to the left of and around Calling Low Farm. From here a diagonal traverse of broad pastures takes us through a small woodland to a broad track across farmland to a stile in a wall. More fields follow until we reach the minor road descending to Conksbury Bridge, which we will encounter a little later in the day. A sign here tells you that Monyash lies but two miles away, when in point of fact we have covered a little over three.

A minor road branches right to a car park serving a nearby picnic area, and a right turn at the car park takes us to a stile at a wall corner, and then by a succession of obvious stiles and paths to reach the road descending into Youlgreave, an attractive village perched on the ridge between Bradford and Lathkill Dales, and once a prosperous lead-mining centre. The youth hostel here is a handsome three-storey building originally constructed for the Co-operative Society in 1887. Just opposite a Conduit Head presented by the Youlgreave Friendly Society of Women provided the village with its first piped water supply. The church (15th century) with its eight pinnacles has one of the best towers in the Peak, and from near the youth hostel appears to completely block the street.

Like Eyam and Tissington, Youlgreave is one of many places in the district to perform summer well dressing ceremonies. There are five wells in Youlgreave, all decorated with mosaics of flower petals pressed into damp clay in the form of predominantly religious themes.

South of Youlgreave lies the attractive side valley of Bradford Dale, which connects with the Lathkill at Alport. By retreating from the village for a short distance we can take a minor road on the left to descend steeply into the dale, following a path on the left bank past a bridge and a weir. At a road continue ahead and go down the wide unmade road opposite. This soon bends left, but where, later, it swings right, uphill, go ahead through a stile and continue down the valley to a minor road leading in turn to a main road, which we must cross to a gate and a stile.

Follow the ensuing path, starting by a stream, but shortly leaving it to follow a fence and then a wall for almost one kilometre (about half a mile) until we reach a lane on the edge of Alport. Continue ahead once more to a road, at which turn right and go down to a bridge. Immediately after the bridge go left through a stile to enter Lathkill Dale. Alport is a picturesque place of seventeenth and eighteenth century cottages, an ancient bridge, and a mill and mill cottages in an attractive setting – well worthy of a short break and potter about.

The stretch of the Lathkill which we now encounter serves only to prepare us for what lies up-river, and marks the point where words fail and the senses are obliged to take over. As far as Conksbury Bridge the path keeps to the west (true right) bank of the river, passing en route Raper Lodge which featured in the film *The Virgin and the Gypsy* starring Franco Nero, and based on the book by D. H. Lawrence, who was no stranger to this area. Youlgreave, too, found a place in the story, being described as Congreave.

Near Conksbury Bridge, the Lathkill flows slowly round wide bends

At Conksbury Bridge, an old packhorse bridge carrying the Bakewell to Youlgreave road, we cross to the river's opposite bank, gaining the path by a gate. The immediate impression is of a wide open dale, its river passing by nonchalantly, as if tomorrow would do. On a quiet spring day peace abounds, and it is difficult to imagine that this place once echoed to the sound of industry as the hillsides were plundered for their lead. Adits and other mine trappings, like the ivy-clad retaining wall of the Mandale Mine engine house, hide themselves among the wych elm and beech that has assumed the responsibility of masking man's redundant endeavours. Dippers and grey wagtails patrol the river margins, its course punctuated by weirs as if to inject a little pace into an otherwise placid progress. But above all else it is the clarity of the water that impresses itself upon us, flowing over a carpet of luxuriant greenness that tells of the Lathkill's curious habit of drying up during prolonged rainless weather. Shadowy trout dart about effortlessly, while the occasional early morning heron stabs at its breakfast long before the hordes arrive.

Would that the author was sufficiently well versed in matters botanical to identify unaided the diverse spread of plants that flourish here, many on the limit of their range – stemless thistle, bird cherry, mossy saxifrage, herb robert (lover of lime), meadowsweet, meadow cranesbill, butterbur, red and white campion, wood anemone, dog's mercury and the strong smelling ransoms or wild garlic. Nor, without the aid of a net, could he describe the butterflies that present themselves so generously in spring and summer that the dale has become the annual venue for a butterfly monitoring exercise.

If one's mind is attuned to these themes of nature, Lathkill Dale is a full orchestral score, a symphony at full tilt; less accomplished walkers will know a pretty tune when they hear one, for in Lathkill the melody is all around, the rippling river, the call of birds, the hum of flower-loving insects.

Beyond Lathkill Lodge we enter the nature reserve at a point where the dale narrows into Palmerston Wood, the trees emphasising the narrowness and forcing an intimacy with the river that has us constantly eyeing the water for the sight of trout or the much-hoped-for flash of iridescence that was a kingfisher.

Our path continues without deviation, and finally emerges from the cover of trees into the upper dale where the prominent white scars of limestone start to feature on the steep dalesides. To the left Cales Dale enters near the remains of an ancient sheepwash constructed by the monks of One Ash Grange more than seven hundred years ago. Keeping right, we press on into Ricklow Dale wherein the River Lathkill emerges fully grown from the dark womb of Lathkill Head Cave, a place for the curious, but not after rain. To our right a keen eye will spot a dry waterfall where once a tributary stream tumbled into the dale, and ahead we are pressed tightly between the downcast boulders of Ricklow Quarry before emerging on to an open plateau, a sudden and green-carpeted conclusion to the confines of the dale just left.

In no time we reach the B5055, and face a contemplative ten minutes stroll back into Monyash.

Variant: Walkers not certain of their ability to complete the full circuit should consider entering Lathkill Dale from Cales Dale and pursuing as much of it as they feel able before retreating to Ricklow Dale.

A start from the B5055, where there is room to park a few cars, is also popular, but misses the pleasant pastureland leading to One Ash Grange.

The whole route can, of course, be reversed, with equal pleasure.

Walk 50: Dovedale

Map: OS Outdoor Leisure Map: Sheet 24: The Peak District – White Peak area

Start: Hartington village. GR 128604.

Distance: 9 kilometres (6 miles)

Ascent: Negligible: minor undulations

Type of walk: Largely riverside and pastoral strolling, of no great difficulty.

Dovedale dingle dawdle

It is among the clefts and dingles of our landscape that John Ruskin feels "the traveller finds his joy", and nowhere has more of these much-prized, jealously-guarded sanctuaries than the White Peak. As Roland Smith comments in his excellent guide to *The Peak National Park*: "Castellated white walls of naked rock rise above native ashwoods, while in the dale floor the rivers exhibit that tantalizing habit of limestone streams, sometimes disappearing mysteriously from sight, only to reappear some miles downstream."

Dovedale is understandably a most popular place of resort, and this walk, from the charming village of Hartington, visits its northerly section before returning via a side dale and attractive country lanes. Like many of the White Peak villages, Hartington has its village pond, near which a limited number of cars may be parked.

Leave the village centre and turn right, heading along the main road as far as the public conveniences, beside which a public footpath sets off into Dovedale via Beresford and Wolfscote Dales (Peak District and North Cheshire Footpath Society signpost). Go beside the toilets to a gate, beyond which a broad well-graded path runs on across low pastures to meet a farm access track at a stile. Cross the track to a squeeze stile, beside which there is a sign which asks visitors to avoid widespread trampling of the grass in the field and keep to the line of the path, here waymarked.

Beyond the first marker post the path ends, but the route descends a grassy field with a dilapidated wall on the left, to another signpost. Here, cross the wall and continue to a gate at the far side of the pasture. Once across the pasture, the way continues ahead, keeping to the right of Pennilow, a small grassy hill on the left. At the base of Pennilow we rejoin a more defined track.

The path runs on down to another wall and stile at the edge of woodland which marks the start of Beresford Dale. Here we make our first acquaintance with the River

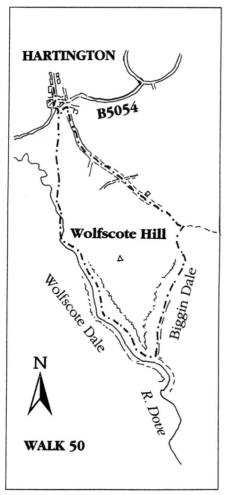

HARTINGTON

B5054

Wolfscote Hill

Wolfscote Dale

Biggin Dale

N

R. Dove

WALK 50

Dove, the dale having closed in and its sides steepened dramatically. A series of weirs enliven the water, adding white-water sparkle and colour to its sombre shade.

Shortly, the path crosses the river by a footbridge and continues delightfully along its bank, now the true right bank. At a ford we cross the river again by a narrow footbridge. Once across the foot-bridge turn right to follow the riverbank as the dale opens out into a broad pasture-land, and leads on to a squeeze stile at the entrance to Wolfscote Dale. A most pleasant walk ensues, following the river deep into the wooded confines of Wolf-scote Dale.

At the end of the dale below the crags of Peaseland Rocks, you come to a wall with a gap stile, beyond which a cave is visible in the distant cliff face ahead. Here turn left before reaching the wall, into Biggin Dale, another secluded valley of great beauty and tranquillity.

The path through Biggin Dale largely follows a wall and the dale stream which from time to time encroaches on the path-way. Part way up the Dale go right through a gate and enter Biggin Dale Na-ture Reserve which is being managed by English Nature.

Towards the head of the Dale swing round to the left on a public bridleway (signposted: Hartington), setting off through a gate. A brief stretch of green pasture leads to another side valley (sign-posted: Public Bridleway to Hartington), rising gradually to a gate. Turn left here, and at the gate, continue ahead on to a walled track.

The track eventually arrives at a crossroads where the signposted route to Hart-ington continues ahead. This is a pleasant, time-worn back road passing through a series of fields delineated by pearl-grey limestone walls in various states of repair.

Finally, as Hartington village comes into view, leave the path at a bend, and go left through a squeeze stile to follow a public footpath down towards the village. When you reach the first buildings, go left along a public footpath beside a wall, and through a couple of stiles that lead you back towards the toilet block at which we started. Once through the last squeeze stile, go immediately left across another stile to reach the toilet block, there turning right to return to the village centre.

Bibliography

Along the Pennine Way, J.H.B. Peel (David and Charles, 1979)

The Companion Guide to Northumbria, Edward Grierson (Collins, 1976)

Davenport's Illustrated Hollingworth Lake Guide and Visitor's Hand-book to Blackstone Edge, J.B. Davenport (1860)

Hadrian's Wall, David J. Breeze and Brian Robson (Penguin Books, 1987)

A History of Cumberland and Westmorland, William Rollinson (Phillimore, 1978)

History, People and Places in Yorkshire, Arthur Gaunt (Spurbooks Ltd., 1975)

The Journeys of Celia Fiennes, Christopher Morris, ed. (Cresset, 1949)

Lancashire and the Pennines, Frank Singleton (B.T. Batsford Ltd., 1952)

Lancashire Countrygoer, Jessica Lofthouse (Robert Hale, 1962 and 1974)

Legends and Historical Notes of North Westmoreland, Thomas Gibson (Unwin Bros., London, 1887)

Millstone Grit, Glyn Hughes (Futura Publications Ltd., 1975)

On Foot in the Peak, Patrick Monkhouse (Maclehose, 1932)

The Peak National Park, Roland Smith (Webb and Bower, 1987)

The Pennine Mountains, Terry Marsh (Hodder and Stoughton, 1989)

The Pennine Playground, Walt Unsworth (Penguin Books, 1984)

Pennine Way Companion, A. Wainwright (Westmorland Gazette, 1968)

Pennine Way Management Project: Final Report, Mollie Porter (Peak National Park and Countryside Commission, 1990)

Pennine Way North, Tony Hopkins (Aurum Press, 1989)

Pennine Way South, Tony Hopkins (Aurum Press, 1990)

Portrait of the Howgills and the Upper Eden Valley, Michael Ffinch (Robert Hale, 1982)

Portrait of North Yorkshire, Colin Speakman (Robert Hale, 1986)

Portrait of Yorkshire, Harry J. Scott (Robert Hale, 1965)

The Roof of Lancashire, Herbert C. Collins (J.M. Dent & Sons, 1950)

Striding through Yorkshire, Alfred J. Brown (Country Life Ltd., 1949)

A Tour Through England and Wales, Daniel Defoe (J.M. Dent & Sons, 1928)

Walking in the Yorkshire Dales, Colin Speakman (Robert Hale, 1982)

Yorkshire Dales: limestone country, Tony Waltham (Constable, 1987)

The Yorkshire Dales, Geoffrey N. Wright (David and Charles, 1986)

The Yorkshire Pennines of the North-West, W.Riley (Herbert Jenkins Ltd., 1934)

We publish a wide range of other titles, including general interest publications, guides to individual towns, and books for outdoor activities centred on walking and cycling in the great outdoors throughout England and Wales. This is a recent selection:

Peak District Walks

HERITAGE WALKS IN THE PEAK DISTRICT - Clive Price *(£6.95)*

CHALLENGING WALKS IN NORTH-WEST BRITAIN - Ron Astley *(£7.95)*

WALKING PEAKLAND TRACKWAYS - Mike Cresswell *(£7.95)*

MOSTLY DOWNHILL, Leisurely Walks - White Peak - Clive Price *(£6.95)*

MOSTLY DOWNHILL, Leisurely Walks - Dark Peak - Clive Price *(£6.95)*

Cycling with Sigma

CYCLE UK! The Essential Guide to Leisure Cycling
- Les Lumsdon *(£9.95)*

OFF-BEAT CYCLING & MOUNTAIN BIKING IN THE PEAK DISTRICT
- Clive Smith *(£6.95)*

MORE OFF-BEAT CYCLING IN THE PEAK DISTRICT
- Clive Smith *(£6.95)*

50 BEST CYCLE RIDES IN CHESHIRE
- edited by Graham Beech *(£7.95)*

CYCLING IN THE LAKE DISTRICT
- John Wood *(£7.95)*

CYCLING IN SOUTH WALES
- Rosemary Evans *(£7.95)*

CYCLING IN THE COTSWOLDS
- Stephen Hill *(£7.95)*

BY-WAY BIKING IN THE CHILTERNS
- Henry Tindell *(£7.95)*

Country Walking . . .

RAMBLES IN NORTH WALES - Roger Redfern

EAST CHESHIRE WALKS - Graham Beech

WEST CHESHIRE WALKS - Jen Darling

WEST PENNINE WALKS - Mike Cresswell

STAFFORDSHIRE WALKS - Les Lumsdon

NEWARK AND SHERWOOD RAMBLES - Malcolm McKenzie

NORTH NOTTINGHAMSHIRE RAMBLES - Malcolm McKenzie

RAMBLES AROUND NOTTINGHAM & DERBY - Keith Taylor

RAMBLES AROUND MANCHESTER - Mike Cresswell

WESTERN LAKELAND RAMBLES - Gordon Brown *(£5.95)*

WELSH WALKS: Dolgellau and the Cambrian Coast
- Laurence Main and Morag Perrott *(£5.95)*

WELSH WALKS: Aberystwyth and District
- Laurence Main and Morag Perrott *(£5.95)*

WEST PENNINE WALKS - Mike Cresswell

TEASHOP WALKS IN THE CHILTERNS – Jean Patefield

WATERWAY WALKS AROUND BIRMINGHAM – David Perrott

- all of the above books are currently £6.95 each, except where indicated

Long-distance walks:

THE GREATER MANCHESTER BOUNDARY WALK - Graham Phythian

THE THIRLMERE WAY - Tim Cappelli

THE FURNESS TRAIL - Tim Cappelli

THE MARCHES WAY - Les Lumsdon

THE TWO ROSES WAY - Peter Billington, Eric Slater, Bill Greenwood and Clive Edwards

THE RED ROSE WALK - Tom Schofield

FROM WHARFEDALE TO WESTMORLAND:
historical walks through the Yorkshire Dales - Aline Watson

THE WEST YORKSHIRE WAY - Nicholas Parrott

- all £6.95 each

The Best Pub Walks!

Sigma publish the widest range of "Pub Walks" guides, covering just about every popular walking destination in England and Wales. Each book includes 25 - 30 interesting walks and varied suitable for individuals or family groups. *The walks are based on "Real Ale" inns of character and are all accessible by public transport.*

Areas covered include

Cheshire • Dartmoor • Exmoor • Isle of Wight • Yorkshire Dales • Peak District • Pennines • Lake District • Cotswolds • Mendips • Cornwall • Lancashire • Oxfordshire • Snowdonia • Devon • Northumbria • Snowdonia • Manchester

… and dozens more - all £6.95 each!

General interest:

THE INCREDIBLY BIASED BEER GUIDE - Ruth Herman
This is the most comprehensive guide to Britain's smaller breweries and the pubs where you can sample their products. Produced with the collaboration of the Small Independent Brewers' Association and including a half-price subscription to The Beer Lovers' Club. *£6.95*

DIAL 999 - EMERGENCY SERVICES IN ACTION - John Creighton
Re-live the excitement as fire engines rush to disasters. See dramatic rescues on land and sea. Read how the professionals keep a clear head and swing into action. **£6.95**

THE ALABAMA AFFAIR - David Hollett
This is an account of Britain's rôle in the American Civil War. Read how Merseyside dockyards supplied ships for the Confederate navy, thereby supporting the slave trade. The *Alabama* was the most famous of the 'Laird Rams', and was chased half way across the world before being sunk ignominiously. *£6.95*

PEAK DISTRICT DIARY - Roger Redfern
An evocative book, celebrating the glorious countryside of the Peak District. The book is based on Roger's popular column in *The Guardian* newspaper and is profusely illustrated with stunning photographs. *£6.95*

I REMAIN, YOUR SON JACK - J. C. Morten (edited by Sheila Morten)
A collection of almost 200 letters, as featured on BBC TV, telling the moving story of a young soldier in the First World War. Profusely illustrated with contemporary photographs. *£8.95*

FORGOTTEN DIVISIONS - John Fox
A unique account of the 1914 - 18 War, drawing on the experience of soldiers and civilians, from a Lancashire town and a Rhineland village. The book is well illustrated and contains many unique photographs. *£7.95*

ROAD SENSE - Doug Holland

A book for drivers with some experience, preparing them for an advanced driving test. The book introduces a recommended system of car control, based on that developed by the Police Driving School. Doug Holland is a highly qualified driving instructor, working with RoSPA. *£5.95*

TRAINING THE LEARNER DRIVER - Don Gates

The essential guide for all those intending to teach a friend or relation to drive. Written by a drivng professional so that you'll know that you are teaching just the same way as a driving instructor. *£6.95*

WE ALSO PUBLISH:

A new series of investigations into the Supernatural, Myth and Magic:

GHOSTS, TRADITIONS AND LEGENDS OF OLD LANCASHIRE
- Ken Howarth *(£7.95)*

SHADOWS: A northern investigation of the unknown
- Steve Cliffe *(£7.95)*

MYSTERIES OF THE MERSEY VALLEY
- Jenny Randles and Peter Hough *(£7.95)*

Plus, superb illustrated books on Manchester's football teams:

RED FEVER! From Rochdale to Rio as United Supporters *(£7.95)*

MANCHESTER UNITED - Moments to Remember *(£6.95)*

MANCHESTER CITY - Moments to Remember *(£9.95)*

Many more entertaining and educational books are being regularly added to our list. All of our books are available from your local bookshop. In case of difficulty, or to obtain our complete catalogue, please contact:

Sigma Leisure,
1 South Oak Lane, Wilmslow, Cheshire SK9 6AR

Phone: 0625 - 531035 Fax: 0625 - 536800

ACCESS and VISA orders welcome - call our friendly sales staff or use our 24 hour Answerphone service! Most orders are despatched on the day we receive your order - you could be enjoying our books in just a couple of days.